INSIDE
TODAY

INSIDE TODAY

THE BATTLE FOR THE MORNING

Judy Kessler

Villard Books
New York
1992

Library of Congress Cataloging-in-Publication Data
Kessler, Judy
Inside *Today:* the battle for the morning
by Judy Kessler.
p.   cm.
ISBN 0-679-40764-2
1. Today show (Television program) I. Title.
PN1992.77.T6K4   1992   791.45′72—dc20   92-53657

2 4 6 8 9 7 5 3

First Edition

F o r e w o r d

Around 1950, Sylvester "Pat" Weaver, Sigourney's father, had an idea. He wanted to create a television show for the ungodly hours of seven to nine in the morning, a show made of news, entertainment, and everything else from weather reports to household tips. The *Today* show would shrink the world into an enlightening package for the American viewer to wake up to—listen to, if not watch—and eventually become hopelessly dependent upon.

He did it. The *Today* show debuted on January 14, 1952, presided over by its first host, Dave Garroway, and the now infamous chimp, J. Fred Muggs. Over the years that followed, it became an American institution, a presence that millions of Americans came to feel was as essential to their lives as their first cup of coffee. *Today* grew into a singular phenomenon that melded the personalities on camera with the ever-growing capabilities and sophistication of the medium. More than anything, it grew into a family—the *Today* show family—to which the audience became uniquely attached. This added an unintended dimension to Pat Weaver's original creation. As it neared middle age, just shy of its fortieth birthday, the *Today* show would have all the makings of the best soap opera on the air.

Pat Weaver once said, when *Today* was at its peak, "You couldn't kill that show with a baseball bat." He came very close to being wrong. As the competition grew, as *Good Morning America* gained strength in the morning, the dynamics of morning television changed drastically, and the *Today* show came dangerously close to being killed, not with a baseball bat, but by its own hand.

Because of a series of bumbling miscalculations, bad judgments, and outright mistakes, *Today* would lose Jane Pauley, one of its mainstays—not to mention one of America's favorite newswomen—and nearly crumble. Deborah Norville would be in and then out in what seemed like minutes, while Bryant Gumbel would persevere, playing a role in the embarassing debacle that few viewers would be aware of. In spite of the close ties between the cast and the audience, what really happened during this near-tragic era for *Today* has not, until now, met the public eye.

I was among the multitudes of Americans who grew up on the *Today* show. Hugh Downs, Barbara Walters, John Chancellor, Frank Blair, Frank McGee, Tom Brokaw, and Jane Pauley were all part of my family. Not only did I love the show, I was captivated by the mystery of how it got done. It seemed that no matter what happened the night before, *Today* somehow managed to bring you not only news of it, but guests to talk about it, by morning. I never knew how they did that. Eventually, I would find out firsthand— often the hard way—after I became a member of the *Today* show staff in 1980. What I learned was more bizarre than I could have imagined.

This book is the inside story of all this: not only how the show gets on the air every day—sometimes magically, sometimes horrifically—

but also what really happened during the most tension-filled years of *Today*'s life. By virtue of the fact that *you* are, after all, a part of the *Today* show family, you have every right to know.

—Judy Kessler
Los Angeles, California
February 1992

Acknowledgments

There are certain people without whom, for various reasons, this book could never have been completed, and I am grateful to each of them: Many of my colleagues from the *Today* show were generous with their time and thoughts, among them Joe Angotti, Coby Atlas, Rona Barrett, Cynthia Bernbach, Emily Boxer, Tom Brokaw, Karen Curry, Allison Davis, Janice de Rosa, Nancy Fields, Steve Friedman, Scott Goldstein, Marianne Haggerty, Bob Jamieson, Janet Jamieson, Ann Schlitt Kolbell, Amy Krivitzky, Mark Kusnetz, Elizabeth McDermott, John Palmer, Jane Pauley, Janet Pearce, Joanne Penizotto, Michael Pressman, Merle Rubine, Marty Ryan, Willard Scott, Andrea Smith, Ron Steinmen, Mark Traub, and Adrienne Wheeler. Landon Jones of *People* helped me immeasurably; thanks also to Michael Gartner, Kevin Goldman, Peggy Hubble, Betty Hudson, George Merlis, and Ellin Sanger.

I am equally grateful to those who spoke with me but wished to remain anonymous.

There are those who have helped me beyond words and far beyond the boundaries of this book: my parents, Harry (Ackie) and Charlette Kessler; my sister, Leida Sanders; my aunt, Nina Kessler; my sister, Wendy Lesch; Dr. Idell Natterson; Dr. Wilbur Schwartz; and my friend and adviser Norman Lear.

I would never have undertaken this project without the encouragement and insight of Doe Coover.

Without the support of Diane Reverand, my editor and publisher, it would never have come to fruition.

It would never have been completed without the help and love of many of my friends, among them: William F. McIlwain, Gary Herman, Ursula Obst, Sheila Silver, Esther Margolis, Rick Kessler, Miriam and Henry Warshow, Chris Conrad, Sharon and Paul Boorstin, Anne Taylor Fleming, Karl Fleming, Kathy Nishimura, Roxanne Jones, Patricia E. Bauer, Ann Daniel, Joel Siegel, and Mark E. Pollack.

Esther Newberg has been superb, above and beyond the call of duty.

Jane Centofante was spectacular as a researcher. Thanks also to Emily Chiang and Linda Kamberg de Martinez.

Others made it possible for me to get to the point of even attempting this, among them: Deborah Aal, Alana Emhardt, Robin Green, Medora Heilbron, Rich Heller, Connie Kaplan, Tom Papke, Judy Polone, Mildred Richards, Dr. Jerome Schofferman, James P. Schreiber, Dr. David Wellisch, and Dr. Arthur White.

Contents

Part I

THE FALL

(1978–1984)

One

YOU CAN'T GET
THERE FROM HERE

How could I have ever suspected that Priscilla Presley, years after she had given birth to Elvis's only child, Lisa Marie, and after her voluminous shiny jet-black beehive had mercifully disappeared from her head, and she had run off with Elvis's karate instructor, Mike Stone, and after she had left him too, for another man, Michael Edwards, who later admitted *he* had fallen for Lisa Marie—how could I have ever imagined that Priscilla Presley, of all people, would someday change my life?

I couldn't have. Now, more than twelve years after the fact, I learn that Priscilla Presley was the reason—the sole, unadulterated reason—that I got my job as talent coordinator of the *Today* show at the beginning of 1980.

This, justifiably, requires some explanation. I was a baby boomer, a short, dark-eyed Jewish girl with thick black hair, who grew up in Seattle, came of age on the cusp of the Women's Movement, graduated from Stanford, floundered for a while—caught between the seemingly conflicting goals of marriage and career—and then by various quirks of fate and happenstance eventually landed squarely in the lap of *People* magazine and the nascent world of "infotainment journalism" as an intrepid, if inexperienced and naïve, reporter, just days after the magazine came into existence in 1974.

From that moment, when I first set foot on the twenty-ninth floor of the Time & Life Building on Fiftieth Street and Sixth Avenue in midtown Manhattan, my life would be affected by a sequence of unlikely celebrities.

The first big one was Danny Kaye. Danny, the father of Dena, one of my closest friends at Stanford, was the one who opened my eyes to the realities of the *mondo bizarro* of celebrity journalism into which I had inadvertently arrived. He gave me my first big scoop, handed it to me on a golden tray, not long after I started my job at *People*.

I knew him from visiting his home in Beverly Hills with Dena from time to time when we were in college. We would fly to L.A. for a weekend—Dena would have her ever-present bottle of Wish-Bone low-calorie Italian salad dressing in her purse, something she simply could not bear to be caught without, even on a thirty-minute airplane ride, the same way her mother, Sylvia, carried her own silk sheets with her even to the finest hotels anywhere in the world. When we were there Danny would usually invite a group of friends to the house on Tower Road to cook one of his famous Chinese dinners for them.

I got glimmers then of a Danny Kaye who was not exactly the man my whole family had revered for a lifetime—the same way we had revered the venerable *Today* show, now that I think of it—but a man who was often rude, yanking cigarettes out of his guests' mouths at dinner and embarrassing them with crude language, a man who was intensely manic in his moods, yet charming and funny and talented nonetheless. But these were only glimmers.

Then one day Dena called me at *People* and said, "Judy, wait till you hear this. Daddy is going on a Unicef tour, sixty-five cities in five days. He's flying his own Learjet, and *you* are the only reporter he is going to let go with him."

Well, I thought, what a way to start. Without even trying, I had just landed a great story, a perfect picture story for *People*, an exclusive—without even lifting a finger. I went to Dick Stolley, the managing editor, and told him the news. "An exclusive," he said smiling, as pleased as I had hoped he would be. "That's great. We'll make it the lead story, four pages for next week. You'll have to write it the minute you get back."

Even before I got on the plane with Danny, along with the head of Unicef, who was traveling with us, and the photographer *People* had assigned to the story, I knew I had a disaster on my hands. Danny was surly and mean from the beginning. When I introduced him to the photographer, they shook hands, and in that split second, a look of fury flooded Danny's face. At first, I thought he was joking. Then I heard, "Why don't you cut your goddamn fingernails, you almost killed me." The photographer shriveled like a dried mushroom and turned white. I let my eyes slide slowly towards his fingernails. They were practically nonexistent. The photographer was a nail-biter.

We piled into the cramped Learjet with Danny at the controls. On our first stop, Philadelphia, I realized that Danny's love for children was outweighed by his impatience with them and that he had nothing but disgust for their parents. When a baby started crying, Danny snapped at the child's mother, "Why don't you go out and diaper that kid?"

I stood there clutching my reporter's notebook, grasping for quotes, my heart sinking and my blood pressure rising each time I tried to record the words that were unabashedly making their way from Danny's mouth to my disbelieving ears. My God, I thought to myself, how on earth am I going to do this story?

And then Mrs. Jones showed up. She was a pure, natural blonde, like the Breck shampoo girl, cheeks beyond pink, closer to magenta, round, wide eyes. She looked as if she had just stepped out of *Little House on the Prairie*.

In fact, Mrs. Jones was the head of the Foundling's Hospital in Toronto, and her expectations were understandably high. She had been eagerly anticipating this night. She was here to meet one of her idols, a hero—in her eyes, no less than a saint—the one and only Danny Kaye. I braced myself for what was to come.

As I watched, beseeching the gods for a turning point, a colorful incident, a good anecdote, a story, *anything* I could tell, Danny lurched forward and grabbed Mrs. Jones. "Don't turn your cheek, Mrs. Jones," he growled. "Kiss me on the lips."

A bright red hue crept from the bottom of her dimpled chin to her already crimson cheeks, spreading slowly across her smooth, broad forehead. I became certain that Mrs. Jones was going to pass out. I heard Danny say with impunity, "I bet you're one of those women who hugs with her ass sticking out, Mrs. Jones. How about ordering us a bottle of pussy fuisse?"

At that point, I accepted the fact that there would be no story, that my short career in journalism was probably over. My good friend's father had given me a break that had perversely transformed into the first *crise de conscience* of my brief professional life. I couldn't deliver what I had promised without losing my friend in the process. I decided I would face the music, return to New York, and break the news to Dick Stolley. At least I owed it to him to tell him he had four blank pages in the front of the magazine for the coming week.

Back on the twenty-ninth floor, I told Stolley what had happened. "There is absolutely *nothing* we can tell," I said. "He behaved abominably and it isn't even printable, certainly not for *People*."

Stolley listened. He seemed calm, in spite of the fact that he had a very large hole at the front of his magazine. "Well," he said finally, "just sit down and write me a memo telling me everything that happened."

I was relieved and glad to get it off my chest. I had been so unnerved by the unexpected events that even the tiniest details had stuck in my head with glaring intensity. I systematically went through my notebooks and wrote down all the unusable quotes, the unbelievable descriptions, the unprintable words. The memo to Stolley went on for eight pages. Relieved the whole thing was over, I turned it in and went to lunch.

When I came back, Stolley was standing there with Bill Ewald, my senior editor. They were grinning. "It's hysterical," said Ewald. "A great piece of writing."

"Great job of reporting," said Stolley. I flushed. Adrenaline pumped through me, propelled by shock and fear. What were they talking about?

"We're going to run your memo," they said. Upset and confused, I meekly told them they couldn't do that. They made it clear to me that they could. They edited my memo, changing words like "ass" to words like "bottom," and my memo became the first piece ever to run in *People* magazine in the first person—Mrs. Jones and all.

Dena never spoke to me again, and Danny's last description of me, *to* me over the phone, was the same unflattering word Bryant Gumbel would be accused by *Spy* magazine of calling Jane Pauley some sixteen years later.

At about the time of the Danny Kaye fiasco, in late 1975, directly across the street from Time, Inc., at NBC in Rockefeller Center, the Today show was in a state of chaos similar to my own. According to its producer, Paul Friedman, the solid old show, having been on the air now for twenty-four years, was going through "an unhappy time, a period of great trauma." Barbara Walters was about to leave to begin co-anchoring the news at ABC; the laid-back host, Jim Hartz, had just been told that Tom Brokaw would replace him; the newsreader, Lew Wood, was going to be demoted to weatherman; Floyd Kalber had been assigned to read the news; and there was no one yet to replace Barbara Walters. Gene Shalit was the only familiar face in the entire *Today* show family.

In mid-1975, for the first time in its history, *Today*'s ratings had begun to slide. By August 1976, this is the way a worried NBC executive described the situation: "It's as if three-quarters of a baseball team had been killed in a plane crash and you had to put together a squad with new talent who had never played together before."

_____

My own career proceeded dismally. In the summer of 1976, the year of the Bicentennial, *People* would do a special issue asking various celebrities to dress up as major historical figures: Flip Wilson was Benjamin Franklin, Susan Ford was Martha Washington, Art Buchwald was Benedict Arnold, Sonny Bono was Nathan Hale. My dubious assignment was to get the respected NBC newsman John Chancellor to dress up and be photographed as Thomas Jefferson.

This was going to take some doing. How was I going to get John Chancellor dressed up in tights, short pants to the knee, and a ruffled blouse on a one-hundred-degree day in New York with 95 percent humidity? First, I rented an air-conditioned limousine for the trip to the site we had selected for the picture: the Jumel Mansion in Harlem. At Stolley's suggestion, I bought a silver ice bucket, filled it with ice and two bottles of Dom Perignon, and arranged to pick up Chancellor at his house on the Upper East Side of Manhattan in the limo, which was now replete with the ice bucket and champagne. I brought the Jefferson costume with me, wondering if he would ever put it on.

We finished the two bottles of champagne on the forty-five-minute ride to the Jumel Mansion, which, unfortunately for Chancellor, was *not* air conditioned at all. He was a sport, though, content from the champagne, and cheerfully wriggled into his tights in the dripping heat. We managed to get the picture—Chancellor as Thomas Jefferson wadding up copy after copy of the Bill of Rights.

I had been at *People* for almost two years now and the more assignments like this I had, the more certain I was that this was *not* what I wanted to do with my life. What I thought I wanted to do was to get *out* of print and *into* what I believed was the magical, more glamorous world of television, a transition which everyone I knew told me was virtually impossible to make.

If Elvis had not died, I never would have made it. Ironically, his death triggered a sequence of events that led me to Priscilla Presley and ultimately to the *Today* show. The path was convoluted. It began with Tony Orlando's nervous breakdown back in 1977.

The odd thing about celebrity journalism—it may be true of life in general—is that the lives of people who would otherwise never have touched yours become intertwined with yours in mysterious ways. It would never have occurred to me when I first heard Tony Orlando and Dawn's recording of "Tie a Yellow Ribbon" that this man's life would ever have anything to do with mine, let alone that he would one day credit me with saving it.

Tony Orlando was devastated when his friend, Freddie Prinze, committed suicide by shooting himself in the head in January of 1977. Having cradled Prinze, who looked astonishingly like him, in his arms as he died at UCLA hospital, Orlando started becoming unraveled himself by July. Most of us can relate to the pain of such tragedy, but Orlando was a celebrity. After he fell apart, he needed to get back on track in public. So his public relations man, a gentle, good man named Frank H. Lieberman, contacted *People* about doing a story.

Now that I had unwittingly established my credentials with the Danny Kaye story as the innocent, harmless reporter who, like the Spider Woman, would deviously go in for the kill—not that I had ever intended to—I was called upon by my editors for the job.

We began with a series of conversations with Tony and his wife, Elaine. They were nice people and we liked each other. At first, it seemed that Tony just wanted to talk and the three of us spent hours taping rambling conversations and getting to know each other. Tony, like so many other celebrities, had been heavily into drugs and had overdosed on fame and his newfound place at the center of the universe. While Prinze's death might have been the thing that put him over the edge, it also seemed to have shaken him back to reality and now he was pulling the pieces back together.

On August 16, 1977, about a month after our heartrending talks began, Elvis Presley died. Tony knew Elvis, and Frank H. Lieberman knew Elvis's longtime girlfriend, or, as *People* would soon refer to her, "his last live-in lover," Linda Thompson.

So when my phone rang at midnight on the night Elvis died, I was puzzled, if not surprised. I had by this time acquired a role with the Orlandos and Lieberman that fell somewhere between shrink and trusted friend. The conversation sounded to me like an undercover police operation:

"Judy, it's Frank."

"Hi, Frank." (Not: "Why are you calling me at midnight, Frank?")

"I can get you Linda Thompson."

"That's *great*, Frank." (Not: "Who is Linda Thompson, Frank?")

"You know she lived with Elvis for the last five years until just a few months ago . . ."

"Sure, Frank." (Not: "She did?")

"Here's the number in Memphis. Call her now. Bye."

I shrugged to myself and dialed the number. Linda was awaiting my call. The next day I was in Memphis with Linda at the house Elvis had bought for her next to Graceland and she was pouring her heart out to me, while she also let it be known that she had certain aspirations for an acting career, having already appeared as a regular on *Hee Haw*.

I flew back to New York and the next week ELVIS—HIS LAST LIVE-IN LOVER RAPS was *People*'s cover line. I had scored another big one.

At the *Today* show, the major changes had now taken place. Everyone was installed in their new positions and the *Today* family was re-establishing its identity. Brokaw was now the center around whom everything and everyone else would revolve. Jane Pauley, with her vague but perceptible likeness to Barbara Walters and only four years of local news experience under her belt, had won the job sitting next to Brokaw over four other women: Catherine Mackin, Linda Ellerbee, Betty Rollin, and Betty Furness. The president of NBC News, Dick Wald, made it clear that things were going to be different: "We're going back to the notion of having one host," he explained, before Jane was even selected. "Brokaw will be the central figure around whom everything revolves, including the new woman."

A new philosophy was also emerging for *Today*. The executives at NBC decided the time had come for a tougher, more sophisticated show, one that would appeal to a better-informed public.

This vision did not stop Paul Friedman, the executive producer, from hiring a bunch of *Today* cousins who would be dropping in for frequent family visits. He hired Frank Field to do health and medicine, Betty Furness for consumer reports, Dick Schaap to report on sports, and Stan and Floss Dworkin on gardening. After all, the increasingly popular host of *Good Morning America*, David Hartman, alias "Lucas Tanner," was beginning to acquire a substantial following, and *he* was joined on a regular basis by Rona Barrett, Jack Anderson, Howard Cosell, F. Lee Bailey, and Helen Gurley Brown.

In spite of the fact that *Today* still had a strong ratings lead, things were starting to heat up in the morning. By the time Elvis's live-in lover rapped, 10 percent of all the homes in America were watching morning television. The *Today* audience ranged between four and six million people in an average minute, which translates into valuable network dollars. *Today* had long been not only the linchpin of the NBC News operation, but a strong drawing card for advertisers, producing an average revenue of $15 million a year.

The Tony Orlando cover story ran in October 1977. Tony was pleased with it. By the time it was on the newsstands, he was drug free and feeling good, ready to make his comeback. On one talk show, he even gave me credit for saving his life. I don't know why, unless it was because the *People* article gave his career a needed boost. He invited me to his comeback performance in Las Vegas and I sat at a table with Betty and Susan Ford, and he referred to me as part of his family.

When Tony is pleased, Frank H. Lieberman is pleased, and I heard from him again not long after the cover story on Tony ran. He had turned into a valuable contact and here he was again, dropping another gem into my lap:

"Judy," he told me on the phone. "Priscilla is ready to talk."

"No shit!" I replied. The much-sought-after Priscilla Presley had not given an interview in years. Now she too was pursuing a career in acting and apparently wanted to let that be known in *People*. In fact, she was scheduled to make her acting debut on a Tony Orlando television special.

Frank gave me her phone number in L.A., and I had no trouble getting in touch with her. We set up all the details and agreed to a few conditions. It would be a cover. It would be exclusive. She did not have to talk about Elvis. (She talked.) I would fly to California to do the interview, which I did the following week.

Priscilla's well-secured house sat on the hill of a canyon in Beverly Hills, not far from Danny Kaye's. I was to meet her at four o'clock, and I arrived on time in my rented car. I pressed the buzzer that was staring out at me from its little box at the top of her driveway and the gates swung open. I drove through and there was Priscilla, standing there to greet me.

I was astonished at how beautiful she was. Her pale skin was flawless, her blue eyes were almost transparent, and her straight, honey-colored hair bore little resemblance to any picture I had ever seen of her—so soft and shiny, it was impossible to imagine it had ever been piled into what had appeared to be a geodesic dome on the top of her head.

This was a new Priscilla, new at least to me. She was soft-spoken, gracious, and polite. We walked into the house and suddenly it occurred to me that, although the soft, warm, seductive California air was over seventy degrees outside, I was still wearing my New York clothes: heavy coat, wool muffler around my neck and winter boots— hardly a match for Priscilla, who looked as if she belonged on the cover of *Vogue*, not *People*. She offered me a glass of champagne, which I gratefully accepted. When she brought it to me—I don't know why this still sticks in my mind—it had a fresh ripe strawberry floating in it, delicately forcing the rising bubbles in the fine crystal glass to encircle it. Something about the strawberry in the champagne symbolized everything to me about California—and Priscilla—at that moment.

Since I was going to spend as many days as I needed in Los Angeles to get my story, we sat there and sipped our champagne, and talked. There was no need to do anything more. She introduced me to her love at the time, Michael Edwards, a model and actor who lived with her. She seemed to be extremely dependent on him. After the few initial minutes we had alone together, Edwards would be present constantly for the rest of the trip—it became a challenge to get a picture of Priscilla without him in it. And who but Frank H. Lieberman himself was in charge of the photography?

Still, the true shock of the week I spent there was when I first laid eyes on Lisa Marie. It was like seeing Elvis as a child, his hooded eyes, his pouty lips—*his* face, in fact, with Priscilla's coloring. I did get my story, although I was exhausted and saturated with everything Presley by the time I did. I had grown tired of chasing Priscilla around and coddling yet another celebrity, which I did even though she hardly demanded it. Mission accomplished, I left, oblivious to the fact that this story would be my salvation, my ticket out of *People* and into television.

When the Priscilla story ran at the very end of 1978, things at *Today* were not getting better, even with Tom and Jane now well in place. Things were getting worse. The show seemed to be stuck in quicksand, asleep. *Today* had hardly changed in twenty-five years and was still staffed in a large part by people who had been there all that time.

In the nearly three years Jane had been on the show, she had not made much of a mark. At one point, NBC had even considered putting Brokaw into *NBC Nightly News* and hiring Phil Donahue as host. After that, actor Alan Alda was actually offered Brokaw's job. He turned it down.

Nothing at all seemed to be working very well. *Good Morning America*, with its soft, friendly, reassuring approach, had doubled its audience, and *that* finally jolted NBC out of its long winter nap. Surveys were constantly ordered. Lists of new hosts and hostesses were drawn up repeatedly. Things got so desperate that at one of the endless meetings of *Today* producers, NBC executives, and NBC president Fred Silverman, someone actually suggested jokingly that it would make sense to pool all the money available to hire a hit man to get rid of David Hartman.

In the end, the network's solution to the rising challenge of the ABC show, nicknamed *GMA*, was to assign a young, hot, and above all *unique* producer to repair the failing *Today* show. His name was Steve Friedman (no relation to Paul). He was thirty-two years old when he arrived at the show in New York in April 1979, after earning an unequaled reputation at NBC in Chicago and Los Angeles—unequaled in many ways. People called him brash, loudmouthed, loathsome. He was pudgy and streetwise, as far from the image of a polished network television producer as anyone could be. He would come to be known by some of his colleagues as "Jabba the Producer." But everyone—fans and detractors alike—agreed that when it came to television, Steve Friedman was brilliant.

At first he was brought in as second banana under then executive producer, Joe Bartelme. Within months, as the ratings continued to deteriorate, Bartelme was out and Friedman was in as executive producer.

Quickly, Friedman brought *Today* back into the race, by redefining the whole show as well as the roles of Tom and Jane. They were relieved to have Friedman there. Despite network pressure to do otherwise, Friedman was committed to keeping them both.

In December of 1979, I was invited to Tom Brokaw's house for dinner on Christmas Eve. Tom, his wife, Meredith, and I had been friends when we all had lived in L.A. a decade earlier. He had been a local anchorman for NBC and I had worked briefly for *The Washington Post* in its L.A. bureau. Tom left L.A. for Washington to become White House correspondent for NBC, and I left L.A. for New York, but we had always stayed in touch. That December, I ran into Meredith at lunch in a Manhattan restaurant, we chatted briefly, and she invited me to dinner.

There must have been forty people at the Brokaws' that night, but when I walked in the door of their tasteful Park Avenue apartment, only one person stood out—he popped out at me like a jack-in-the-box, so totally different was he from everyone else in the room. He was chubby, almost fat, with a round moon-shaped face, rumpled hair, metallic rimmed glasses, and a very sweet smile. That was the first time I saw Steve Friedman. Within moments, Meredith introduced us and when Friedman asked me what I did, I told him I worked for *People*. Although I thought I detected a sparkle in his eye at my response, I couldn't figure out a graceful way to ask him for a job.

The holidays came and went uneventfully. Some time during the first few weeks in January, I walked into my office at *People* and my red message light was gleaming. I had no idea at that moment that it signaled the end of my quest. I was becoming more convinced each day that I would be at *People* until one of us folded—whichever came first. I did not want to spend the rest of my life at *People*, but I could not quit with no place to go and I was failing miserably at my attempts to get into television.

Just weeks before, a friend had set up an audition for me as an on-air reporter at ABC. I figured I had nothing to lose. When I arrived, they asked me to wait in the control room. I had written a short, entertaining piece which I would read from the TelePrompTer for my audition. My heart was pounding wildly against my chest. I was nervous. Public appearances were not my forte. It occurred to me that perhaps this was not my calling after all.

I was right. When they called me to alight from my control-room perch for the taping, I fell down the steps and landed sprawled on the floor, at which point at least eight crew members kindly rushed to my aid. I wasn't physically hurt, but my psyche was demolished. When I tried to deliver my piece, my mouth was so dry my upper lip stuck to my front teeth and I could not talk; my bruised hand was shaking so much I could not pick up the glass of water they had set in front of me. When I somehow managed to utter the last word I saw on the Tele-

PrompTer, I fled like a criminal from the scene of the crime. I never called them and they never called me.

Now, curious, I picked up the phone to see who *had* called. The message was simple: Call Steve Friedman at NBC. So I did.

Blunt as ever, Friedman said, "You wanna come over and talk to me about a job?"

I was speechless. We made a date. It was actually possible to go from the lobby of the Time & Life Building underground all the way to NBC, so when the day of the appointment came, I did not even have to take my coat.

When I walked into Friedman's office, he smiled. His feet were propped up on his desk, his collar was unbuttoned, his shirttails were hanging out of his pants, his tie was draped around his neck like a muffler. After all, by four o'clock in the afternoon, Friedman had already put in a twelve-hour day.

"How would you like a job?" he asked me.

"Doing what?" (Not: "I'll take *anything* you've got.")

"Booking talent."

"God, I'd love it." (Not: "What does *that* mean?")

He ran down the list of all the advantages of the job, as if he had to convince me. I was wild with joy. But it was not a done deal. He told me I would hear from him soon.

When I did, he asked me to have lunch with him. I could only assume that the news must be good. Otherwise, why would he take me to lunch? But I was wrong again.

"They won't let me hire you," he told me.

"Who?" I asked, contemplating which method I would employ to kill myself.

"The Suits," he replied.

"Who are they?" I asked.

"The guys on the twelfth floor, the executives," he said. "I told them it was between you and another girl. The problem is she has television experience and you don't, so they're making me offer it to her. She asked for a week to think it over," he added, "but I can't imagine why she wouldn't take it."

Neither could I, but she *didn't* take it. She was offered a better job at *GMA*, and so I got my job in television.

Just recently, when I was interviewing Friedman for this book, I found out the *real* reason he hired me.

"You know why I hired you, don't you?" he asked me.

"Why?" I replied.

"I said, 'I want to get the person who got Priscilla Presley for *People*. Whoever that person is, *that's* who I want for this job.' And I found out it was you."

I had no idea what was in store for me.

T w o

LET THE GAME BEGIN

March 31, 1980. It is like a well-choreographed ballet—sort of. At precisely 4:00 A.M., before the dawn has even begun to break, the petite, demure, beautiful blond Princess (Jane Pauley) is awakened by the delicate "ping-ping" of her alarm clock. She crawls out of her cozy bed, showers, applies her own makeup, does what she can with her troublesome hair, descends to the street outside, and is whisked off by the shiny black limousine that has been parked there, waiting to carry her away.

Just across town, at 4:15 A.M., in total darkness still, the boyish, dark, and handsome Prince (Tom Brokaw) awakes. He dons his preppy blazer and pinstripe shirt, ties his tie, combs his hair, tiptoes through his apartment and out the door, careful not to disturb his sleeping family, and climbs into his awaiting car.

As the sun feebly attempts to rise, like two lovers destined to meet, (in this case by their NBC contracts), their respective drivers bringing them ever closer, they will converge upon 30 Rock, the NBC studios, within moments of each other, where the roly-poly King (Steve Friedman) awaits them. By five o'clock in the morning, Friedman has already gone over the show's routine, made the necessary changes, written the open to the program, and is in the process of consuming his third diet Coke of the day.

After her makeup is touched up at the studio and her hair is rearranged, Jane takes her place behind the desk of the *Today* set, sipping coffee out of a mug, nibbling at a muffin, sifting through the morning papers. Tom sits down next to her, with his coffee and a bagel, and begins to study the day's material. The familiar New York skyline, painted on canvas, looms behind them.

At exactly ten seconds before 7:00 A.M. Eastern Standard Time, on the sixth floor of the RCA Building, in studio 6B, the stage manager holds up his hand. *Today* is about to begin again—the eleventh week of its twenty-eighth year. The stage manager drops his fingers, one by one, as he quietly chants, "And in five . . . four . . . three . . . two . . . one."

The familiar sunburst explodes on the screen, the *Today* theme music builds, and the two fresh faces smile flawlessly into the beckoning red light of the camera.

But, alas, a ballet this is not. About five minutes into the program, in the tense blackness of the control room, the heartbeat of the *Today* show, Friedman looks over to see that one of the monitors is malfunctioning. Where he is supposed to see what is happening on *GMA*, he sees nothing at all, nothing but snow. Exasperated with the lousy quality of the often faltering NBC equipment, his blood pressure creeping upward, he slowly, deliberately, removes his newly polished size eleven brown leather shoe from his right foot and, with the precision of a veteran baseball pitcher, hurls it into the screen, smashing it into tiny bits. There will be a brand-new monitor to replace it by morning. (If he had gone through the proper channels, he would have had to wait six months.)

By the time Friedman's shoe and the monitor became one, I had been up half the night myself. It was one month after he had told me I was hired. For me (the booker) there was no limo waiting, but the subway was only a block away from my Greenwich Village apartment.

I had automatically assumed, with a degree of double-edged anticipation, that like the Prince and Princess, I too, would have to get up in the middle of the night, it was part of the mystique. So I was taken aback when Friedman had told me not to show up until 9:00 or 9:30—I wondered if I wasn't being excluded from the mainstream. I watched the first hour of the show on my TV at home and arrived at the *Today* show offices one floor above the studio a few minutes after 9:00.

My timing was perfect. They came up on the studio elevator right after the show—all three of them: Jane and Tom and Steve. Jane and Tom still had their makeup on, not a hair on either head was out of place. Steve, with his tie loosened, his collar open, and his jacket flung over his shoulder, looked as though he'd been through the ringer. At least his right shoe was back on his foot.

Of course, I already knew Tom. Jane was friendly; she smiled and said hello as though I had been working there forever, and Steve motioned me to come with them. We walked down the stark, shabby, mustard-yellow corridor, heading for Friedman's office.

Although I had been there once before for my interview, I hadn't noticed the details. They reflected his essence: A dart board hung on one wall; on another, a photograph of Wrigley Field, the home of his passion, the Chicago Cubs. A basketball sat on top of his desk next to a well-worn, skid-marked hardball and a leather mitt. Next to them was a baseball cap with moose horns that he wore whenever the mood struck him. A baseball bat leaned ominously against the wall in the corner of the room.

Above the desk was a poster-size picture of Steve with a serene, Madonna-like smile, wearing a hooded silk robe. He looked like a victorious fighter after a bout. I would later learn this was a shot of the outcome of one of the momentous "Battles of the Bulge," major starvation matches in which he partook regularly, betting money on who could lose the most weight over a predetermined period of time. Friedman thrived on competition—the more intense the battle, the more driven he became. In his office as in his life, television and sports were symbiotic partners.

He sat down behind his big wooden desk and plopped his feet up, stuck his hand in his mitt, reached for the hardball, and began tapping it into his leather palm like Captain Queeg. Tom and Jane sat down on the couch against the wall, so I did too. From the window you could see Rockefeller Center and all of midtown Manhattan behind it. If you fell out the window you would land directly on the skating rink.

A few writers dribbled in and I was introduced. They smiled and greeted me politely, but the winds of change had blown in with Friedman and I detected a modicum of defensiveness towards me on the part of the old guard. After all, some of these people had been there nearly thirty years, since the first day the *Today* show had gone on the air, on January 14, 1952. I was a member of a new generation, the first person Steve had hired in New York.

I sat quietly and listened. They talked about tomorrow's show, a conversation which I soon discovered took place every day of the week at this time: What was the big story? Who should lead the show at 7:10, the first spot after the news at the top of the program? It was the middle of the Iran hostage crisis, three weeks before the U.S. attempt to free the hostages in Tehran would fail. They decided to go after Henry Kissinger for 7:10.

Steve reached over to his right and picked up the thick, black grease pencil next to The Book. In 1980, The Book was the key to the *Today* show. It always rested next to him, open, on a shelf tilted forward like a music stand. About twenty inches long and fifteen inches wide, with a black vinyl cover, it looked like an oversized corporate checkbook. Instead of checks, it contained plastic pages divided into squares defined by permanent black lines. There was a square for each segment of the day—eleven in all—each day of the week, each week of the year. As segments were booked—as guests committed to appear on the show—Steve scribbled them in the appropriate square with a grease pencil. That way they could be erased as quickly as they were written in. Easy come; easy go. Things came and went like that on *Today*. I personally was responsible for at least one square a day—the crucially requisite celebrity.

Over the 120-minute period each morning, the show would range from politics (usually at the beginning) to music (usually at the end) and virtually everything and anything else in between. There were certain givens. A segment pegged to the top news story of the day would open the show: the eruption of Mount Saint Helens the night before, or the release of the U.S. hostages in Tehran after 444 days. The celebrity slot was usually at 8:37, in the second half of the second hour, right after the news and the weather, (which was now presided over by the jovial weatherman Willard Scott, who had come to *Today* only weeks before I had).

On a scale from heavy (ten) to light (one), the beginning of the first hour would be a ten, while the last segment of the second hour would drop considerably, sometimes nearing zero, as when, for instance, homemaker Dian Thomas would teach the audience something like how to keep the salt in their salt shakers dry.

No show was complete until all the squares in The Book for that day were filled. Generally, the first five or six (the first hour of the show) were geared towards the male viewer—hard news, politics. If a celebrity made it into the first hour, it would probably be a macho man like Arnold Schwarzenegger or Chuck Norris, or a sexy Sophia Loren that the male producers couldn't resist. The remainder of the boxes were filled with things that would appeal to the housewife who stayed home after the rest of the family had left: celebrities, cookbooks, feature stories, household tips.

Steve, who never squandered an ounce of time or energy, had his own special lingo for The Book. If you booked, for instance, the man who had had a near-death experience, he would simply put down "Dead Guy." Or, if you booked the bigamist who was recently discovered to have thirty-eight wives, he would write down "Married

Guy." The woman who was caught in a frightful blizzard and was found a week later, unconscious, but alive, was (what else?) "Frozen Lady."

The group disbanded at nine-thirty. Steve tucked in his shirt, buttoned his collar, tied his tie, and put on his jacket as he did every morning at this time for the meeting on the twelfth floor with the "Suits." There, in spite of his aversion to the network bureaucracy, he would discuss the next day's show with other news division executives, exchanging information and plans so that everybody knew who was doing what.

Momentarily reenergized, Friedman took my arm and walked me back down the shabby hallway. About halfway to the elevator he stopped in front of a closed brown-painted wooden door that looked like the door to a closet. "This is your office," he told me, turning the knob, pushing the door open. "Book those guests—we need to fill that book!" With that, he turned and continued down the hall.

It wasn't exactly what I had envisioned. The office was stark and cold, claustrophobic. It was more than fifteen feet long, but there were no windows, and it felt as if there were no air. It had an old linoleum floor and two scratched clunky desks, one behind the other, each with an old phone atop it. There was one electric typewriter precariously perched on a rickety metal stand. I stared into the room. I did not know what to do, but I decided I would try to be as productive as I could, considering the fact that I still was not certain exactly what my job was. So I chose the desk closest to the door—I figured at least that way I could get out fast in case of fire—and I sat down and tried to think. Then I reached for the familiar security of the typewriter, inserted a piece of paper, and began to write Steve a memo about some of the people I thought we should book.

At the time, I was big on mothers and daughters, fathers and sons, fathers and daughters, mothers and sons—a classic ploy I had learned at *People*. If we could get them together, the whole package would be larger than the sum of its parts. Besides, they would make good guests, and Mother's Day was just around the corner. Father's Day was not far behind. With a negligible surge of confidence, I started to make a list:

> Lee Grant and daughter Dinah Manoff
> Paul Newman and daughter Susan Newman
> Carl Reiner and son Rob Reiner
> Eddie Fisher and daughter Carrie Fisher, or (a twofer)
> Debbie Reynolds and daughter Carrie Fisher

Having run out of offspring, I had turned to my next list, classic "untouchables" that I already knew by heart from my tenure at *People*—the ones you could *never* get but *always* wanted: Elizabeth Taylor, Jackie O., Woody Allen, Barbra Streisand, Frank Sinatra, Greta Garbo—when Friedman came back in.

"What's that?" he asked me, ripping the page out of the typewriter, crumpling it up, and skillfully slam-dunking it into the wastebasket.

"I was writing you a memo," I said, wondering why he had just destroyed it.

"Don't *ever* write me memos," he told me. "We don't have time for that. We have two hours a day of live television to do. My office is always open. What you do is you come in, or you pound my door down if you have to. That's the only way to get things done."

I would quickly learn the differences between the world of the written word, which I had just left in the Time & Life Building at Fiftieth and Sixth, and the world of television at 30 Rock, into which I had entered, almost directly across the street.

For one thing, everybody at Time, Inc., had smoked—it certainly seemed that way, at least. How could you be a magazine writer without a cigarette dangling from your lips and dark, shadowy circles lingering beneath your eyes while you sweated over your typewriter? (We didn't have computers yet.) I had always promised myself that the minute I got a new job, I would quit smoking.

The first day I started working at NBC, dressed in a new white silk suit from Saks I had splurged on, a group of staffers gathered to talk in an open area outside of Tom Brokaw's office in the middle of the afternoon. My resolve to quit smoking faltered immediately, and I couldn't resist the temptation to light a cigarette. "What?!" said Brokaw, looking at me strangely, with an air of disbelief. Before I knew it, he reached over and slapped the cigarette out of my hand. As it flew through the air like a fizzling Scud, it came dangerously close to igniting my new outfit. Mortified with embarrassment, I reflexively crushed it into the worn, dull green carpet with my new Ferragamo pump. In that instant, it occurred to me that nobody else in the room was smoking. That was the last time I would smoke a cigarette, in public anyway.

At *People,* "closing" nights, the two nights before the magazine was put to bed, were often harder to get through than doing the stories themselves—unless you happened to get an assignment like spending the weekend at Three Mile Island after the nuclear disaster.

On Fridays and Mondays, you would often have to stay until dawn, waiting for your editors, and your editors' editors, and *their* editors, to come back from their expense-account dinners to begin editing your piece. Nothing really got going on those nights until ten or eleven o'clock. Dinner for the lowlier members of the staff would be catered around 9:00 P.M. (about the time Jane Pauley was going to bed), and at that time they would break out the wine—and there was always plenty to go around. That was what you did while you waited for your story to be edited, and then for the edited copy to be retyped and corrected and checked for facts. One of the few high points of the evening while you waited was to try to come up with a winning "contents" line for your story. The best one I can remember had to do with a selfless Indian swami called Rama. The contents line read: "The woes of the world weigh down upon the Swami Rama." Still, it was little consolation—closing nights invariably dragged on. It might be four or five in the morning before you were free to leave.

There were many nights that I left work as the sun was coming up. I probably passed half the *Today* show staff on more than one occasion coming to work on those mornings just as I was leaving, the rhythms of the two places were so diametrically opposed.

It was not just the rhythms that were different. I was getting a clearer picture of broadcast journalism. After only one day at NBC, I could already detect that I was about to enter a different, but equally crazy, world.

The object of the game was to fill The Book completely for each day's show by the time the show went on the air—but with luck and perseverance, much sooner. Different tasks, each with varying degrees of difficulty, fell to different people. The *Today* show had always been, first and foremost, a news show. The segments tied to breaking news events obviously depended on what was happening at the moment. If it was a crisis, all the better, from the standpoint of news, at least. It seemed that the *big* things inevitably happened at night, Eastern Standard Time. Anything that occurred after the networks' evening news was fodder for the morning shows. The trick was not only *who* to get, but *how* to get them on the air by morning. If, for example, the Soviet president Leonid Brezhnev died after 7:00 P.M. E.S.T., you had to have a guest, someone like the Soviet ambassador or the U.S. secretary of defense, to talk about it by dawn—which sometimes gave you only a matter of hours. That segment, the most pressing, would lead the show as soon as the news was over, at 7:09 A.M. It had better not be empty.

Bookers or producers who dealt with breaking news events often spent endless hours in the dark of night on the phone, being yelled at by people they had awakened in their frantic quest for a prospective guest. Sometimes they would find it necessary to set out in the wee hours of the morning to corral the guests they needed before the sun came up.

Fortunately, this was not my particular job. My mission was slightly different. In essence, it was twofold: The easier and less important part was that I was supposed to find human-interest stories everyone would be irresistibly drawn to, be utterly compelled to watch on *Today*, and be forced to talk about later—from the baby who needed a bone-marrow transplant within days or she would die, to the first quadriplegic in history to climb to the top of Mount Everest alone. Friedman always said he wanted guests that people would talk about for the rest of the day over the watercooler at work or at the checkout counter of the grocery store. His dream was to overhear Middle America repeating the question, "Did you see that guy on the *Today* show today?" I was constantly looking for those, scanning everything from *The Whole Earth Catalog* to *Mother Jones* to local papers from around the country, searching anywhere I could think of for the guest who would cause the sacred words *"Today* show" to be echoed from the tallest skyscrapers of Wall Street across the golden wheatfields of the Midwest to the snowcapped peaks of the Cascade Mountains.

It was my job to help make that happen, not just with heartbreaking babies and larger-than-life heroic figures—that would have been easy by comparison—but by booking big, no, *humongous*, celebrities. That was my main responsibility: the one-of-a-kind, impossible-to-get, biggest-name stars in the world. And I needed at least one for every single day of the week, except for Saturday and Sunday.

In itself, this task was formidable but not impossible. The problem was, virtually every valuable guest I wanted to get, *needed* to get for the *Today* show, was being hotly pursued by the other networks at exactly the same time, especially the burgeoning *Good Morning America*.

As it turned out, it was not a job, it was war. This was not simply a matter of having an assignment and doing it, but simultaneously fighting an ubiquitous enemy who was after exactly what you were after every second of the day. It was a battle which was fought on every conceivable level: wits, power, clout, luck, and sometimes even sheer physical prowess. Both shows were constantly vying for political leaders—presidents, heads of state, diplomats, senators—not to mention authors, scientists, and artists. And with each passing day, the importance of entertainment celebrities was increasing exponentially.

I did not merely have to get Elizabeth Taylor, Paul Newman, the pope or whomever else, I had to get them before *GMA* got to them, in spite of what *GMA* was doing to get them, by whatever means I could employ. (CBS was not yet a serious contender, since it was on the air only one hour a day.) If a guest did one show, they could not do the other, because neither show would deign to be second—this was a cardinal rule. If you did not get them first, you did not get them at all, a circumstance which placed an inordinate amount of pressure on the person whose job it was to procure the guest in question.

The hottest guests—from the White House to the movie studios—were worth their weight in the rating points they ensured your show if you got them. Since rating points meant money, the hottest celebrities, the untouchables—Liz Taylor, Jackie O., Paul Newman, along with everyone else on my infamous list: Sly Stallone, Robert Redford, Diane Keaton, Woody Allen, Barbra Streisand, Jim Garner—could literally be worth millions of dollars to the network that won them.

There were various ways to go about getting celebrities. The first and best source was the list of upcoming movies, plays, and record albums that the performing stars were willing to promote. Many of these could be booked well in advance. If, for example, the film *On Golden Pond* was coming out, it wasn't hard to figure out that you would want Katharine Hepburn, Henry Fonda, and his daughter, Jane. Nor was it hard to figure out that everyone else would, too.

The announcement of a new film release was, to the talent booker's ear, like the deafening "bang" of a starting gun. Like a racehorse, you had to get out of the gate as fast as you possibly could. You had to try to grab the star before the other guy got him. If you happened to know a particular star personally—well enough, say, to call and ask a favor, which didn't happen often—that was all the better. Otherwise, this was a complex process, which often involved the industry publicists, or press agents—the public relations people whose job it was to plot the public course of their clients' careers, to decide what they would and would not do; the people who, as one observer noted, parceled out their clients like winning combinations in the state lottery.

There was a publicist for each movie studio, one for every Broadway play, record label, and television company. Then there were those extremely powerful figures who headed the most famous PR firms in the country, who were usually the bane of the booker's existence. These people represented the untouchables: Pat Newcomb from Rogers and Cowan who, over the years, had handled everyone from Robert Redford to Warren Beatty, Jane Fonda, and Barbra Streisand; Dick Guttman of Guttman & Pam, whose clients included Clint Eastwood, Jackie Bisset, James Garner, Roger Moore, Christopher Reeve, and Arnold Schwarzenegger; Pat Kingsley of PMK, who ran the public lives of Candice Bergen, Mary Tyler Moore, Sally Field, Cher, Tom Hanks, Goldie Hawn, and Jodie Foster, to name a few.

By the time I arrived on the scene, the morning-show competition had become so intense that the publicists had acquired an inordinate and unwieldy amount of power. They decided which show their client would do, often making outrageous demands in the process: which show would give their client more time, their movie more "parts"—two or three, or even as many as five days on the show devoted to it, as opposed to just one? (Things were getting so intense that GMA had actually offered five parts—one whole week—to get the stars of *Ordinary People*, including Mary Tyler Moore and Tim Hutton.) What else would each show be willing to promise? It was a poker game. You never knew how high your competition was willing to go or what they were able to offer.

Relationships and contacts were obviously important. The names and numbers in your Rolodex were the key to a booker's success. If you could get Priscilla Presley on the phone at home, that was an obvious plus—if she would talk to you, that is. But you still had to cultivate the dreaded publicists. I knew most of them from my six years at *People*, but this situation was different. *People* had been the only game in town, as far as celebrity magazines went, anyway. Here, the publicists could pit one show against the other and make you writhe in agony to get what you wanted. Pat Kingsley, whose *modus operandi* has been compared to that of the KGB until the 1991 putsch, rarely returned a phone call, unless she wanted a favor—which usually meant putting on a lowly client in whom you had no interest.

Wining and dining the publicists was also part of the job, even though it seemed it should have been the other way around. An appearance on *Today* was worth a fortune in advertising for a client's project. Conversely, a hot star tied to a hot movie was worth a fortune to the show that got them. With the meteoric rise of *GMA*, for the first time in nearly thirty years of morning television, the publicists had a choice of which show their client should do.

There were many things to consider. First, there was the very basic question of ratings. Each rating point is the equivalent of 921,000 households, while a share point signifies the percentage of the homes using television sets who watch a particular show. The show with the higher rating was generally the preferable show to appear on, at least from the guest's point of view. If more people watched, more people would go to see the movie or whatever the star was promoting. Although in the first months of my induction into television, the ratings were too close—within only a few tenths of a rating point of each other—to be a significant factor, that would not be the case for long.

There was also the question of hosts. *GMA* was setting a new pace, a pace designed to intensify the growing schism between news and entertainment. *Today* had always been the hard-core news show, and that had been its enduring strength. With David Hartman, a well-known actor himself, as the host of *GMA*, the ratings were exploding. Show business was taking on a new meaning for the morning. Hartman and Brokaw were diametrically opposed. While Hartman's strength was in entertainment and show business, Brokaw's was in politics and news. Brokaw could bring in the political guests, but *GMA*'s successful new emphasis on show business seemed to be what was drawing new viewers—the younger female viewers who were so appealing to advertisers. Brokaw was an uncompromising journalist to the core, but for him the shift towards entertainment posed a conflict. "David comes as an actor," he explained at the time. "He is not expected to be a journalist. He is an intelligent man. But there is less burden on him to be serious."

Serious or not, Hartman had undeniable and valuable clout with the stars, and it was paying off. Not only did he know many of the most sought-after celebrities personally, even those he did not know felt an affinity with him because he was a fellow actor. Besides making my own job harder, this was a source of severe irritation for Steve Friedman, who in typical style had by now begun referring to David Hartman by one of his endearing pet names. For Hartman it was "Potato Face." Friedman fully grasped Potato Face's role in the steady rise of *GMA*, even though Potato Face was by no means the *Today* show's only obstacle.

GMA was in the Entertainment Division of ABC, while *Today* was under the auspices of NBC News. This imposed certain limitations on *Today*, especially when it came to entertainment guests. A news show does not pay for interviews per se or pander to the demands of the interviewee or the publicist, which were becoming more outrageous every day. Since *GMA* was not in the News Division of ABC, the producers and bookers did not suffer the same journalistic restrictions when it came to pulling out all stops to lure the most precious guests. They could offer money if they wanted to and other perks without any breach of ethics—an extra plane ticket or two for a spouse or a friend, a weekend on the town, whatever it took to lure their targets—while *Today* could only offer a hotel for the night before (and possibly the night of) the interview, rarely extra tickets, unless they could somehow be justified, and certainly no cash, with the exception of an occasional payment of the AFTRA minimum if a celebrity who belonged to that union—a singer, for instance—actually performed on the show.

In television there was always more money for entertainment than for news, so *GMA*'s budget of $20 million was considerably larger than *Today*'s $16 million.

The power of the money was not limited to show business guests alone. During one Super Bowl, an experienced sports producer from *Today* was in Los Angeles attempting to book players from the winning team. To his surprise he couldn't get a single guest, something that had *never* happened to him before. He finally found out that *GMA* had already booked all of the players by providing their wives with cars and drivers for their entire stay in southern California. There was simply no way *Today* could compete with that.

Of course, there was also the other side of the coin. As hard as it was to get the guests you wanted, it was even harder to avoid the ones you did not want. The morning shows were an ideal forum for virtually any subject or guest, from sex to politics to sports to the arts and entertainment and everything in between.

For every hard-to-get movie star I lusted after, there were hundreds of more-than-willing guests to fend off. Both phones, on both desks in my office (all four lines) rang constantly. What I heard when I answered them never ceased to amaze me. It was never Pat Kingsley offering me Candice Bergen or Dick Guttman offering me Clint Eastwood, but people offering me things like the family full of Franks. The father, Frank Fernandez, had six boys, all of whom he had named Frank, which meant, if you included the twelve grandsons who were also named Frank Fernandez, there were nineteen Frank Fernandezes in all, and I could have *all* of them. For free! Was this any way to win a war?

——

The challenge facing Steve Friedman was enormous. For nearly thirty years, NBC had had a monopoly on the hours between seven and nine in the morning with *Today,* as they had with *The Tonight Show (Starring Johnny Carson)* from eleven-thirty to twelve-thirty at night. Together these two shows brought in nearly 40 percent of NBC's total profits. They were the very cornerstone of the powerful network. Even when NBC dropped to third place in prime time in 1980, the cornerstone of the network remained solid. When NBC began to lose its hold on the morning hours—when *GMA* actually beat *Today* three weeks in a row in February 1980—it looked as if the network might be falling apart. The very foundation of NBC appeared to be crumbling under Fred Silverman, its president.

The ascent of *Good Morning America* was a boon to morning television in general. In less than five years, the number of people who watched *GMA* had nearly tripled, and its audience consisted of younger women than *Today*'s—it was demographically ideal. Yet *To-*

day had held onto its own viewers. While the margin between the two shows had diminished greatly, now that there was an alternative to what many perceived as the effete, elite *Today* show, more people were watching television between seven and nine than ever before.

In Friedman's eyes, this meant only one thing: *Good Morning America* was a vicious foe which had to be destroyed—and he took his adversaries personally. "I view them as trying to take my mortgage away, stop me from eating," he declared. "I view them as the enemy."

Steven Michael Friedman was a streetwise kid who grew up in a Chicago neighborhood where baseball spelled success: If you could play ball, you were something, and if you couldn't, you were nothing. On the streets of Chicago, you played ball to win, which is exactly what Steve Friedman did from the time he was a little boy. He always wanted to be a baseball player. Not the way most boys want to be baseball players. Friedman was dead serious.

Fate had been against him. For one thing, he had been cursed with bad knees. On top of that, he had not been good enough. By the time he was seventeen, Friedman had been forced to admit sadly that his baseball career was over.

By the time he was eighteen, television had replaced baseball as Friedman's consuming passion—he was particularly smitten by *The Jack Paar Show*. At the University of Illinois, he had wisely listened to an adviser who had warned him, "You gotta learn news because it never gets canceled," and that was the beginning of Friedman's career in television news—better known as broadcast journalism. In his mind, television and sports were one and the same, a concept that would set the tone for the *Today* show for the seven years of Friedman's reign.

"Television, football, baseball, hockey, boxing. They're all the same game," he explained to me years later (after I had seen his philosophy in action firsthand) in his office at NBC, where he had become, by then, the executive producer of the *Nightly News*. It was the bottom of the eighth inning of a no-hitter during the 1991 World Series. As I spoke with him, his eyes darted back and forth between me and the game on the monitor. His philosophy had not changed. "You try to outthink, outwork, and outhustle the people," he said. "You're not nice. Once you have them on the ropes, you kill them."

I could see from the day I first met him that Steve Friedman was an enigma. This streetwise kid with the tough-guy exterior had a mysteriously strong charisma that not only attracted his followers to him like a magnet, but made them want to go to extraordinary lengths to please him. He gave everybody a chance. What you did with it was up to you. He was also a shrewd and talented producer who knew his own strengths and weaknesses.

As soon as he became executive producer of *Today* he appointed Marty Ryan, a friend and colleague from NBC in Chicago, to the job of senior producer. They complemented each other superbly—the two of them were total opposites. Marty looked like an ad out of GQ. Aquamarine eyes, fair skin, hair greying slightly at the temples, chiseled features, soft sexy lips, all encompassed by a pervasive quietness. He seemed shy when you first met him, but he was just self-contained; he was competent but not aggressive. His job was to run the show under Steve, handle the action in the control room, and do whatever else Steve told him to do.

With Steve Friedman, the *Today* show did not run in a normal, organized, "dotted-line" fashion, but then with Steve Friedman nothing was ever exactly what anyone would call normal. Everybody from top to bottom—from the director, producers, writers, on down to production assistants, went directly to Steve if they wanted to. His door was open to everyone.

Marty balanced Steve well. While Steve ranted and raved and hurled his shoes through monitors and smashed wall clocks with his Chicago curveball, Marty stayed composed—his expression never changed. He rarely smiled, he never flinched, he was an excellent line producer. He just did his job, and he did it very well.

Friedman approached the war he was fighting with the resolve of a Marine Corps captain. He had a calculated battle plan, which revolved to a large degree around the composition of his staff: He knew in order to attract younger female viewers, he needed a younger, hipper staff. He also wanted to hire more women, which he did as soon as he could. Most of them were his age or younger (in their twenties or early thirties), and he selected them all very carefully. He had an uncanny instinct for finding talented people, people who were unique in some way. He brought in women like Cindy Samuels, a cherubic but gritty, sharp, young mother of two boys who besides being *Today*'s resident expert on the sixties, soon became the presiding political conscience of the show. When it came to political and social issues, her strength was unequaled.

Steve also hired Karen Curry, another outstanding female producer. Totally different from Cindy, she was decidedly high fashion. Everything about her was ultrahip, from her thinking to the way she dressed. Tall and striking, part *Harper's Bazaar*, part *Rolling Stone*, she could carry off things like purple hair, if she was in the mood, black velvet capes, and antique clothes—and she could pull off this same style in the pieces she produced as well. Karen had a blazing imagination and a flair for the dramatic which she instilled in every segment she did, whether it was science, hard news, or a Broadway musical—or even the annual Christmas show.

Friedman knew he had to breathe new life into the aging, stumbling *Today* show in other ways, too. He wanted the program to be fast-paced instead of slow and leisurely; he wanted it to be on top of the news—on top of everything, in fact—on the cutting edge. He wanted to change *Today* from what he perceived as a rural white show to an urban, multiracial one.

At the same time, without sacrificing the fact that the foundation of the *Today* show had always been news, Friedman saw the handwriting on the wall: He was convinced that for *GMA*, there was no business *but* show business—he believed *Today* was unbeatable in news—so his strategy was to stay strong in news while he fought *GMA* on its own turf. He knew what he had to do was beat them at their own game.

Still, while Friedman was building the strength of his troops and honing his game plan, the show had to go on for two hours every day, and it involved a delicate balancing act. When a guest was booked, Steve would give the spot a time and date—for a movie it would be opening day, if possible; for a book, the day of publication. Then he would assign a writer to the spot and decide who would do the interview. Certain things were understood: Brokaw would get the heavier political interviews, almost always the lead interview of the day—everyone accepted the fact that Jane wasn't always equipped to handle those as well. On the other hand, Jane would get a lot of the human-interest stories and the "plain old folks." Steve Friedman knew that one of Brokaw's shortcomings was a tendency to interview everyone from the president of the Girl Scouts of America to Charlene Tilton as though they were all Watergate conspirators. Beyond that, things would be split up so Tom and Jane had, more or less, an equal amount to do between them.

For me, actually booking the guests was only the beginning of a long process. When a guest was booked, arrangements for transportation and hotels had to be made; the writer had to be told everything about the booking; if the segment was to be taped, a camera crew had to be ordered; everything had to be coordinated between the publicist, the guest, and the show. Overlooking anything, even the smallest detail, could be disastrous.

Of course, it wasn't only a problem of booking the guest. What happened after the actual booking and before and during the show itself, was often a more legitimate worry. The possibilities were awesome. One thing I quickly learned about live television was that it was not safe to breathe until it was all over. Too many things could go wrong. And did. Beginning in the greenroom.

The greenroom, which is not really green, was where the guests waited before their appearance on the show. They were supposed to be there a good half hour early—which meant anytime from 6:00 A.M. on—ready and waiting, after having their hair fixed and their makeup applied. The greenroom was supposed to be a comfortable place to wait. It contained a couch and some overstuffed chairs, from which the guests could watch the show on a monitor until the time they were collected by the production assistant to go into the studio a few minutes before they were to appear. There was always a gigantic institutional-size metal urn of notoriously bad coffee percolating for their consumption, presided over by another permanent greenroom fixture, Gloria Casanovas, better known as "the coffee lady." Next to the coffee was an ever-present large cardboard box filled with a variety of cheap glazed donuts, bran muffins and bagels, and sundry pieces of fruit.

Not long after I began working at *Today*, I learned one of the hazards of the greenroom—and there were many. I had booked one of my favorite music groups, the Pointer Sisters, for a live appearance, not yet having absorbed the common inside knowledge that as difficult as it was for most guests to appear on a live show at this ungodly hour of the morning, it was an even more outrageous feat for performers in the pop-music industry. For one thing, their rock-concert-oriented schedules were such that their work the night before probably did not end almost until the *Today* show began. For another, voices are not usually at their optimum level anytime before noon at the earliest.

I was happy with the booking and so was Steve. The Pointer Sisters, who had a new album out that was quickly becoming a smash hit, had even agreed to sing. When I had important guests appearing on the show, I went to the studio to make sure everything went smoothly. Anxious to meet the Pointer Sisters, I arrived well before they were scheduled to appear. I knew they would have to have their hair and makeup done first, so I allowed them time for that.

When I walked into the greenroom to meet them, it looked more like the sleeping car of the Southern Pacific Railroad. My beloved Pointer Sisters were sprawled on the couch and over the chairs, snoring noisily only moments before their segment. I knew I should wake them but I was not at all sure how to go about it. I considered smelling salts, but instead I started unobtrusively making noise. I banged on the coffeepot and knocked it around a bit, and then I started coughing. It worked. They woke up, but even then I couldn't imagine how they were going to pull this off. Their music wasn't exactly low key and at that moment I couldn't perceive their being able even to stand up, let alone sing "I want a man with a slow hand . . ." To my grateful surprise, they made a complete and astonishing recovery. And they were even better than I had hoped.

The greenroom was really the jumping-off place, the last stop before the studio, the place where all the nerves and anxiety about being on live television spewed forth. The greenroom lent itself to the unpredictable. More than one guest has thrown up in the greenroom over the years. Nature has called from the greenroom in other ways too. One day a guest excused himself to go to the men's room moments before he was to appear and when he did not come back, the female writer for the segment panicked about what to do, sped into the men's room to retrieve him, and dragged him back out in the nick of time. There is no time for waiting—or anything else, really—when a show is done live.

By the time a guest arrives in the greenroom, it is usually too late to do anything to stop him from going on. Once, a well-known country-western star arrived in the greenroom obviously drunk. The bewildered production assistant virtually had to carry him to the studio and place him carefully into the chair on the set. Needless to say, the interview was a disaster.

Sammy Davis, Jr., lost his shoes in the greenroom during one *Today* appearance, when Gloria, the coffee lady, walked off with them. She adored Davis and when she spotted him in the greenroom, Gloria, who was anything but bashful, walked up to him and said in her thick Spanish accent, "Meester Davis, I'm sach a fahn of yours." Then glancing down at his expensive Gucci loafers, she said, "I *loave* your shoes. Can I tray them on?" The obliging Davis slipped out of his loafers, Gloria put them on and disappeared down the hallway. Davis left the studio shoeless that day.

Some guests made it to the greenroom but not to the studio. Jodie Foster had agreed to appear on *Today* with the understanding, she thought, that she was not to be asked about John Hinckley, the obsessed fan who shot Ronald Reagan and later admitted he had been pursuing her. Bryant Gumbel had understood Foster's concern about bringing up the Hinckley matter again and had assured her that Hinckley would only be mentioned. But as Foster sat in the greenroom before her interview, which was to be post-taped, she was watching the monitor and happened to see the taped introduction to it. Not only did it show John Hinckley, but it showed President Reagan falling to the ground after he was shot and James Brady, his press secretary, lying in a pool of blood. In that instant, Foster changed her mind about doing the interview. "I don't really need this in my career," she said calmly, and abruptly left the greenroom—and the building—without another word, either on or off the air.

Actor Michael Douglas almost had a heart attack in the greenroom when he walked in before he was scheduled to appear to promote his film *Fatal Attraction*. Glenn Close, who had maniacally pursued him in the film, had hidden behind one of the greenroom overstuffed chairs on all fours. When Douglas came in, she pounced out from behind the chair and tackled him, knocking him to the floor, where they spent several minutes rolling around to the surprise of those who showed up after them.

And then there was my experience with the Dutch actor Rutger Hauer, who became one of the most infamous bookings of my fledgling career. Steve had made it clear to me that part of my job was to discover new talent, and get them on the show on the cusp of their success so that when they became famous, people would remember they first saw them on the *Today* show. This was easier said than done, as my attempt with Rutger Hauer proved.

Hauer was costarring with Sylvester Stallone in the movie *Nighthawks* and was relatively unknown in the U.S. I saw an early screening of *Nighthawks* and loved it. I thought Hauer was strikingly handsome and an excellent actor, too. Shakily trusting my own judgment, I decided to bet that he would become a star with this film. I went to Steve and got his okay, and I quickly arranged to fly Hauer in from the coast that night. He would appear on the show the next morning, leaving no possible margin for *GMA* to steal him away with a better offer.

Steve gave the interview to Tom. For some reason, Jane had a lot to do in the rundown for the show that day, or she would probably have gotten it. Tom did not have much taste for interviewing movie stars unless they were extremely famous.

The morning of the interview I went into the studio early so I could meet my discovery and watch the segment from the control room. When I laid eyes on Rutger Hauer in the greenroom, I choked. His beautiful blond locks had disappeared, replaced by a bleached platinum spiked punk hairdo—the first of its kind back then. It turned out he was filming *Blade Runner* at the time, a movie in which he played some sort of unhuman being.

Brokaw took one look at him and reacted as though Hauer really was an alien. Besides his bizarre hairdo, Hauer had a glazed look in his eyes. I knew I was in trouble. To this day, Brokaw is convinced that Hauer was stoned—he might as well have been. Every time Tom asked him a question, the answer—if there was one—was incomprehensible and bore no relation to the question. The questions got tougher and tougher. As they stared each other down, Brokaw became increasingly hostile and Hauer did not respond well to that at all. After a few minutes of sinking slowly, nearly drowning with my discovery, Brokaw cut the interview short and went to a commercial. He never let me forget it. The following Christmas he sent me a picture of Rutger Hauer, signed, "Thanks. Tom." Both Brokaw and Friedman told me years later that the Hauer interview was one of the things that convinced Tom he had to leave the *Today* show.

Still, during my first months on the job, I had successes I would not fully appreciate until later, when every difficult booking—or loss of one—would take on a meaning I could not have grasped early on. Just weeks after I began working at *Today*, I managed to get the inimitable

Bette Davis, a committed "Potato Face" fan, to do ⁻ ͻ *Today* show—barely.

I knew I was starting out at a disadvantage because of Hartman, but Davis was valuable and I wanted to get her. I also knew I had Gene Shalit, *Today*'s film critic, to use to my advantage. Shalit, who had been there since 1973 and was the senior member of the *Today* show staff, had not only an affinity, but a great talent for getting along with stars of Davis's stature.

I had heard that Davis was about to receive an award at Birmingham-Southern College. A group of "Legendary Women" were being honored: Ann Getty, Pauline Trigere, CZ Guest, Iris Love, and Bette Davis, among others. It was the opportunity I had been waiting for. The event in itself was hardly momentous, but it was important to Davis and provided a reason to ask her to do the show—something a booker was always looking for. I found out that her good friend and sometime publicist was a woman by the name of Mildred Collins, so I called Collins to ask if there was any way we could get Bette Davis to do an interview for the occasion.

When the handsome, blond, well-spoken Collins answered the phone in her deep-voiced, husky southern drawl, we liked each other instantly. We talked for nearly an hour. Mildred was one of those people who, like me, had grown up on the *Today* show and felt the kind of loyalty to it that was familiar to its disciples. When I realized this, I asked her if she thought she could help me lure Bette Davis away from David Hartman and convince her to do the *Today* show for a change—as a favor to me.

Although her reply was noncommittal, I knew that she would try. "Well, Miss Davis likes David Hartman a lot and she's incredibly loyal, but I'll certainly ask her," Mildred told me.

She called me promptly the next day. "Davis says she'll do it," Mildred said, and I could tell that she was pleased. She had obviously been instrumental in the decision. "But she *has* to be through by one o'clock to go to the plane to get to Birmingham on time."

I was delighted. I promised Mildred that it would be no problem, we would certainly get finished well before Davis had to leave for her plane. We would tape the spot in Davis's room at Manhattan's Lombardi Hotel the next day, at noon. Gene Shalit would do it. We were set. I had scored my first big coup. Or so I thought.

The next day Mildred ordered Bette Davis's favorite lunch, egg-salad sandwiches, from the deli, so they could eat them at the hotel since they were on such a tight schedule. Davis was nervous about missing her flight, but Mildred reassured her. She knew the *Today* show was reliable, that we would be on time. When we said we were going to do something, we would do it.

The doorbell to the hotel suite rang precisely at noon, and Mildred opened the door. Standing there was the mustachioed, furry-headed Gene Shalit, holding the bag of egg-salad sandwiches that Mildred had ordered from the deli, which he had managed to grab from the front desk on his way up to the room. The good news was that the egg-salad sandwiches were there. The bad news was that the camera crew was not. Unlike the sandwiches, the crew had not been delivered. The seconds were ticking away. Instantly, Shalit put in an emergency call to NBC.

"They'll be here in fifteen minutes, I promise," he told Davis.

"Well, we'll never get it done and we have to make the plane and they have to set up and it takes forever," said Davis.

"Nope, we'll get it done," Shalit insisted.

"There is no way," Davis insisted.

I was beginning to agree with Davis, but within moments, the bell rang again and the crew came in.

"You'll never get it set up in time," muttered Davis.

When everything was set up, with only a few precious moments remaining, Davis insisted that Shalit read the entire list of legendary women being honored, and all of the literature accompanying it. He handled it beautifully. When you're taping something, as we were in this case, you are in control—anything you want can end up on the cutting-room floor.

Shalit read the list like lightning, coddled Davis sufficiently, and got the interview he wanted. Mildred had made me a hero, and Davis got to her plane on time.

For a while, I was on a roll. I had not yet learned how difficult things could get. For the most part, everything seemed to be going along swell. When the musical *The Pirates of Penzance* came to Broadway, I booked the entire cast of the show, which included Linda Ronstadt, Kevin Kline, and the popular teen singing star Rex Smith. Not only did we have them all as guests, but Karen Curry produced a whole week of the show in which we recreated the set of the smash hit. Each star performed on *Today*, the audience got to see the most popular pieces of a sellout Broadway show, and Steve Friedman was ecstatic, which I would soon learn was a rare occurrence.

I also managed to book Elizabeth Taylor in those early days of my career, thanks to Mildred Collins. It was a rare and glorious feat, the full magnitude of which I could not even begin to comprehend at the time. Little did I know when Mildred, who was representing Taylor's film, *The Mirror Crack'd*, asked me if I wanted Taylor (I grabbed her instantly), that the megastar would one day become the bane of my existence.

You never knew what would happen next. The possibilities were endless. A guest could sound great when you spoke with him before the interview and fall apart completely the minute he sat down on the set. Once Brokaw was interviewing an Italian filmmaker who had discovered that when the clouds were just right on Mount Rushmore, an Indian's head was outlined in the mountain's shadows. He had brought an astounding piece of film to demonstrate his discovery. In spite of the fact that he spoke very good English, when the interview began, he forgot every word he knew. When Brokaw asked him a question, he answered it in Italian, which made it necessary for Brokaw to answer his own questions—in English. The terrified filmmaker just nodded his head and said, "*sì, sì*," as Brokaw's question-and-answer monologue accompanied the Italian filmmaker's striking footage of the mountain.

So many things on live TV were dangerously unpredictable. The gamble was whether the spot, if it was as good as it optimally could be, would outweigh the potential risks. Jim Fowler, the wildlife expert and veterinarian, who had access to a wide array of fascinating wild animals, was a case in point. Besides the fact that wild animals are, after all, wild, they tend to become even more so on the set of a television studio. The first time Fowler was a guest after I began working there, he brought a rare owl onto *Today*. Again Brokaw was the lucky one. In the middle of the interview, the owl took off and disappeared into the rafters of the cavernous studio, where he remained long after the show was over. Brokaw, trying to improvise as he groped for something to say to Fowler now that the subject of his interview was gone, shrugged and said, "I just hope it doesn't nest in Gene Shalit's hair." A special team of experts had to be brought in later to retrieve the bird.

At least the bird had shown up for the spot, which was not the case once with Dick Van Dyke. I had booked Van Dyke because of a television movie he was doing. He was scheduled for the usual celebrity spot, at 8:37. Van Dyke was a pro, he had appeared on *Today* many times, and I never anticipated a problem . . . until 8:30 came and he wasn't there. Friedman was screaming, "Where the hell is he?" from the control room and I had absolutely no idea and no way of finding out. By 8:35, my heart now stuck permanently in my throat, I realized he was not going to come. That was when I learned that in desperation at a time like that, you pulled a tape that was hanging around the control room and ran it, no matter what it contained, which is exactly what Friedman had had to resort to.

It turned out that Van Dyke had slept through his wake-up call, as well as a series of frantic attempts by his publicist to rouse him from his bed at the Plaza Hotel. By the time she did, the show was over. I was afraid, for a moment, my career was too.

Even the pros were not spared on *Today*, like the time in 1980 when NBC correspondent John Hart was in Poland to cover Lech Walesa and the Solidarity movement. It was to be the lead story for *Today*. Hart was reporting from Poland and Brokaw was in the studio in New York.

In the control room, moments before the program went on, Friedman spoke to Hart on the phone.

"What should Tom ask you?" Friedman asked Hart.

"Tell him to ask me how it's going in the countryside," replied Hart, who was exhausted and dazed after being up for almost two days straight.

What Hart had meant to say to Friedman was exactly the opposite of what had come out of his mouth in an instant of tired confusion. There was no way that Friedman could have known that.

Friedman reached down and pressed the button on the panel that would allow him to communicate into Brokaw's earpiece. "Tom," he said, "ask him how it's going in the countryside."

Brokaw complied, as the camera went to him. "How is it going in the countryside, John?" he asked Hart.

"How should I know, Tom?" replied Hart. "I just got here—I'm in Warsaw."

At that moment, Friedman looked up at the monitor that showed Brokaw. He swears to this day he could see the steam coming out of Tom's ears. Brokaw handled it as professionally as ever, but it had not made his heart soar.

Anybody who goes on television live lays himself on the line. Once when David Hartman was discussing a complicated legal case with a lawyer, she fainted dead away in the middle of her explanation. And during an interview on *Today*, Barbara Walters once asked the author of a book on Albert Schweitzer how the good doctor was doing. "Not very well," the author had helplessly replied. "He's dead."

There was nothing quite like morning television, really nothing at all. Not only did you have two hours a day, five days a week—520 hours a year—of live, unadulterated television to produce, but it was a phenomenon unto itself.

The cast of *Today* was like a family to those who watched it, and the *Today* show family was real. Tom and Jane and Gene and Willard weren't portraying anyone else—not Murphy Brown nor Archie Bunker. It was probably impossible to fool anyone at that hour of the morning.

The relationship between the viewer and the *Today* show family was unique and oddly intimate. After all, you got dressed in front of these people every morning. You brushed your teeth, ate your breakfast, screamed at your kids, and got ready for the day ahead while you watched them, and it felt like they watched you.

That gave you certain rights: More viewers complained about Jane Pauley's hair than any other single subject. Piles of letters arrived at NBC daily that dealt with Jane's hair and nothing else. Viewers behaved as though they knew every member of this family personally. They cheered them when they agreed with them and booed them when they did not. They rooted for them when they were down, got mad at them when they misbehaved, and worried about them when they were sick, or even when they just did not look so good.

The president of NBC, Fred Silverman, was not an average viewer, though, and he did not respond like one. All Silverman saw was that *Good Morning America* was moving rapidly along a successful upward path. He attributed this to their glitzier feeling and their softer touch, and he attributed it to one more thing he thought was quite ingenious: having an actor familiar to the audience as the host of the show.

Silverman was not very happy with either Tom or Jane. Tom believed Silverman had always wanted to get rid of him, and Jane would soon learn the hard way exactly how Silverman felt about her.

Three

POTATO FACE RULES

It was what I called the Universal Question: What's Jane Pauley *really* like? From the first moment I began working on the *Today* show, wherever I went, whatever I did, everyone would ask me that, from Gay Talese, seated next to me at Elaine's, to CBS president Tom Wyman seated next to me at a CBS black-tie dinner, to the taxi driver taking me home from work.

I would reply, truthfully, "The thing about Jane Pauley is that she's exactly what she appears to be." Had I been disposed to elaborate, I would have added: She's really nice—she's just pure Jane, the wholesome, shy, pretty, decent, good, self-deprecating—but underneath it all, strong-as-steel—Midwestern girl from a humble background. Her silver-haired, James Stewart–like father, Dick, was a traveling food salesman and her mother, Mary, was a plain, unpretentious housewife. She seems to have been blessed with a life heavily weighted in the good-fortune department from the day she was born Margaret Jane Pauley on Halloween in 1950.

I could have gone on: In person, Jane is even prettier, more petite, more personable, and certainly sexier, than she appears to be on the air. Besides her flawless fair skin and peachy-pink cheeks, and twinkling, magnetically inviting blue-green eyes, she has long, shapely legs you rarely catch a glimpse of on *Today*. Jane's television image never oversteps that crucial boundary that has kept "attractive" and "appealing" from spilling over into "sexy" or "threatening" for those touchy, delicate hours of the morning.

Had I been in an especially talkative mood, I would have even thrown in more about her background: She grew up in a rural suburb of Indianapolis with her parents and her older sister, Ann, to whom she was extremely close. When Jane graduated from Indiana University in 1972, with a major in political science, she had never studied journalism or ever been on TV. She had already racked up a good deal of time in front of an audience: She was a competent—even good—public speaker, who stumped for New York mayor John Lindsay during his 1972 presidential campaign. Before that, she had played the washboard in her sorority jug band, The Kappa Pickers, where she sang with a Hoosier twang—which was as close as she would ever get to her secret desire to be a torch singer.

Jane's *real* gift, the one singled out by every television producer or executive who ever had anything to do with her—beginning with the news director of WISH-TV in Indianapolis, Lee Giles, who hired her for her first job in television despite her complete lack of journalistic experience—was the way she transformed in front of a camera. When Jane looked into the camera, with its red light glaring back at her, the camera dissolved like a helpless man reduced to a puddle by a beautiful woman.

These newspeople detected her special talent at the first brief glance: There was virtually no distance between Jane and the viewer. Jane was in *your* living room, talking directly to *you*. In spite of the fact she hadn't studied anything related to it—not acting, not communications, not even journalism in any form—she possessed this boggling talent that could not be taught or learned. Still, she had no experience, and when Giles made up his mind to hire her, convinced of her extraordinary ability, he had to promise the general manager of the station that she would be hired on a ninety-day probation.

With only an occasional glitch here and there, Jane Pauley's broadcasting career soared. Even the little glitches seemed to propel her towards stardom. When she was passed over for a co-anchor position at WISH, another station, WMAQ in Chicago, offered her an even better job. In 1975, she became co-anchor with veteran newsman Floyd Kalber. Then, in spite of the fact that the Chicago audience resented the coupling of this young, unseasoned blond reporter with the experienced, well-respected Kalber, and in spite of the fact that syndicated columnist Gary Deeb declared that Jane had the IQ of a cantaloupe, and that people complained that she had been hired for looks, rather than substance, Jane Pauley, with her ever-present lucky stars shining down on her, prevailed. Cantaloupes and good looks notwithstanding, she won the *Today* job in 1976 for a six-figure salary, scarcely a year after she had left WISH for Chicago.

She had packed up almost overnight, leaving everything, including the boyfriend she had acquired in Chicago, behind. After all, at twenty-six, fairly naïve and undeniably unworldly, with only a few years of broadcasting experience under her belt, she had just been awarded one of the most sought-after jobs in television.

But she was hardly affected by the formidable prospects awaiting her or the seductive lure of New York City and the world of big-time broadcast journalism. Jane did not really change at all, except for the fact that she now had to go to bed shortly after dark and get up before the break of dawn.

She lived a surprisingly quiet life, rarely leaving her one-bedroom, unpretentiously furnished Manhattan apartment. Jane had always been down-to-earth, very private, not very social. She had never been a big party goer. In fact, she did not go out much at all.

Not long after Jane took her place next to Tom Brokaw, who treated her with a combination of brotherly affection and a paternal eye, he noticed something out of the ordinary had begun to occur. His friend,

Garry Trudeau, the handsome, witty, successful, eligible, Pulitzer Prize–winning creator of the cartoon strip *Doonesbury*, had started calling Tom with unprecedented frequency. Then one day, when they were scheduled to fly to Chicago together for the memorial service of a mutual friend, Garry insisted on coming to the studio to pick Tom up, instead of meeting him at the airport, as Brokaw had suggested.

That's when it finally occurred to Brokaw that something was going on. "Gary had asked me a lot about Jane and he was real interested in her, so he came and he sized her up from the back of the studio," Brokaw told me, thinking back. "She was very wary of this—I told her he was coming, and she thought, 'just what I need—a hotshot *toonist* in my life.' "

Once again, as she had done in a different sense with Steve and me, Meredith Brokaw played matchmaker. "Jane needs an interest in New York," she told Tom. "We ought to invite Jane and Garry over to the house for dinner."

And so they did. Jane and Garry spent the evening discussing frozen foods—a natural topic for two single people. According to Tom, that was it. It was a marriage made not in heaven, but on Park Avenue in New York City, based on a strong foundation of love and Stouffer's frozen lasagna.

Meanwhile, on the opposite coast of the United States, in Hollywood, California, the land of purple blooming jacaranda trees, glimmering black-bottomed swimming pools, cigar-puffing moguls in Rolls-Royces, and every conceivable form of show business, the career of one formerly obscure blond, personable Hollywood actress was finally taking off—in television commercials no less—and her stunning success did not go unnoticed by NBC president Fred Silverman.

Mariette Hartley had become loved and instantly recognizable—a household word, even—almost overnight, from her role as James Garner's irreverent wife in the hot new series of Polaroid commercials. She was not too young, she was not too blond nor too sexy, she was self-possessed and came across as if she was not only shrewd, funny, and clever, but might even have a real brain in her head.

The commercials became more and more popular, the chemistry between Garner and Hartley was golden, and quickly she became a highly sought-after, desirable commodity—exactly what Fred Silverman had been looking for to spice up the gurgling, sinking *Today* show.

Jane Pauley and Garry Trudeau were scheduled to be married on June 14, 1980, near Trudeau's house in the country in New Haven, Connecticut. Jane had been at *Today* for nearly four years now, and her contract was about to expire, but nobody—on the staff, at least—doubted that it would be renewed. She had already notified the network that she would be taking three weeks of the vacation due her for her impending wedding and subsequent honeymoon.

Just about the time Jane tossed her bouquet to the women of the wedding crowd and set off on her first journey as Margaret Jane Pauley Trudeau, Mariette Hartley blew into the dingy *Today* show offices at NBC in New York with all the grace of a charging water buffalo in the middle of the bush. In no time at all, she would become as irritating to the *Today* show staff as the pea under the princess's mattress.

It was not all her fault. She had been plopped there blindly, seduced from the flashy world of Hollywood show biz by her biggest fan at NBC, Fred Silverman, to fill in for Jane, with not a soul to help or guide her. At the time of her arrival, Silverman was not even there to greet her—he was on vacation in Hawaii.

I had seen Mariette on those Polaroid commercials, and liked her, too, but what I had seen was clearly not what we were about to get. As naïve as the rest of the staff about Silverman's true intentions, I was anxious to meet Mariette and do what I could to make her stay a pleasant and successful one.

Unfortunately, as it turned out, Mariette arrived with a not entirely welcome entourage: her husband, Patrick Boyriven, and her two small children were fine, but Arlene Dayton, Hartley's overbearing, heavy-handed manager—without whom Mariette could not even go to the bathroom—stuck to her like glue, flailing her demanding, stifling attitude about like a whip. For this particular job at least, Mariette would have been better off without her.

The staff knew nothing more than the fact that Hartley would be replacing Jane while she was away on her honeymoon. We had no reason at all to anticipate trouble, but within days of her arrival, rumors started flying. Before long, the word was out that Silverman had every intention of hiring Hartley to replace Jane to prove his theory that the David Hartman factor at *GMA*—the equation of actor equals host—was responsible for the show's meteoric rise. Silverman had apparently found his Hartman in Hartley. We did not like this at all.

Still, before we had become convinced that this was in fact Silverman's intention (which neither Friedman nor Brokaw knew anything about), we tried to be friendly. After all, in the Polaroid commercials Hartley was likable enough and there seemed to be no reason not to give her a chance.

The whole notion was wrong from the start, however. This was a *news* show, not a Hollywood sitcom. These hallowed halls had been the home of respected journalists—like John Chancellor, David Brinkley, Barbara Walters, and more! The blond, boisterous actress and her aggressive manager were totally out of place here. No one doubted that Mariette Hartley was good at what she did. A live morning news show was simply not what she did.

You could tell the direction that it was going from the first day she filled in for Jane. It was June 9, 1980. Tom and Mariette sat side by side at the familiar desk on the *Today* show set. She confirmed to the world that she was as uncomfortable as she looked.

TOM: Good morning all, I'm Tom Brokaw. Let me introduce you to
        Mariette Hartley, if I may. Jane Pauley is off on three weeks'
        vacation . . .

MARIETTE (INTERRUPTING):   Vacation! She's getting married. That's
        hardly a vacation . . .

TOM: Anyway, Mariette, it's nice to have you with us, without your
        Polaroid along . . .

MARIETTE (INTERRUPTING):   Do you know this desk is just about as
uncomfortable as I always thought it would be? Now, if I can just
get my red lights and my words straight, we'll be okay. . . .

She couldn't and we weren't. She had never even read from a
TelePrompTer or done a live show of any kind. She didn't know how
to play to the cameras, or even where to look. And there was no one
there to show her.

Like the rest of us—producers, writers, bookers, even secretaries—
Hartley had been thrown into the churning, cold, unfriendly, waters
and left to either sink or swim. The difference was that a successful
Hollywood actress was not used to that kind of treatment. This was the
NBC News Department and that was the way things were.

Under these circumstances, Hartley had an even more difficult time
handling her assignments. The worse she got, the better Jane looked
and the more we missed her. I watched the drama unfold, perplexed.
She suggested silly stories, joked when it seemed she should have been
serious, sallied about with Arlene Dayton, and slowly alienated most
of the staff.

I tried to be friendly at first; it was my job to book entertainment
interviews for her and to find her some "folksy" features to do, and that
is what I did. After attempting repeatedly to get through Arlene to the
wilting Mariette while wondering what the motive behind her presence
there really was, I did what everyone else finally did—I gave up trying
to be nice and simply did my job.

The more trouble she had, the worse things got. Friedman saw it
coming. Balancing the staff's loyalty to Jane with the fact that he had
had nothing at all to do with the selection of Hartley, and the fact that
he was also still the executive producer of the show, he did what he
thought was best: He gave her only those kinds of pieces he thought she
could handle—among them were a piece on the real high school
depicted in the movie *Fame*, which was a hit at the time, and a story
on a blind golfers' tournament, about which she would publicly com-
plain after she left the show.

I booked a spot with Blackstone the magician, who was appearing on

Broadway at the time, for her. She liked him. It was the kind of performance she was good at, and she felt comfortable ad-libbing with him. Willard joined them both. He was the perfect foil.

First Blackstone made a few things disappear. Then he sawed her in half, with a solid steel blade, live in the studio. As if he needed an encore, he managed to steal Willard's watch and then his shirt—right out from under his size-fifty jacket—to the astonishment of the bemused, now half-naked weatherman.

Blackstone brought out the best in Mariette. Everyone liked the performance so much that Friedman told me to book Blackstone again two more times before Hartley's three weeks were up. By the time Blackstone came back the second time, I think Friedman was hoping that he might saw Hartley in half for real.

Day by day, Hartley's "audition" deteriorated. As Friedman saw the trouble she was having, he pulled the reins in more, to avoid the deeply embarrassing moments that only live TV can provide. You could sense her discomfort on the set next to Brokaw and it made you even more uncomfortable than she was. She was digging herself in deeper by the minute. Friedman felt he had to be careful about what he gave Mariette to do. "I can't have her talking about heroin or SALT Two," he told us at one of our weekly staff meetings. "And I can't give her Henry Kissinger or some senator to interview either. She's not used to this, and people just coming in like that tend to be gaga about public figures—and the interview becomes a filibuster. She does very well with the one-legged football players and the blind golfers. Let's leave it at that."

Hartley understandably felt abandoned and disliked. She believed we were out to get her, before it was even true. Perhaps it became a self-fulfilling prophecy. Even Jane's assistant, Ann Schlitt, says she tried to be helpful at first, but she accidentally told Hartley she liked the Kodak commercials (they were Polaroid).

In the beginning, Brokaw made a feeble attempt, but he gave up quickly, too: "I tried to be civil to her, and I introduced her to one of my daughters, Andrea, and they went to the theater, and we tried to make her comfortable and happy, but it was just clear that she hadn't read a newspaper or watched morning television for a long time, and she kept coming up with ideas that we had been doing for a while," he said.

Hartley saw it differently: "I came from California, which meant I consulted channelers, consorted with beach balls, and had bikini brains," she said. "I was not only from California, but I was a woman from California. I was not only a woman from California, but I was an actress from California, the triple crown of imbecility."

After struggling through a few days with Hartley on the air and Arlene Dayton off, Brokaw gave up the fight. One day he realized the whole thing was a setup. "Jane had gone away and Fred Silverman was pushing Mariette very hard. I think that he was determined to get rid of me as well. I felt very protective towards Jane. I thought that it was just unfair to let her leave town and then try to take her job away," he recalls.

Brokaw defends himself against Mariette's charges that he tried to undermine her. "I didn't sabotage the woman as she's accused me of doing," he insists. "I just thought she was absolutely wrong for the *Today* show. She was much too hot as a personality, she didn't care about the issues that we were concerned about. Her big contribution was flapping her skirt at Willard, so I was just trying to hang onto the dignity of the program. Mariette and her manager just swept in like they were going to take over the show. I thought, the hell with that."

Willard, champion of the underdog, felt sorry for Hartley, and he had a slightly different perception of the situation: "I saw things done from the control room that really tripped her up," he says. "She hadn't done live television before. Nobody helped her. They let her hang. I saw them go out of their way in a couple of instances to really screw her up."

Before Hartley's stint was up, Arlene Dayton pulled Ann Schlitt aside and told her not to worry, that they didn't want Jane's job. As it turned out, Jane's contract was renewed before she returned from her honeymoon. She got not only a two-year guarantee but a substantial raise as well.

Still, after she left the show, Hartley insisted time and again she had been sabotaged by the staff of *Today*, which by then she referred to as the *Titanic*, and that Silverman had indeed offered her Jane's job: "NBC president Fred Silverman told me he would change my life," she told *Parade* magazine only weeks after she had left the show, "and he proceeded to offer me a five-to-seven-year contract to replace Jane Pauley as cohost of the *Today* show."

Several years later, in her autobiography, *Breaking the Silence*, her recollection of events changed substantially: "To put it mildly, I was not terribly accepted," she wrote. "I was filling in for Jane Pauley while she was on her honeymoon, and there were rumors that I was to replace her. No one knew the true story including me."

Steve Friedman says that to this day he has no way of knowing what happened for sure. "We assumed that Mariette was there to replace Jane while she was on her honeymoon. Nobody told us it was a tryout or that she was promised a job. I don't know that she was. Fred Silverman swears to me that she was promised nothing, that they were looking at Mariette as a person for the network and that *Today* was done as a vehicle. I think all the stories about Mariette Hartley were probably made up by Mariette Hartley. As far as I knew she was there to replace Jane for five weeks."

And then there is Jane's point of view: "I came back from my honeymoon and found out that Fred Silverman had offered Mariette Hartley my job. He called me to tell me he didn't and she swore that he did, and you tell me what is the truth."

Whatever the truth, one thing was certain: the celebrity fever that had parlayed *People* magazine into a gigantic publishing success, and transformed *GMA* to number one from an inconsequential second place in the morning race, had begun to insinuate itself wickedly into virtually every form of the media, and it was not about to spare the *Today* show.

Journalism was changing, tilting sharply towards the stars. Celebrity names spelled ratings and money. The bigger the name, the more the take. Those who bucked this new system would lose. It simply wasn't economical.

Celebrity journalism, this new amalgam of celebrities, information, and entertainment, now referred to as "infotainment," was firmly establishing its place in history. Nowhere was it more apparent than in the changes this phenomenon brought about on the venerable *Today* show.

The Hartley debacle had signaled the future. Right on its heels came the Rona Barrett affair, a move precisely consistent with the incipient consumption of the *Today* show by show business.

Miss Rona was stolen right out from under the noses of ABC executives in a plan masterminded by Fred Silverman's protégé, Brandon Tartikoff, who had been handpicked and groomed for the job of president of NBC Entertainment—which he had been awarded in January 1980—by Silverman himself.

Rona Barrett, the petite, made-over, blond, inside-Hollywood entity who purveyed a brand of gossip which she insisted (and sometimes rightly so) was industry news, had had a lifelong desire to be a legitimate newsperson, but had always teetered precariously on the wrong side of the border between Hollywood gossip and entertainment news. Still, she had undeniably been a boon to the ratings at GMA, where she had appeared once an hour and drawn viewers with her inside track into celebrities' lives and affairs—be they sexual or business.

At the beginning of 1980, when Rona's contract with ABC was about to expire, Brandon Tartikoff got a brilliant idea: He would hire her away to be cohost of the *Tomorrow* show with Tom Snyder, a late-night hour-long show which was enjoying a moderate degree of success at NBC and was about to expand to ninety minutes. Snyder was in New York. Barrett would appear from the West Coast, at NBC in Burbank. Tartikoff's plan was twofold: He would also use her on the *Today* show the same way she had appeared on GMA, reporting Hollywood "news" and doing celebrity interviews.

This particular combination made it possible to pay Barrett what she required, which was more than NBC News alone could afford. The bulk of Barrett's salary could be paid out of the Entertainment Division, since the *Tomorrow* show was under its auspices. NBC News—specifically *Today*—would then only have to supplement a small portion of her salary and Rona could enjoy all of the frills and accoutrements of the Entertainment Division (which was where the money was) to which she had already become accustomed at ABC.

Everybody was pleased with the deal, with the exception of Tom Brokaw, whom Barrett insists had hated her since his days as a local anchorman in L.A. when she had appeared on a show he was hosting. Rona Barrett was happy because she would now be what she considered to be the true Queen of the Morning. She had, after all, been so desirable she had been stolen from one show by the other. Barrett herself admitted in her autobiography that she had always aspired to royalty of a kind, having felt inferior most of her life to legitimate Hollywood stars. Friedman was happy because he was convinced that she would help the ratings. Jane Pauley had no problem with Rona either. So when Tom Brokaw made it clear from the outset he wanted nothing to do with Miss Rona, emphasizing the fact that he would *never*, under any circumstances, even introduce her on the air, Jane agreed to do it.

Brokaw grudgingly admitted he understood that there was a place for Rona on the *Today* show, but he had no qualms about saying he didn't want it to be *his* place. He did not want to be associated with Miss Rona in any way at all. He was worried about going too far in the direction of what he referred to as "cheap gossip and the other devalued coin of the moment."

Reflecting on that time, he sees it this way: "Part of the problem was that I came from a traditional hard-news background and brought those instincts to the *Today* show, and then the rules began to change in the morning and we never had any kind of strategy sessions. No one would come down from on high and say, 'Hey, listen guys, we've got to take a look at what we're doing here.' So I was just finding my way through it as best I could while being loyal to my own instincts and my own interests. And I just knew that I didn't want my career wrapped up in Rona's."

There were already murmurs that Brokaw wanted to leave *Today* when his contract expired—but that would not happen for over a year.

Silverman was still disgruntled. He showed his dissatisfaction by publicly describing the *Today* show now as a "mausoleum." In some ways Friedman agreed with him. He knew the show was dull, but he did not blame it on Tom and Jane. He was in the gradual process of carrying out his overall plan, but he could not do it all overnight. He was bringing in a new director, Julian Finkelstein, whom he had known, worked with, and admired when he had been at NBC in Burbank, and he ordered a new, more upbeat set (minus the familiar New York skyline), which would finally materialize the following November at a cost of $160,000.

Friedman was making other changes, too: There would no longer be a separate newsreader—Brokaw would read the news; he was counting on Willard Scott, the weatherman, to add the essential quality of folksiness to *Today*, something that was an obvious strong suit for *GMA*. Bryant Gumbel, who had become known and liked as a network sportscaster, would also do three sports segments a week on the show; and, above all, an attempt would be made to emphasize that *Today* consisted of one big happy family: Tom, Jane, Gene Shalit, and Willard. They would all be sitting more closely together than ever on the new set.

Brokaw's feelings notwithstanding, the Barrett deal was a coup for NBC and *Today*. Rona would start on *Tomorrow* with Tom Snyder in October 1980. Three months later, she would begin appearing on *Today*.

I remember the day Rona came to New York to meet the staff. She was my height (five feet two inches), but there was something about her that looked like a caricature. Maybe it was the way her blond hair appeared to be molded like clay around her head. Even off camera, she moved as though she only wanted you to look at her from one angle; on camera, she had always insisted she only be shot from one side. She was intriguing to watch in action—the way she interacted with the staff, especially the men. She was obviously adept at manipulating them to get exactly what she wanted.

After Rona Barrett's deal was made, everything went swimmingly—for about two minutes. Barrett and her staff got fancy offices at NBC in Burbank—unlike anything on the *Today* show or in the News Department anywhere at NBC, where space was always at a premium. They even built a private bathroom for Rona—in Hollywood private bathrooms were status symbols—and that became a joke around the office because the ladies' room was just a few feet down the hall.

The ratings improved as Brandon Tartikoff and Steve Friedman had hoped they would, helped by NBC's airing of the blockbuster television movie *Shōgun* with Richard Chamberlain, as well as the World Series, which was also a huge ratings draw. It had always been a common assumption that the better a network did in primetime, the better it would do in the morning—the theory being that people would leave their TV dials where they had been the night before.

Almost as quickly as it had come to fruition, the Barrett deal began to crumble. Rona's debut interview for *Tomorrow* was with Mary Tyler Moore. There was no doubt that Rona Barrett was *good* at celebrity interviews. George Merlis, the executive producer of *GMA* at the time that Barrett had been hired away by *Today*, explained the Rona Barrett quotient: "Only Rona would have asked certain questions. Only Rona would have asked Gregory Peck about his son's suicide. Only Rona would have asked Rock Hudson about the hoax marriage where invitations were sent out for the marriage of Rock Hudson and Jim Nabors. Only Rona would have asked David Bowie about his bisexuality."

The Mary Tyler Moore interview was in keeping with Rona's reputation. It was taped and ready to go early, before it was scheduled to air. But then a tragedy occurred: Mary Tyler Moore's son committed suicide only moments before the air date, and she had discussed her son at length in the interview with Rona when he was still very much alive. Understandably, the interview could not be aired as it had been taped. It was pegged to the film *Ordinary People*, and too much of it had centered around her son. It could not be used at all. The idiosyncratic, egocentric Snyder exploded. After only a few weeks, the already precarious Snyder-Barrett bubble had burst.

Snyder was mad at Rona now. It had taken Tartikoff's cunning, manipulative ability to convince Snyder he should share his show with Rona Barrett in the first place. Now Snyder decided abruptly that she wasn't a cohost, but merely an insert. According to Coby Atlas, who had been Barrett's writer and producer at *GMA* and went with her to the *Today* show—and would become the first female senior producer of the show six years later—"Snyder got scared, and whatever Tartikoff had convinced Snyder to do for the good of the show fell apart the moment Snyder realized he had to do it."

Things went slightly better for Rona on *Today*, but only slightly. Brokaw stuck fast to his refusal to introduce Rona. Jane made the introduction graciously, twice a day, three times a week, when Rona appeared at 7:50 and again at 8:20.

That was not the only problem. There was an added technical difficulty. Rona Barrett had always insisted that she be shot not only from the right side, but with the "contours" taken out of the camera, and she was not about to change now. Doing this blurred the video, dissolving lines and wrinkles and making everything slightly fuzzy, so that it gave Miss Rona an almost ethereal quality. She looked as though she were broadcasting her report directly from heaven. The problem was that as you watched the show, as your eyes went from Jane, who was computer focused as sharply as a tack, to Rona, who was in a kind of Vaseline blur, it was a shock to your system until your eyes adjusted.

By April, less than six months after she had begun, Rona Barrett walked off the *Tomorrow* show. Things had become unworkable between the two incompatible personalities and, fairly or unfairly, Rona got the worst rap. Everyone on the *Tomorrow* show claimed she had been impossible to work with. Although Snyder was certainly no angel either, he was surrounded by old friends who were part of what was known as the "Burbank Mafia" from his years in L.A.—Steve Friedman and Tom Brokaw among them.

Rona declares she was lied to from the start. "From the first day and night it was a disaster," she told me more than a decade after the fact, still intensely bitter about the way she was treated by the men at NBC. "They lied to me." She is certain of this. "They were supposed to bring aboard a new producer and instead they kept Tom Synder's girlfriend on, so it was not an equitable situation."

Both Friedman and Grant Tinker (who had replaced Silverman as president of NBC by this time) were willing—and perhaps even anxious—to keep Rona on *Today*. The deal that Tartikoff had made now backfired. Most of Rona's salary had been coming from the *Tomorrow* show. She had been making $500,000 a year when they had stolen her from *GMA*, and besides that, ABC had been paying for her staff. The overall NBC deal had paid her over $500,000, but now that the burden for Rona's salary was entirely on *Today* and therefore NBC News, they offered her less than $150,000 a year and an additional $40,000 for her seven-member staff. Rona contends this would have left her in the hole.

"It was fucking insulting. Insulting!" she yelled angrily, as she recalled the way she had been treated. "When I said to Grant, 'I'll stay on the *Today* show if you want me, but you're going to have to make it more equitable,' he said, 'Oh, I don't want to get into that.'

" 'If you can't get into it, who can?' I asked him."

So Rona quit. "He tracked me all the way down to the beauty parlor. He had everybody at NBC chasing me to find me when I quit, to beg me to come back, and he caught me with my hair in rollers at the beauty salon."

Tinker was not willing to budge; Steve made no effort to fight for Rona, and Tom Brokaw just sat back and watched, smiling. To this day, Rona believes she was treated unfairly. "I wasn't asking for five million dollars," she says, "or even a million. But that was the convenient issue. That is what they told everybody. 'Rona's impossible, she wants too much money.'

"I feel like the Barbra Streisands and the Goldie Hawns and everybody else in this town. The minute they ask for something that's rightfully theirs—or should be—they're difficult, impossible bitches."

She is certain that there was a conspiracy against her, led by the powerful Hollywood agent Ed Hookstratten, who handled both Brokaw and Snyder, and later, Bryant Gumbel as well.

"Think about it," she told me, when I asked her about what had happened. "Who handled Tom Brokaw? Who handled Tom Snyder? Who handled most of the NBC News people? Ed Hookstratten. When the thing with Tom Snyder fell apart they blamed me. It was, 'Let's get Rona.' Brokaw hated me. From day one he never wanted me on NBC."

Steve Friedman says he let Rona go for a reason that will pain her to this day. As hard as she tried, she could not seem to escape the gossip corner into which she had been boxed. That was the very thing Steve wanted from her, and had she been willing to give him pure Hollywood gossip, he would have fought much harder to keep her.

"Rona and I had a strong relationship," he told me. "But she didn't want to do what made Rona famous, she wanted to do industry business. And when the *Tomorrow* show got canceled, I wasn't going to pick up the full bill for that kind of reporting, so we came to a parting of the ways."

In spite of the difficulties with Mariette Hartley and Rona Barrett, the year had not been all bad. With the ongoing hostage crisis, the Soviet invasion of Afghanistan, the political conventions, and the fact that it was an election year, *Today* had made some headway. When it came to covering news events, it was still the hands-down winner. *Today* always managed to get news scoops, sometimes even beating out *Nightly News*. Billy Carter had divulged his Libyan connections on *Today* and Gerald Ford had let the Republican convention know that he might be interested in becoming vice president again.

So for a time the ratings flip-flopped. *GMA* would win and then *Today* would outdo them (usually because of a major news event, as they did during the Republican Convention coverage, for instance), which would put *Today* back on top again, if only fleetingly. It went on like that for a while. With the new viewers that *GMA* had attracted and the fact that the year was crammed with compelling news events, the total viewing audience was the largest it had ever been.

At GMA, David Hartman's ego was expanding faster than the audience. He was enjoying his newfound stature and was rapidly acquiring a stronger hand in the show, to the dismay of many of those who worked with him. In the course of his precipitous rise, he had mistreated many people on the show. It had gotten so bad that the staff had been delighted during one Hartman interview when Muhammad Ali had referred to Hartman as "The Great White Dope." It was becoming more widely known that Hartman treated the people—especially the women—he worked with poorly. Sandy Hill, his first cohost, got fed up with him and left in 1980. When Joan Lunden replaced her, one staffer explained that the reason Lunden would get along well with Hartman was that she would be no threat to him whatsoever: "She's risen because she's a pretty girl with an empty head who doesn't bother anybody. If you told her to jump off the Brooklyn Bridge, she'd ask you what time she should be there and when the limousine would pick her up afterward."

Even at CBS, things were finally beginning to percolate. The network had never been a serious contender in the morning race because the *CBS Morning News* was only an hour long, from seven to eight. For over a quarter of a century it had shared the two-hour period with *Captain Kangaroo*. In spite of this, when Charles Kuralt was named to take over the show in October the ratings went up a whole point, which for CBS translated to a 40 percent increase.

For me, things were going well. After less than six months, Steve called me in and offered me a one-year contract, which I interpreted as a vote of confidence. Bookings like Elizabeth Taylor, Bette Davis, and Linda Ronstadt, along with John Travolta, Peter Ustinov, Roger Moore, Jack Lemmon, and Billy Joel, quickly paid off for me. I even managed to get Paul Newman's daughter—unfortunately without her father. Now Steve gave me an assistant, who could do the time-consuming technical aspects of the job. Her name was Nancy Fields, and she looked like a dark-haired Raggedy Ann doll with her painted-on lashes and big oversized glasses. Nancy worried for me, panicked when she thought something was wrong—and then took care of it. She fended off the unwanted phone calls ingeniously, and was, without a doubt, the most loyal person in the world. She had been at the *Today* show quite possibly longer than any other human being— she had been secretary to many of the show's producers for almost thirty years. For me she was a blessing.

Nancy organized my life at work in a way I hadn't known was possible. I had been so overwhelmed by trying to handle my work load by myself that I was using not only both desks in my office but both telephones as well.

Now Steve gave me a new office, too. It was perfect, I thought. Right next to his, overlooking the skating rink, warm and cozy, with a carpet on the floor and wooden shutters on the window, my own TV set, a couch, a refrigerator, and Nancy Fields parked right outside, willing to do anything for me. I thought I had it made. I had made it through my initiation and I thought I knew what I was up against.

What I didn't know at the time was that ABC had just hired a champion booker—the Mother of All Bookers, perhaps—a woman by the name of Ellin Sanger, who took her job no less seriously than finding a cure for cancer. She would quickly become my nemesis, like a little black cloud parked permanently above my head, outsmarting me at every turn. There was nothing she would not do to get a guest, and although I did not know it at the time, I would learn my lesson the hard way.

But at that moment, at the end of the year, we on the new staff that Steve had hired were finding our way and liking it. We liked our new incarnation—we were the loyal disciples of Steve Friedman, patriotic warriors in the battle for the morning.

December 12, 1980. It was an icy cold night in Manhattan and I was sound asleep, nestled safely in my cozy down comforter, when the piercing ring of the telephone by my bed split the air, jarring me back into reality. I reached for the phone, groping in the darkness, wondering why it had rung. This call would be my initiation into the symbiosis of crisis and morning television.

"Judy, this is Mark Kusnetz." The soft, vaguely familiar voice tried to ease its way into my consciousness. "Why is Mark Kusnetz calling me?" I wondered hypnotically, trying to make the transition from the security of my protective sleep to the voice that had invaded it.

"John Lennon has been shot. He's dead."

"What?" I mumbled, trying to absorb what I thought he had said, but it was difficult to make the connection. Mark Kusnetz, the handsome, sensitive writer, the writer on the show who was closest to Tom Brokaw, was aware that what he was doing—imparting this dreadful news in the middle of the night—was painful, but he had a job to do.

He went on. "He has just been shot by a crazy man in front of his apartment." A pause. There was no time for emotion now. "We have to put a show together," he said.

It was a little after midnight and Mark Kusnetz had just arrived at 30 Rock, in a state of semishock that graciously allowed him to function. The minute the news of the shooting had come over the AP wire in the NBC News offices, Don Snyder, who manned the overnight news desk, followed the normal procedure of notifying top executives. Since the *Today* show would be the first on the air, he called Friedman first, who in turn called Cliff Kappler, his third in command, under Marty Ryan. (Kappler lived in town, while Ryan lived forty-five minutes away, and there was no time to waste.)

Friedman had done what he had to do—he had put the people he wanted in charge—and decided to grab a few hours of much needed sleep before coming into the studio at the usual time, around 4 A.M.

It was Kappler who broke the news to Kusnetz and told him that he was in charge. Now Kusnetz had less than seven hours to get a show together about the death of John Lennon, which would be the way millions of Americans would learn for the first time of the senseless murder.

It was the first time I had experienced this from the other side—I had always wondered as a viewer how the show had gotten on in the morning when what I was watching on the TV screen had not even happened by the time I had gone to bed.

I was about to find out firsthand.

"Who do you know who knows Lennon? Who are your Beatles contacts?" Kusnetz asked me solemnly. "I need you to make some calls."

Phase one had begun: lining up guests for the show; starting from scratch, seeing whom you could reach at this hour; trying to get them to talk, arranging logistics if they agreed; and then putting them all into some kind of order that made sense for a two-hour show.

Now I was awake. I grabbed my brown leather book, which was filled with my most precious contacts and phone numbers I had culled from my Rolodex at work, and I looked quickly for the names—record company executives, managers, and agents—I thought could be helpful.

"Shall I come in or call from here?" I asked Kusnetz.

"Make the calls from home," he told me. "That will save time. We'll stay in touch by phone. Then we'll see where we are."

Kusnetz had already called Cindy Samuels, who was on her way to the office. Of all of us, she was the quintessential child of the sixties. She was more tuned in to the Beatles' generation than the Beatles themselves. She had the heart, the soul, and the consciousness that characterized the era that most of the new members of the *Today* staff had grown up in.

What made the Lennon crisis so intense and set it apart for us was that it was the first major tragedy that really belonged to us. President Kennedy's assassination was traumatic, but this was a man our own age. It was the first time we had lost one of our own, perhaps the first time we had felt our own mortality, and it took on a significance in proportion to that fact. The impact was profound.

It occurred to me then that a situation like this brought out the best—and the worst—of what our job was. It was one of those tragic moments that transformed caring, sensitive human beings into fighting animals seeking the same prey. It did not matter at that instant that

Paul McCartney had suffered a shocking personal loss. If you could find him, you would somehow reach down deep inside yourself to find the words to beg him to do your show. After all, this was television, the despicable part of it at that, when reporters would stick microphones in the face of a grieving mother whose child had just been killed, or ask the victim of a stabbing, whose throat had just been slashed, how she felt about her assailant.

These were the pivotal moments of morning television—as much as you hated to admit it, the most exciting times, the times that caused your adrenaline to flow. When tragedy struck, when the unexpected happened, it was not only news, but fodder for morning television ratings, because that was the place the public could always learn more about what had happened.

We did not really care who we got that night. We needed bodies to fill the airtime, and the better known those bodies were, the more famous, the better. With time as important as it was, anybody who could talk about John Lennon—or give us some insight into what had happened—would do, whether it be a reporter who knew him, a psychiatrist who could talk about the crazy man who shot him, or a musician who could talk about the impact of the Beatles' music. Anything. There was no time to be picky.

We did not get McCartney.

I reached two of the people I wanted, one of whom was a well-known manager and the other an executive at CBS Records. I was lucky to have their home numbers. One was awake and aware of what had happened. I woke up the record executive, and she burst into tears when I told her about Lennon, but I got the numbers of producers and executives in London from her and called them in to Mark and Cindy. Then I headed for the office myself.

Meanwhile, Mark and Cindy had already summoned the writers they wanted to put taped pieces together and do whatever else needed to be done. Other staffers came too, as they heard the news, if only for their own comfort, or to pour coffee for their colleagues.

Everyone was scrambling to see whom they could come up with. As we reached different people, the rundown for the show kept changing. Although it must appear smooth and seamless when it aired, changes could be made throughout the show if we wanted. If we got a better guest for the 8:10 slot—if Paul McCartney had suddenly agreed to talk, for instance—we could have put him in as late as 8:09 and thrown out what had been there.

There was electricity crackling in the air, spurred by the ironic combination of excitement and sorrow. It was the magnetic, bonding electricity of a shared trauma. We were all distraught, but we were drawn together not only by our pain, but by a common job to do.

Kusnetz did his job well, but he had to solve the question of how to put the show together, and what to do in an extremely short period of time. There were two things he knew that had to be done. First, the news aspect of the story, which had already been set in motion by the news desk, had to be taken care of completely. NBC correspondent Steven Frazier was already out with a crew, covering the news events that were unfolding at Lennon's apartment (the legendary Dakota on Seventy-second and Central Park West) and the hospital where Lennon had been taken.

The more creative job, our job, was the "show" side, the features that would make the show unique: the guests, the taped pieces—whatever we could come up with. As Kusnetz pondered this problem, he suddenly realized what he needed: pictures of John Lennon—pictures that captured the essence of both the man and the music of the Beatles.

Logistically, things were tough at three o'clock in the morning. Libraries and bookstores were not possibilities. NBC itself could be of little help. Aside from available videotape of former appearances, the NBC archives had little to offer in this instance. Resources were limited—we had to be creative. Kusnetz knew exactly where to get what he needed. He had his own collection of Beatles books. So he took off for his apartment in the eerie, quiet darkness of Manhattan, grabbed his books, an oddly consoling action, and returned to the office to get them prepared for air.

The show was set before the sun came up. We had gotten a Beatles record producer in London, a colleague in Copenhagen, and a reporter from *Rolling Stone* in New York. We had put together several taped feature pieces on Lennon and the Beatles, and those would round out the show. Somehow it had gotten done in the nick of time, as it always did.

At seven that morning, the *Today* show told the unsuspecting people watching it—those, like me, who had been asleep when it happened—about John Lennon's death. The viewers were not the only ones who watched riveted to the screen. His work done now, Kusnetz along with the rest of the staff could let down and feel the despair of the tragedy that had somehow eluded us while we worked. Exhausted and frazzled, Kusnetz entered the dark control room to watch the show he had helped create. The two hours floated by, surrealistically, in keeping with the mood of the previous night, and then the end of the show began to roll: Picture after picture of John Lennon—Kusnetz's pictures—lingered on the screen, as the song "Imagine" played mournfully in the background. His emotions began to rise. At that moment, he glanced up at the monitor that showed the camera aimed at Jane. The director could not use this shot, because tears were streaming uncontrollably down her face. She put her head down on the desk and cried like a child as Brokaw stood by and stared at her with a stricken look on his face.

"It was as if they had put my youth in a box and closed it," Jane recalled many years later. At that moment, in Mark Kusnetz's words, "Jane had become totally unglued."

Brokaw kept it together. Later he told me how certain he was of the importance of that show in another sense. In his mind it was the thing that brought together the relatively new staff of *Today*, those of us whom Steve Friedman had hired, in a strong and permanent way. We were in this for the long haul now, but as we would soon find out, Brokaw himself was not.

F o u r

BYE-BYE BROKAW

I met Tom Brokaw in 1971 when I worked for *The Washington Post* in L.A. My boss, Roy Aarons, had introduced me to a group of journalists in L.A. that included Tom and Meredith Brokaw; Steve Roberts, a reporter for *The New York Times*; his wife, Cokie (who is now an ABC news correspondent); Karl Fleming, who was then head of the *Newsweek* bureau in L.A., and his soon-to-be wife, Anne Taylor Fleming, a writer. We all became friends—we had a lot in common.

But Brokaw was outstanding. By the time I met him, he was already the anchor of the eleven o'clock news on KNBC, the local affiliate in Los Angeles. To me, he appeared to be the perfect man: great looking, with his dark hair and intense brown eyes, all underscored by his irresistible boyish quality; athletic, curious, interesting. He was smooth as ice, but smart as well.

As if that weren't enough, he had what appeared to me to be the perfect wife, Meredith, who had not only been his high-school sweetheart, but Miss South Dakota as well. So of course, they had the perfect family: three beautiful daughters, Andrea, Jennifer, and Sarah. All this might have been simply too much to bear if the Brokaws hadn't been so nice.

If you went back a few years, you could find a few tiny flaws in Brokaw's otherwise perfect life. He had not been a perfect football player (at Yankton High School, in South Dakota, where he grew up), and he certainly hadn't been a perfect student. He dropped out of college twice, in fact—from the University of Iowa, and then the University of South Dakota. But he did go back and he did finish, getting his degree from USD in political science, in 1962.

He came from a modest family; his father was a foreman on a U.S. Army Corps of Engineers dam, and his mother worked too, in the post office and later in a shoe store. Tom was the eldest of three boys, and like the rest of his family, he did his share. By the time he was fifteen, in 1955, he got himself a job after school as an announcer—he was more like a disc jockey—at a Yankton radio station. When he graduated from college, he got a job as a television reporter for the local NBC affiliate in Omaha and then went on to a better job in Atlanta in 1965. A year later, he landed the job in Los Angeles.

In the City of Angels, Tom and Meredith had what seemed to many to be the perfect existence. Brokaw quickly wrapped L.A. around his little finger. Besides having looks and overabundant charm, he was an excellent reporter and a good anchorman. He could handle any kind of story from politics to the arts. He knew everybody there was to know. They were on the A-list for every important party in town.

At thirty, in spite of the fact that he worked all day and anchored the eleven o'clock news five nights a week, he never ran out of energy. He loved skiing, tennis, and jogging, he was a fanatic about mountain climbing, and above all, he was ruggedly adventurous. The more daunting the challenge, the more he liked it; the higher the risk, the happier he was. In 1970, on a whitewater rafting trip down Idaho's Salmon River with several guys, the raft struck a log and overturned, and one of his close friends was killed. Brokaw was understandably shaken, but even that did not stop him at all.

No matter how sophisticated he became, as he ascended rapidly in the world of television, he still had that bit of country boy in him and he was hopelessly in love with the great outdoors.

After seven years in Los Angeles, the Brokaws were ready to settle there for good. They had decided to build themselves an imposing house on the beach in Malibu (which they would never even move into) when the call from on high came. Brokaw had covered civil-rights stories in Atlanta (which often ended up on *The Huntley-Brinkley Report*), and stories in L.A. that included the assassination of Senator Robert Kennedy, the 1971 earthquake, and the gubernatorial campaigns of Ronald Reagan and Edmund Brown, Jr. He had grown impressively as a journalist. He was fascinated by politics and was an astute political reporter. His talents did not go unnoticed by the executives at NBC.

In 1973, the big break came—the chance to go from local TV to the network: Brokaw was asked to become White House correspondent for NBC. Even though it meant taking a pay cut from $100,000 to $65,000 a year, he clearly saw himself as a "political junkie." So Mr. Brokaw went to Washington, where Watergate was the story of the hour, not only captivating him, but helping him hone his political talents even more. He had it all: the glamour, knowledge, and clout of Hollywood and the savvy and political contacts of Washington—a pretty powerful package.

When *Today* host Frank McGee died in 1974, Brokaw was considered for the job, but he saw himself first and foremost as a journalist, and he adamantly refused to do commercials on *Today*. Jim Hartz took over instead. The network finally caved in. Brokaw was invaluable. They needed him and they knew it. So in 1976, he got his way; he began as the sole host of the troubled *Today* show on August 30, 1976. And he did not have to do commercials.

Now that he had established beyond a doubt his credentials as a journalist, Brokaw would soon make a further transformation. Like almost everyone who hosts the *Today* show—from Dave Garroway to Barbara Walters to Hugh Downs—he would become a celebrity himself.

I refer to it as the *"Today* show host syndrome." It seems to go with the territory. You cannot spend ten hours a week on TV in a job that forces you to interact with everyone from the president and vice president of the United States to members of the cabinet to the biggest sports heroes in the world to foreign dignitaries to heads of state to the most famous movie stars, musicians, and artists, without gaining a stature that automatically catapults you into the same arena as those you're covering.

Brokaw had the kind of charm that could win people over in droves. Andrea Smith, his first assistant at *Today* (who later became a producer on the show), gave up a chance for an on-camera job just to work with him. Andrea was perfect for Tom. She once spent an entire year making a collage of Brokaw's life. She was like a comedian, sort of a cross between Bette Midler and Lily Tomlin, pretty, with dark straight hair, a narrow face, and a wonderful sense of humor.

She never regretted her decision to take that job. Not only did she get to go with Tom to cover trips like the space shuttle and the aftermath of the shooting of Anwar Sadat in Egypt, she got other perks as well. Brokaw appreciated Andrea, and was the kind of boss who went out of his way to make the people who worked for him happy.

One day, when Robert Redford was coming to New York, Brokaw wanted to do something nice for Andrea. He had an idea that he knew would make her happy, and he called her up to tell her. "I have a big surprise for you, Andrea," he said. "Robert Redford's coming to town and he wants to keep it real quiet, but I'm going to let you pick him up at the airport."

Andrea was so excited that she forgot one crucial thing: She forgot she could not drive. She was contemplating her options, maybe even a crash course in driving, when her phone rang again. It was Brokaw. "I just realized you can't drive for shit."

"You mean I can't pick up Robert Redford?" Andrea said.

"I'll tell you what," said Brokaw, thinking. "I'll send a car for him and you can be in it."

Then there was the time in 1979 when Tom Brokaw saved John Chancellor's life. They were at an NBC luncheon for Governor John Connally of Texas (whose press secretary at the time was James Brady), when Chancellor began choking on a piece of Gouda cheese that had gotten lodged in his throat. Fast on his feet as always, Brokaw grabbed him and performed the Heimlich maneuver, successfully dislodging the cheese. Chancellor not only survived, but never forgot it. He repaid Brokaw a few years later, when he stepped down as anchor of the *Nightly News* six months earlier than his contract had stipulated, so that Tom Brokaw could take over.

Brokaw grew in many ways during his tenure at *Today*. But after five years, what he had grown, more than anything else, was frustrated. Interviews like the one with Rutger Hauer and another vapid one he did with *Dallas* star Charlene Tilton about a new diet she was on (which she made clear in the interview was the thing around which her entire life revolved) finally had a role in driving him away.

Brokaw's desire to leave was increasing every day. He saw a future for himself beyond the *Today* show. Since his contract would not be up until December 1981, he had plenty of time to contemplate his next move. Before he had barely even begun to think about it, the other networks started coming to him.

A veritable onslaught of network executives began to woo Tom Brokaw. First it was CBS. They desperately wanted him to leave NBC for their network. When ABC got wind of this, they got into the game as well. All this had a profound effect: "ABC started talking to me and put on a kind of four-wall operation," recalls Brokaw. "They were really selling hard about coming to ABC, and that just raised my sights in a way about the other things that I could do with my life."

So the ball was in motion, and the rumors were flying. Only one thing was certain. If Brokaw did decide to leave, his departure would have a very detrimental effect on the rallying *Today* show.

———

By the time the networks began flirting with Brokaw, I had been at the *Today* show almost a year—a year which I would someday look back upon as my Golden Year—the best year I would have at *Today*.

In spite of the growing pressure of the competition, I had landed some good guests. One of the most memorable was Richard Burton, whom I was able to convince to do the *Today* show largely because of Burton's affinity for Gene Shalit. Burton was an exquisite guest, but when Shalit seized the opportunity to ask him to read from the Manhattan phone book, the interview skyrocketed to the sublime.

It had been totally unplanned. Shalit had said to Burton, "I always heard that if Richard Burton got on stage and read the yellow pages, he would fill the theater."

"I did it once, at the YMHA," Burton had replied.

At which point Shalit produced the only phone book around (which happened to be the white pages) and handed it to him to read.

Burton reached for the book dramatically, and began reading it as though it had been written by Shakespeare. He had opened it, by chance, to the *H*'s: "Hoffman, Lauren," he read, his piercing blue eyes looking upward, the color beginning to flush his face. Then, softly, passionately: "Six-six-oh, two-one-seven-one."

He went on: "Hoffman, Theodore . . ." Then, in a louder voice, "Eight-two-eight, one-three-two-one." And then, as only Burton could have done, he created a play within a play: "Are the Hoffmans related, these two Hoffmans," he pondered seriously, "or are there so many Hoffmans in the world that they actually live in the same city and are only ten lines from each other? These Hoffmans, are they old? Are they young? Is one female? The other is obviously a man."

And finally, *sotto voce*, "I think we should arrange for them to meet."

Burton's performance had been unforgettable, a one and only. Even my Bette Davis coup and the two-part interview Mildred had finagled for me with Elizabeth Taylor paled by comparison. Nobody complained about them though. And things had actually picked up, ratings-wise. *Today* now looked as though it might even have a chance at coming back and beating *GMA*.

After nearly a year and what must surely have been five million phone calls later, I was admittedly tired and I needed a vacation. What I really wanted was a few weeks in which I didn't have to see or talk to a publicist or think about a movie star.

The man I was in love with and about to marry, Harold Hayes, the legendary editor of *Esquire* magazine and also a highly respected authority and writer on wildlife conservation, wanted me to go to Africa with him in February. What a perfect trip that would be—you couldn't get much farther away! I would have to be gone for three weeks—a considerable amount of time—but when I asked Steve if I could go, he said yes, of course I could.

On Fridays, we had staff meetings that were Friedman's creations. They were pep talks more than meetings—General Friedman rallying the troops. We would all sit around the conference table in a room upstairs, several floors above our offices, and Friedman would sit at the head of the table and stick his feet up, and we would stare at the bottoms of his shoes, as usual, with The Book in front of him. Even when the ratings were at their worst, he would launch into a diatribe of how things were changing.

"David Hartman is dead," he would say emphatically, with his Chicago accent. "He's finished. Over. Done. David Hartman is history. *GMA* is dying. And it's up to us to get them now. Now is when we get them."

Then we would talk about ideas. What could we do? How could we get them? We would try to think of special series, ratings grabbers that combined all the right elements: maybe a series on kids in advertising, how to get your kid into advertising; then a series on what *happened* to all those kids who got famous in advertising, like Rodney Allen Rippy of Jack-in-the-Box hamburger fame, who by that time had grown to

the size of a blimp; or a series on child stars—actors who had disappeared, like Dennis the Menace and the Beaver. A mix of pathos and
stardom—this was one of the formulas. Then of course there were
other more predictable ideas that were good for ratings, like a week of
all the women currently starring in the nighttime soaps: You would
have Linda Evans from *Dynasty* one day, Joan Collins the next,
Michele Lee of *Knots Landing*, the next. The possibilities were endless. We just had to think of them—and then execute them, which was
by far the more difficult task of the two.

By the end of the meeting, we would talk about the obstacles we
were up against—not just ABC and CBS, but in our very own building, right there inside NBC. You could not get edit time, there were
not enough edit bays, people had to work in the middle of the night
and all sorts of other crazy hours because of the shortage of equipment
and space. Editors, upon whom the writers had to depend, followed
tight union schedules and didn't make any effort to help, like the time
Friedman needed a freeze-frame for a piece he was doing and it was
one minute into the editor's lunch break. Friedman had had to pin
him against the wall and threaten to beat him to a pulp—and he would
have—if he did not do what he asked him to do.

On top of all that, our very own executives were imbeciles, not only
in Friedman's eyes but in the eyes of many on the staff. They almost
seemed to be against us, making things more difficult for us than they
already were. Steve felt we were mired in bureaucracy and it always
took an enlightened Fred Silverman or Grant Tinker to save the day.
He had no respect for most of the "suits" he had to work with and they
felt exactly the same about him. "They never wanted to do anything,"
he said. "They were very shortsighted and they never wanted to spend
any money. You would have an idea and they would all turn it down
until I went to Fred or Grant, and they would say, 'Oh, that's a great
idea, let's do it.' "

That is why Friedman found it necessary sometimes to do things his
way. He knew in the end it was not how you behaved, but only the
ratings that counted: "If you get a twenty-five share and you're a prick,

they'll call you eccentric," he said. "If you get a fifteen share and you're a good guy, they'll fire you." That was the rule he lived by.

In one of these infamous Friday meetings, Jane Pauley, who had become a good friend of mine by this time, joked about my upcoming Africa trip with me. We were sitting next to each other, writing notes back and forth as we listened to Friedman wail.

"Judy Kessler, African Queenie" she wrote in my notebook, drawing a cartoon of a lady with dark glasses and a safari hat with a rotating fan on top. (She wasn't nearly as good an artist as Garry.) I had told her I was petrified of snakes and was certain I would be killed by a poisonous snakebite in Africa. She reached over and drew a book with a cover that said:

"MY AFRICAN STORY"
Judy Kessler
1947–1981
As Told to Jane Pauley

That didn't give me a lot of confidence.

But as it turned out, Africa was unbelievable, exactly what I needed. I had never known anything at all like the warm, dry, enticing African air which blew so gently over the vast golden plain as the sun beat down from the pearl-blue sky and wild animals paraded past. I saw everything—elephants, hippos, zebras, cheetahs, lions, monkeys, foxes, baboons, wildebeests, warthogs . . . Every once in a while, at first, they would remind me of someone I knew back in New York, but after a day or two, it was hard even to imagine the two so different worlds at once.

It was breathtaking, like a page right out of the Bible. Just to see this untouched beauty brought tears to my eyes, and I quickly forgot about the *Today* show. Harold and I were at the Mara River Camp, a tented camp in Masai Mara in Kenya. One day, after a delicious African breakfast of eggs, bacon, homebaked bread, and Kenyan coffee, we set out in our Land Rover to see what we could see.

We were keeping the *Today* show schedule, almost exactly. You had to get up well before the sun came up so you could be out on the plain at dawn. That was when the animals would be out, in the soft coolness of the earliest morning hours, looking for food (about the same hour Tom and Jane were eating their muffins and bagels and sipping their first cup of coffee, in that jungle on the other side of the world).

As we bumped over the plain in our Land Rover, popping in and out of warthog holes and various other topographical formations, we saw that something was happening nearby. Driving quietly and slowly, we discovered that a lion had snared a zebra, and we watched, enthralled. We stopped the Land Rover and stood there, protected by the metal of the machine, with our heads sticking out of the sun-roof.

The scene was awesome. As the lion tugged at the zebra, and ripped it apart, gripping it with its formidable incisors, I heard a shrieking sound that was not coming from the animals. Here we were, in the middle of the bush, the only humans for miles, I thought. What could this commotion possibly be?

And then I looked up in sheer disbelief. Another Land Rover was barreling towards us almost out of control. Out of its sunroof stuck the head of a woman wearing an odd hat that looked more like it had come from Bonwit than L.L. Bean or Banana Republic. And it went down-hill from there.

"Judy! Judy! Is that you?" the voice shrieked.

This cannot be, I thought. The chances of running into someone you knew in circumstances like this *had* to be infinitesimal.

Again, she yelled. "Judy! It's me! Valerie Jennings, from Fabergé!" She had once arranged an interview for me with Farrah Fawcett that turned out to be a cover story for *People*.

A publicist, no less! I had run into a publicist in the middle of the bush, in the Heart of Darkness, a million miles from home.

While I was riding around Masai Mara, my archrival, Ellin Sanger, was hard at work in New York, laying the groundwork for the interviews she would eventually get with Clint Eastwood, Marlon Brando, Elizabeth Taylor, and Katharine Hepburn, among others.

Ellin was a "hands-on" booker. She made her own rules and played by them. She once trapped a famous star in his apartment, shaved him, dressed him, poured coffee down his throat, and brought him to the studio to do her show—she simply would not take no for an answer. Where I operated on rules of human decency, Ellin's only goal was to get her guest, and she would do it in any way she could. She was shameless, but she was successful.

And she was absolutely relentless. Here is a case in point: Ellin had once worked for Muhammad Ali, so her contacts in the world of boxing were outstanding. It was the night before the prizefight between Sugar Ray Leonard and Tommy Hearns. I had no boxing contacts whatsoever, but *Today* had Bryant Gumbel, who obviously did, and this was his territory. Ellin arrived at the fight with Ken Norton, the fighter, who was to be the on-camera correspondent for *GMA* for the Leonard fight, and Tom Brokaw accompanied Bryant Gumbel. All of them were out to get Sugar Ray Leonard for an interview after the fight.

As it turned out, they were seated together at ringside. In typical style, Ellin's mind was working nonstop as they took their seats. She quickly sized up the situation and immediately went into action:

"Hi, Bryant," she said. "How are you? What's Tom doing here?"

"Oh, we're going to interview Sugar Ray Leonard first, after the fight," Bryant replied smugly.

"Uh-huh," said Ellin, turning to Ken Norton. Then, politely, she made small talk. "Ken, this is Bryant," she said, knowing they obviously knew each other. "Bryant this is Ken. Ken, this is Tom . . ." With that, she literally dove, head first, under the press tables that were set up around the ring. She had spied Juanita Leonard, Sugar Ray's wife, on the opposite side of the ring, and she thought if she could get to her she could enlist her help. She did.

On her hands and knees, as though she were on a holy pilgrimage, albeit under the tables, she made her way over to the other side of the ring, and with her knees killing her, and her back aching, she pulled herself up, crawled out from under the tables, brushed herself off, and introduced herself to Leonard's wife.

Ellin had done it again. Juanita Leonard promised her the interview. And Ellin Sanger got Sugar Ray Leonard first for *Good Morning America*, in spite of Bryant and Tom.

The minute I set foot in my office when I returned from Africa, it was clear that something was different. You could smell it in the air—it was not the sweet, pungent smell of the African continent, but the smell of indisputable disaster.

The rumors were true. The speculation was over. Although it was not official, Friedman was now absolutely and unequivocally convinced that Brokaw was leaving the *Today* show when his contract was up—even if where he was going was yet to be decided.

"That's when I gave up on Tom staying," Friedman told me. "Tom said to me, 'I've done six years. That's what I signed on to do, and I want to do something else.'

"That was it," said Friedman. "There wasn't any amount of money that could get him to stay. He didn't want to do it anymore. He wanted to do something else. After almost six years of getting up at five o'clock in the morning and doing two hours a day of live television, he had had enough."

Friedman also knew that Brokaw's decision would bring the new-found upward movement of *Today* to a grinding halt. "We would have continued to pull ahead with no decline," he insists. "I think we extended David Hartman's life by two years because Tom left."

It certainly changed the mood of the place and threw everything into a state of chaos. Nobody knew exactly what to do, but there was still time to think.

May 14, 1981. Pope John Paul II stood erect in the familiar white Jeep known as the "Popemobile," greeting the throng of thousands who awaited him in St. Peter's Square in Rome.

He picked up a baby girl and hugged her and then reached out for the hand of a pilgrim when the bullets hit him and bright red blood spread through his white vestments. He had been shot by a twenty-three-year-old Turkish terrorist who had left a note in his hotel room saying he had killed the pope to avenge victims of Russian and U.S. imperialism.

The pope survived, and the world was hungry to learn everything they could about the shooting. So Friedman dispatched his troops to Rome. Cliff Kappler would oversee the production, and Steve picked Karen Curry to produce the individual *Today* segments from Rome. She had by now proven to be not only intelligent, adept, and talented, but insightful and artistic as well. So far, she had taken every challenging opportunity Steve had given her, run with it, and run well.

The minute Friedman had heard the news of the shooting, he had called Karen and told her, "I want you to go to Rome." He did not ask if she could or would. Cliff Kappler went with her and so did Tom Brokaw. The NBC people in Rome called in people from Paris and London to help.

They were set up to work at Italian TV where all the necessary equipment was. As soon as Karen landed, she took a cab to the Italian TV offices and started working on footage that had been shot while she was on her way to Rome. While she put her pieces together, Brokaw went around to various locations throughout the city with a crew and did "stand-ups" which would introduce and glue the pieces Karen was working on together.

Karen and Cliff also lined up interviews to do live from Italian TV: among them were a priest from the Vatican and a terrorism expert from Rome. That is when the trouble began. The competition in morning television never stopped, not even in a situation like this.

There was only one studio and one satellite, so there was an agreement between ABC and NBC, as there often was in these circumstances, that the two networks would rotate, each yielding to the other after an interview. This, after all, was live television. There was no room to spare and no time to waste. ABC went first with the priest from the Vatican. The priest had agreed to do both shows and both shows had agreed to use him—they both wanted him. It was an obvious exception to the predominant rule of exclusivity. When it was NBC's turn, with time ticking away, ABC started stalling. They kept the priest in the chair. They would not yield the camera to NBC, trying to stall long enough to keep NBC from getting their interview in time. The tension rose, with the poor priest from the Vatican caught in the middle. What was he to do? The two teams came to the brink of a physical confrontation. Brokaw was on the verge of punching the ABC producer in the face when ABC finally yielded. NBC had lost valuable time, but there was nothing they could do. They had almost lost their "window" of available time to broadcast.

Karen and Cliff were up with no sleep for two subsequent days and nights, but they got their jobs done, and then they returned to New York and continued working as if nothing had ever happened.

———

The official announcement of Brokaw's departure was made in July. After being offered everything from a possible spot on *60 Minutes* to a place on ABC's *World News Tonight* team, Brokaw had finally decided to stay at NBC, thanks to the eleventh-hour intercession of Thornton Bradshaw, the chairman of RCA, who was willing to keep him at any cost.

After spending several sleepless nights at a retreat in Long Island, Brokaw had made up his mind. Chancellor had agreed to step down from his anchor position the following April, and Brokaw would anchor *Nightly News* in New York with Roger Mudd in Washington.

"I've been here for fifteen years," said Brokaw at the time. "I just couldn't find enough reasons to walk out the door." Which was not surprising, considering he was about to become the highest paid TV newscaster in history, with a salary (and benefits) of over $15 million for the seven-year contract he signed.

"It was one of the most emotional things I have done since I decided to get married," he observed.

The whole thing was bad for *Today*, however. It was only July, and everybody knew Brokaw was leaving, even though he would be there for six more months until his contract was up in December. The lag period would eventually do more harm than good. The show would inevitably lose momentum. In a sense, Brokaw would be a lame duck.

Still, with Tom and Jane together, the show held its own when they went to cover the royal wedding in August, reporting every movement surrounding the event, perched right outside of Buckingham Palace. The show was broadcast from London for the entire week. *Today*'s ratings were the highest they had ever been in the history of the show, which is why the mood was understandably good after the wedding was over.

On a hot, muggy Friday, towards the end of August, I was sitting next to Jane in one of our weekly staff meetings, doodling in my notebook and making lists, which I had an increasing tendency to do—I had started seeing lists of celebrity names in my sleep at night—when Jane reached over and tapped my arm. She looked like the proverbial cat that swallowed the canary, which wasn't a Jane-like look. She had a mischievous smile on her face. I knew she was about to tell me something, and I was right.

When the meeting was over, we walked out together and she swore me to secrecy. Then she told me that she was pregnant. I was elated—I knew how thrilled she was—and we went out to lunch to celebrate. But only days later, on August 20, columnist Liz Smith got wind of the news and printed it in her column. PREGNANT PAULEY WILL KEEP PLUGGING, said the headline. So at the next staff meeting, Jane made it official, and everyone was thrilled.

Sadly, a week later, Jane suffered a miscarriage. Again, it was Liz Smith who made the announcement. While Jane was gone from the show during this time, Bryant Gumbel took her place. And he did an outstanding job. "Everybody was so impressed that I sat in for Jane," Gumbel said later. "Five minutes of doing *NFL '81* is a thousand times tougher."

A succession of people from NBC News, including Chris Wallace and Jessica Savitch, had already been auditioning for Brokaw's job. There had been a good deal of jockeying for the position from the moment he had made it clear to Steve in February that he was leaving.

Friedman had known who *he* wanted the minute Tom had convinced him that he was really going to move on. With his producer's instinct, he had pondered the direction television was going and asked himself what he thought the show should be like for the rest of the decade. In keeping with his TV-is-sports philosophy, he had come to this conclusion: "I decided then we were going to wind up doing a play-by-play program. Play-by-play news. Things as they were happening—not after they had already occurred."

And who was the best play-by-play man he knew? None other than Bryant Gumbel. Steve knew he wanted Gumbel well before the day Bryant Gumbel sat in for Jane, but the road was not going to be easy. Bill Small, the president of NBC News, who had replaced Dick Wald in 1979, wanted Tom's replacement to come from the News Division. "You can't hire a sports guy," he had told Friedman bluntly. Small was also partial to Chris Wallace, the son of Mike, who was a former CBS colleague of Small's. Small was not alone in his feelings about Bryant Gumbel. A war of sorts began. Everyone got into the act; besides Bill Small, the advertising people had their own ideas, along with the research people—not to mention Don Ohlmeyer, who was president of NBC Sports and did not want to lose Gumbel—and, of course, Friedman himself. They were all deeply embroiled in the fight over who should replace Tom Brokaw.

Many people felt that giving the plum assignment to somebody outside of the News Division was the same as committing heresy. Especially when that somebody happened to be a sports guy. And that was not the only potential risk with Bryant Gumbel. Nobody quite knew how to weigh the fact that he was black. How would America react to a black man sitting next to a white woman on the *Today* show every morning?

Friedman insists that the sports issue was the bigger problem. "It was 1981, not 1921," he says. At the time, Friedman had called Scott Goldstein, who was the head of the West Coast bureau in Burbank, and would later come to New York as supervising producer, to ask him what he thought.

"Steve asked me, 'What do you think of Bryant doing the show?' " said Scott. " 'What do you think of a black man and a white woman doing it?' I just said, 'I don't have any problems.' Of course Steve didn't have any problems. Whether the viewers did, our attitude was 'Fuck it. You can only produce good shows. And Bryant is a real smart guy.' "

Steve had a different problem. If he decided on Bryant, he would have to convince him, too. "He thought I was kidding," says Steve. "He said, 'I do sports.' " Bryant finally agreed.

In the end, taking all of these factors into consideration, Friedman found what he thought was a happy medium. He would create what he would refer to as the Mod Squad. It would be a troika: Bryant would take Tom's place next to Jane in New York, and Chris Wallace would do the show from Washington. That way Friedman got his choice, Gumbel, while at the same time, he would appease Bill Small, which was one of his prime motivations, by necessity.

"I thought it would be easier to get along with the News Division if I somehow carved out a role for Chris," he told me. "And that is what I did."

His thinking went even further. "I thought Chris had a lot of potential and I wanted to ease Bryant's transition from sports to news— and not make a mistake like CBS did with Phyllis George. I think in Jane's heart she would have rather had Chris Wallace because she thought he was a little safer."

Thanks in a large part to Grant Tinker, who supported Bryant in the face of Bill Small, the Mod Squad would get a chance. Bryant Gumbel would sit next to Jane Pauley on the set of the *Today* show after his contract with NBC Sports was up, beginning on January 4, 1982—two weeks after Tom Brokaw's last day.

October 6, 1981. In Cairo, the day was sunny, warm, and dry— perfect for the big parade to commemorate the day in history in 1973 when Egyptian forces had stormed across the Suez Canal, purging the country of the humiliation it had suffered in three previous wars with Israel, and ultimately leading to a peace treaty with the Jewish state. Anwar Sadat, hailed by his countrymen as "The Hero of the Cross- ing," was the leader who had dared enough to go to war in order to seek peace. Although he was not feeling well that day, he had no choice but to attend the parade.

The attack began around 12:40 in the afternoon. Three uniformed men in the back of a truck towing a Soviet-made 130mm antitank gun blasted the viewing stand at the parade with gunfire. Moments later, President Anwar Sadat lay dying.

It was 7:30 A.M. in Washington when Secretary of State Alexander Haig telephoned President Ronald Reagan to tell him word had come from the U.S. embassy in Cairo that there had been a shooting in- volving Sadat. Reagan was relieved when he was told the embassy believed Sadat had been only slightly injured. It was not until 11:15 A.M. that the White House Situation Room confirmed that Sadat was dead.

At 7:15 A.M. in New York, on the *Today* show, Brokaw happened to be interviewing Henry Kissinger when Brokaw's secretary, Adrienne Wheeler, called Friedman in the control room and asked if he had heard that Anwar Sadat had been shot. She had heard it on CBS radio. Friedman checked the wires and there was nothing. But two minutes later, the news of the shooting hit, and the *Today* show went into high gear.

It was one of those rare circumstances in which the event is ac- tually occurring—unfolding literally before your eyes—while the show is on the air. Nobody knows what is going to happen. You have to go with your instincts and play your hunches, and there is a lot at stake. Do you believe the first reports? How much importance do you give them? Do you go on with the show as planned, or scrap it and go with the news, even if there may not be any more while you are on the air? Who can you get to talk, and how? Will the story go on past the time of the show? Do you make arrangements with the affiliates and the network to stay on the air? These are big decisions that affect everything, including advertising revenues.

Steve called the shots. Marty Ryan and Cliff Kappler scrambled fast, getting everything that was available for broadcast hooked up to the control room: the State Department, the White House, foreign bureaus. Karen Curry was dispatched to the United Nations to get reaction there of the shooting. Friedman knew there were three ways to do television: You can use reports, interviews, or phone calls. He chose to mix and match. He threw out the existing show and went with the shooting of Anwar Sadat, moment by moment, as the events transpired.

The problem was that nobody knew yet how bad things were or what the truth really was. That makes it difficult to put on a news show. To Friedman, only one thing was worse than a bad decision in television, and that was no decision at all. So Friedman went with his gut. Besides throwing out the original show and devoting the entire show to the shooting, he decided to stay on the air after nine o'clock.

The executive producer of GMA, George Merlis, did exactly the same thing. Merlis had the habit of watching his show from home two days a week, and he was in the bathroom shaving and listening to GMA when a news bulletin interrupted the show to say that Anwar Sadat had been shot. With half of his face shaven, he drove to the studio and found the place in chaos. No one knew, of course, how Sadat was, but Merlis's instincts warned him.

"The bulletins coming out of Egypt rang my shit detector," he recalls. "He was wounded, but something was wrong with it and I made the decision to stay on the air." He told the unit manager to let the stations know that *GMA* would be staying on for another hour. And then the *GMA* staff went after every guest *Today* was after: Henry Kissinger (whom *Today* ironically already had at the time of the shooting), Jimmy Carter, Gerald Ford, and Cyrus Vance.

When Karen Curry called in from the UN to the control room to report what she was getting, Friedman told her to go home and pack her bags and get on the next plane to Cairo.

Karen and Tom Brokaw and Andrea Smith got an Olympic Airways flight to Greece, where they changed planes for Cairo. Karen was scared, because this kind of "crash-and-burn news stuff," as she referred to it, was new to her. It was a whole different ball game from doing pieces in the studio or special segments where there was little pressure in terms of time. When they arrived in Cairo, they had trouble with their visas, and for a few panicky moments they weren't sure they would get in. It was getting closer and closer to airtime back in New York. The seconds were ticking away and Brokaw had to get to a phone so that he could check in with the NBC bureau in Cairo and at least get a sense of what was going on there. He managed to do that, and phoned through to the show in New York, getting on the air by phone—no video—just in the nick of time. *Today* air time was 4:00 P.M. Cairo time.

They finally made it to the bureau, which was right along the Nile on a street filled with goats and chickens. The building that housed the bureau also housed most of the other Western television offices and everyone was running around frantically, trying to figure out things to do. Since the NBC bureau in Cairo was substantial, there was no shortage of manpower. The problem was determining who they could talk to and lining up interviews. Then they had to get into a studio, where the equipment they needed for broadcast was, so they went to Egypt TV, which was surrounded by sandbags and armed guards. According to Karen, it looked like it had just been bombed. They began lining up more interviews to do that night so they could stay up through the night and cut them, which would provide some taped spots for the next day, and they also booked people to bring into the studio for live interviews.

For three days, *Today*'s viewers knew virtually everything happening in Egypt surrounding the assassination of Anwar Sadat. When there was no longer a reason to produce segments from Egypt, Karen, Tom, and Andrea flew back home.

———

Less than three months later, on his last day as host of *Today*, Brokaw passed the mantle gracefully. On December 18, 1981, he opened the show as usual:

TOM: Good morning, all, I'm Tom Brokaw, here with Jane Pauley and Gene Shalit . . .

JANE: This isn't *Today*, this is *the* day.

TOM: The day you get rid of me, finally . . . I was just explaining that Mrs. Brokaw showed very good judgment this morning. She woke up and said, "On this occasion I ought to go down and fix you some fresh orange juice and some coffee," and with that she promptly rolled over and went back to sleep, in keeping with the last five and a half years.

After an interview with President Reagan, and a captivating taped piece about Brokaw's five years at *Today*—the places he'd been, like the River Thames, the Pyramid of the Moon in Teotihuacán, Mexico, the Panama Canal, Italy to cover the attempted assassination of the pope, the banks of the Nile, London for the royal wedding, Vienna for the signing of Salt II; and the multitudes of people he had interviewed, a list that was a mile long—Brokaw made a good-bye speech that captured the essence of morning television:

BROKAW: This is hardly the kind of occasion that ends up in bold print in history books, but since you've indulged me in the past . . .

Suddenly, after five years of trying to get him to appear on the show, his friend and skiing buddy Robert Redford surprised Tom with a totally unexpected cameo appearance, walking right onto the set in the middle of Brokaw's farewell speech.

REDFORD: Tom, Rona couldn't be here, but . . .

Stunned, Brokaw replied: "Tab Hunter, ladies and gentlemen, and he'll be auditioning for one of the NBC soap operas down the hall . . . a good friend, going downhill or uphill . . ."

Then he went on with his parting words:

BROKAW: At any rate, I thought my friends here would give me a moment to reflect on what has been a grand experience.

This is one of the most privileged seats in broadcasting, whoever occupies it. The occupant is guaranteed a close-up look at the passage of life, large and small, good times and bad. What makes it especially appealing, I think, is its active nature. In five years I've been able to examine questions, ponder the issues and personalities of our time. It's a privilege and I am grateful.

I'm grateful too, for the continuing interest and support of all of you. More than any other news program of which I'm aware there's a personal bond between here and out there, and I have learned from all of you as well.

I'll miss being here for a lot of reasons. The people with me in front of the camera and those behind the camera are first among them. Gene and Jane and Willard truly are my friends as well as my colleagues, and for those of you who don't see the people behind the cameras, I am simply in awe of them. Think of what they accomplish every week: live television, two hours a day, five days a week, fifty-two weeks a year. And always on time—or almost always.

As for me, after a couple of months of other reporting assignments, I'm off to *Nightly News* with Roger Mudd, and John

Chancellor doing commentary. In the meantime, the next time someone comes up to me and says, "What time do you have to get up in the morning anyway?" I can answer with a smile and say, "Just in time to hear my good friend, Bryant Gumbel say, 'Good morning, this is *Today* on NBC.' "

Five

THE RISE
OF CHICKEN GUMBO

Nobody could seem to get it right: The mail was addressed to Byron Gumbolt, Briant Gumbul, Bryand Gumball, Bryan Bumvel, Brian Gummel, Briant Dumble, Giant Gumball, Byron Gunball, Bryan Gumbell, Byran Gamble—but more than anything, Brian Gumbo. Which is why Friedman called him "Chicken."

Bryant "Chicken" Gumbel came to his new job on the *Today* show with the same attitude with which he approached virtually everything else: Nothing fazed him. There was nothing he could not do. "I've never had a failure in my life," he said soon after he began as host. "Maybe it's because I'm a cocky son of a bitch who thinks he can make anything work."

At the beginning at least, perhaps he should have thought twice. The Mod Squad made its debut on January 4, as soon as Bryant's contract with NBC Sports was up. It was a disaster from the beginning.

In television, it is always difficult when the host of a show changes, ratings-wise and otherwise. Even at CBS the ratings seriously suffered for a time when Dan Rather replaced Walter Cronkite. Unfortunately, to make matters worse for Bryant and me, his starting date was during a week in which everybody (who was a celebrity, at least) was still on their Christmas holiday vacation. That particular year, I learned that most of them were in Aspen.

With fair warning of the upcoming changes, I had started many weeks earlier trying to book some major celebrities for Bryant to interview during his first week on the show. Steve had been adamant about that; we needed somebody big, like Marlon Brando or Katharine Hepburn, to attract ratings for that first week to counter the ratings drop-off that would inevitably occur.

This was the kind of time when I had to rely heavily on my contacts. I needed someone good for Bryant, simply as a favor; there were no movies to be released that week (all the Christmas releases were already out), no record albums, no new plays opening on Broadway. I needed someone to appear on the show when there was absolutely nothing in it for them. They would be doing it, essentially, for Bryant, for Steve, for me, and for the *Today* show—and the only bargaining chip I had was that we would pay them back. The trouble was, the people we wanted did not need any favors.

Contacts were a funny thing. My Rolodex was filled with names and numbers I had acquired over the years: publicists, politicians, agents, lawyers, and home numbers of celebrities I had gotten to know. I had photocopies of every Rolodex card put away in case something untoward happened. What if someone stole it or the RCA Building burned down? Ellin Sanger guarded her information so carefully that she put all of her numbers in a giant phone book which she lugged around with her everywhere in an oversized handbag which was never out of her sight. As a booker your value was precisely this: who your contacts were, how accessible they were to you, how many people you knew, and how effective you were at getting them.

When you spend a week with Priscilla Presley or Farrah Fawcett or Tony Orlando and get to know them, as I had done at *People*, you can call them directly. That is of utmost value. The more of those the better. When you spend endless hours of your day talking to publicists, you get to know them pretty well, too. It's no different from anything else. Often when a publicist was in trouble, they would ask for a favor. Would we put one of their lesser clients on the show, for instance, to help them out? If the guest was tolerable, Steve would generally do it, knowing that he would get the favor back in spades. Usually it worked.

For Bryant's first week, I could not pull it off. I went down lists and more lists, and called every publicist I knew, beginning with the ones I knew the best, the ones who were my friends. I started with the names I really wanted—basically the same old litany of untouchables. After exhausting not only those names, but the next acceptable level of stars, ones who would be okay, but not as good, like Steve Martin, Tony Randall, or James Arness, I ended up asking for anyone that any of my friends could give me. Time was running out. Friedman was not happy.

All the conversations were the same, like the one I had with Dick Guttman. "You've got to help me out, Dick," I began. "I really need someone for Bryant's first week. Who can you get me for the first week in January? It's really important."

Guttman paused, thinking. I could feel the calculations running through his mind. He could not just deliver someone of the stature I wanted. Why would they want to do it? What was in it for them? Why should he even ask them? Even though he was my friend, there were some things he just could not and would not do.

"Judy," he said. "You know there's no way. Nobody will even be in town."

"We'll tape it," I said. "Anywhere. Anytime. You tell me what I need to do."

I was fighting a losing battle. If I could have only given him one motivating reason to convince one of his clients to do the show, besides the fact that we needed a favor . . . Soon it was clear that Guttman wasn't going to go out on a limb to put a famous client on *Today* to be interviewed by someone he didn't know yet, for no apparent reason at all.

Even without the problem of a new host, it was a notoriously difficult week to book. Nobody wanted to ruin a vacation to tape a piece or do an interview with someone he hardly knew. For all intents and purposes, outside of the field of sports, they hardly knew Bryant Gumbel.

Celebrity guests always had preferences about which of the hosts would do the interview. In most cases, Friedman would not allow the guest to choose—unless it was a guest he wanted badly enough that the concession would make sense. He had to balance the show and make it work. He could not have Tom doing five interviews in one hour and Jane doing none, or vice versa. But he also had to make his choices on the basis of who would be best with whom, and who was better at what.

Tom had obviously been the pillar of *Today* in terms of his ability to handle the heavyweights. Jane could be very good, but she could also be very bad. Her most consistent quality was that she was inconsistent, and everybody on the show knew it. Writers often cringed when she ignored questions they had written for her. She would sometimes not be focused or adequately prepared, and then she would lose the entire point of the interview. When she went off on one of those tangents, you could hear voices in the control room muttering, "Earth to Jane, earth to Jane . . ." When things really got bad, when Jane slipped seriously off track, you would hear the familiar warning signal "Oh, no, code blue! Code blue!" Even *The New York Times* could not pass up the chance to write about some of Jane's eminently forgettable moments, like her interview with Michelle Pfeiffer when Pfeiffer was starring in *Grease* 2, and Jane had asked her questions like "How long have you been so incredibly beautiful?"

Now that Tom was gone, there was only Jane Pauley and Bryant Gumbel in studio 6B in New York. To most of the world, in January 1982, Gumbel was still considered to be not only a sports reporter, but an unknown quantity in terms of his broader abilities. Given these choices, and the fact that the ratings were better at GMA, most stars and publicists felt more comfortable and secure with David Hartman.

From the minute the Mod Squad hit the air, the pressure was on. There was an enormous amount at stake. The network was forecasting around $10 million in operating profits for *Today* for 1982, a big chunk, considering the fact that NBC's network TV operating profits would not exceed $50 million that year. Bryant himself was earning more than the $1.5 million a year he had been making when he signed with NBC Sports. A thirty-second commercial on *Today* was commanding $10,000—up considerably from the year before. The same advertisement on GMA cost around $12,000 because of their higher ratings—the audience appeal of a program is reflected in its ratings, and the ratings determine advertisers' demand for commercial time on the program, and the demand leads to the price of ad time. On top of all that, CBS was about to expand its morning news show to two hours for the first time in history, which would finally put it into the race as a viable competitor. In the first week after Brokaw left (two weeks before Gumbel started), GMA had a 5.1 rating, while *Today* had a 4.3. The New York consulting firm McHugh and Hoffman made the following assessment: "Gumbel is a real smart-assy young kid and Jane Pauley is vacuous. They are not strong enough to compete with GMA's entertainment style or play the hard news game with *CBS Morning News. Today* will get squeezed from both sides." Whether that was true or not, everyone was feeling the heat, an ironic backdrop to the upcoming anniversary of *Today*.

January 14, 1982. It was thirty years to the day since the *Today* show had first gone on the air, hosted by Dave Garroway and the chimpanzee J. Fred Muggs, who had been thrown in as an afterthought to lighten things up. The creation of Pat Weaver, the show was meant to give its viewers a taste of what was happening around the country in news and everything else—from weather to sports to entertainment—and to chronicle history as it happened and impart the whole package live from seven to nine in the morning, with intelligence, wit, and humor.

Now, Bryant Gumbel, there at the studio that day with Jane Pauley, Chris Wallace, Willard Scott, and Gene Shalit, was awed to be included in this great company only ten days after his promotion as a host. Most of the original cast had come for the show commemorating the anniversary: Garroway; Jack Lescoulie, his sidekick; Frank Blair, who had read the news for twenty-five years; along with others who had surfaced throughout the show's history—Barbara Walters, who had made her mark, and a mark for women in television, on *Today*; Hugh Downs; John Chancellor; and some of the old "*Today* show girls," like Estelle Parsons and Florence Henderson.

There had been a party at Manhattan's Tavern on the Green in Central Park the night before, in the middle of a blizzard that made the park look even more magical—almost surreal—as so many faces from the past congregated there.

Karen Curry, now well established as Steve's producer of choice for special programs, produced the anniversary show. She had proved her abilities early on with the special Christmas shows she had done two years running, along with her talent to pull things together somewhat miraculously on stories like Sadat's death and the shooting of the pope.

For this show, she had spent hours watching old *Today* shows, selecting and cutting memorable segments that would show how *Today* had truly covered the history of the past thirty years and had reflected the pop culture as well. Karen's favorite segment was a five-minute spot the talented Garroway did during National Donut week one year on a device someone had invented which allowed you to rest your wrist and pinky finger to keep from straining your hand while you dunked your donut.

With the help of two others, Karen had tracked everyone down, arranged to get them together for the show in New York, and created a program that included all of them. Then she prayed that they would all show up and that the whole thing would work. It did.

The anniversary show was a success, a poignant moment in history. It was also the last time that group of people would ever gather together. On July 21, Dave Garroway was dead. He had shot himself in the head.

Several Months Later. Friedman stood at the far end of the large central reception area of the *Today* offices, the hub around which everything outside of the studio and the control room revolved, with his autographed leather mitt on one hand and a baseball in the other, poised once more to vent his accumulating frustrations. He aimed carefully, and threw. There was a loud crash and the tinkling of broken glass, followed by a thud. Bernie Florman, who had been the office manager for *Today*'s entire thirty years, winced, shrugged his shoulders with a newfound resignation, and bent down to pick up what remained of the broken clock that Friedman had just knocked off the wall—the third this week. Carrying it gingerly, Bernie turned around and headed for his office down the hall to order yet another clock, thinking, "It didn't use to be this way."

Bryant appeared in the doorway with his mitt. Steve threw a curve. Bryant caught it solidly, and zipped a knuckleball over to Marty. Cliff Kappler (known as "Spin" because he was Marty's cohort) oversaw the action like an umpire. Karen Curry ducked her head as another pitch zipped by, trying to figure a safe way into her office. Steve picked up the bat. Marty pitched. Steve swung and missed. He put down the bat and redeemed the ball, just as Bryant's secretary, Tricia Peters, passed through. Wrong time. Wrong place. Thunk! The baseball cracked into her head. You could hear it a mile away. Dazed but still conscious at least, she regained her bearings, thinking, "You deserve hazardous duty pay to work at the *Today* show these days." Steve, feeling some remorse now, apologized mildly. The next day, he presented Tricia with one of her favorite things, an expensive Hermès silk scarf.

———

There was something about the chemistry of the particular combination of men who were running the show after Brokaw left that would allow it to acquire over a period of time what many of us saw as a locker-room mentality. Maybe it was because both Steve and Bryant were inveterate baseball fans, or because they both grew up on the streets of Chicago, or maybe it had nothing to do with either of those things. Whatever it was, the tone of the *Today* show—behind the scenes, at least—changed distinctly in the months following Tom Brokaw's departure.

It was not just the balls and bats, but a change in the attitude that pervaded the place. A "boys club" of sorts was forming, at the core of which were Steve, Marty, Bryant, Cliff, and the new director Steve had hired to replace Julian Finkelstein (who went to *Nightly News* with Brokaw) by the name of George Paul, who was considered by many to be a talented director, but who could be cruel and exceedingly demanding of some of the people he worked with.

The metamorphosis was subtle and gradual. There was a lot of snickering and complaining behind closed doors. Brokaw's office door had always been open. For one thing, he had had one of the few tape playback machines, which everyone needed to use to view tapes. "Tom's office was a place you went into and you sat down and you had a conversation with him," remembers Karen. "Bryant's office wasn't off limits, but it was a place you wouldn't just sail into."

"It was like a locker room," recalls one writer. "There was a lot of snickering and 'so she's a good lay' talk, which may or may not have been a lot of talk and no action, but there was a lot more of that kind of swaggering. You didn't have that with Tom. That was not his style. If Tom played around, he wouldn't have given any evidence of it. He was the father of a bunch of women."

Things were even worse in the daily morning meetings, which were not even always in the morning anymore. These meetings to figure out the content of the next day's show were now attended exclusively by men—usually Steve, Bryant, Marty, Cliff, and sometimes Ron Steinmen, the news producer, and George Paul. Here, things descended to their lowest level in terms of the mentality of the men who were instrumental in the show. It was here that Bryant referred daily to many of the women on the show in the most derogatory terms. His worst offense was towards Jane, whom he often referred to behind the closed doors of these daily meetings as "the cunt."

As time went on, he got progressively worse. "Bryant was generally so aggressively nasty towards women that it was shocking," said one of the men who attended the meetings. "He would give his assessment of everyone's bust size and he would say things like, 'You know I could sleep with that one if I wanted to.' There were women unit managers that he claimed to have slept with all over the place and then he would say things like, 'She's not even a good lay.' Then he had the habit of walking around the office and going up behind a lot of women and massaging their back and shoulders. The other thing he used to do was run his hand up their back to see if they were wearing a brassiere."

After I did not deliver for him on his first week, Bryant rarely spoke to me. For his first day, I had come up with nothing. To save the day, *Today*'s Hollywood correspondent, Jim Brown, and Coby Atlas, who had taken Scott Goldstein's job as West Coast producer, had put together a five-part series on Fred Astaire, which was promotable, but had absolutely nothing to do with Bryant. Chris Wallace had gotten an interview with then Vice President George Bush out of Washington. Jane read the news, which left Bryant with little of importance to do on his first day on the job as "boss," except introduce everyone else.

He was understandably unhappy with my performance for his debut. When you got on the wrong side of Bryant, the situation was not easily reversed. He held his grudges tightly. He never forgave David Letterman after Letterman had leaned out his window at 30 Rock with a bullhorn and interrupted Bryant during an interview he was doing outside with the stars of *Miami Vice* by yelling, "I'm not wearing any pants!" And he never spoke to Connie Chung again after she refused to join him on the air one time when she was substituting for Jane, to help him fill in empty air time after a Reagan speech had run short. Chung had refused, saying she would make a fool of herself because she had not paid attention to the Reagan speech, so Bryant was left to vamp by himself. He later admitted he had not been paying any attention to it either. Many people agreed, however, that Chung had shirked her responsibility and left Bryant in an untenable position.

It was more than obvious Bryant Gumbel had little regard for the "Talent Department," which had sprung into existence with Brokaw's departure, and which consisted of me and my new young, feisty assistant, Marianne Haggerty, who had replaced Nancy Fields when she had become ill. Marianne looked astonishingly like the girl on the Sun Maid raisin box, with her ultra-shiny pitch-black hair, white skin, O-shaped red mouth, and wide-open, sparkling brown-black eyes, which always made her look surprised. She was as nervous about doing her job well as she was willing to kill to get what she needed. She was also an excellent baseball player, which upped her stock with Friedman considerably.

As the Talent Department, we were in a no-win situation. The worse the ratings got, the harder it was for us to get anyone, simply because the big stars who had things to promote wanted to go where there were the most viewers. The Talent Department was an easy scapegoat. With each passing day, and each dropping rating point, we were treated with more and more disdain.

Marianne remembered it as intensely as I did. "When we walked in the door there was either a message or someone was intimating that we fucked up. Every day. I don't think there was a day that I didn't feel on edge that we weren't going to get something," she recalled when we looked back nearly eight years later. "Then we'd get into these frenzies and call everybody and make lists to make sure that everything was covered. No matter what we covered, somebody else was getting them."

I took the big names and tried to handle the office politics. There were certain people that Bryant requested, like Don Rickles and James Garner, and I did everything I could to get them. Unless they had a special affinity for Bryant, I usually struck out. Every day, I would make the initial phone calls, using everything I had to secure a commitment from an agent or publicist—or any other way I could think of. Then Marianne would follow through, covering all the movie lists, calling publicists all day long to make sure we were getting what they promised us, and putting our bids in the minute we learned about anything new coming up, even if it was months in advance. More and more we were promised things that would end up slipping away mysteriously to GMA. The bottom line was, everybody was going where the ratings were, and there was not much the Talent Department could do about it.

Steve did not see it that way, though. In his mind, we should have been able to figure out a way to get what we wanted, no matter what it took. It was not *his* fault, it was not Bryant's fault or Jane's, it was *our* fault. And he did not ever attempt to conceal his displeasure. As the pressure on him increased—both from within NBC and from the affiliates—he passed it along to the rest of the staff, not least of all to the Talent Department. As the days went by, the words "Talent Department" were rarely uttered by Steve, Marty, or Bryant, without being preceded by a derogatory adjective. Before long we were generally referred to as the "Fucking Talent Department."

The developing irony was that Steve had brought in women to work on the show, recognizing that women were, in large part, the ones who watched it. The way he staffed the show had looked like a step forward for the women he hired. In ways it was. No one was better than Steve at giving people—women included—every chance to move up. You just had to show him that you were good enough, smart enough, and that you were willing to work your butt off.

Now an invisible wall was going up. "It was a wicked little locker room in which they didn't exclude women but they didn't make you feel welcome," recalled a female writer, who later became a producer.

There seemed to be a vague and general disdain for most of the women on the show, which even Jane Pauley was not spared. "There were times when they perceived Jane as vacating out a lot," said a producer. "Forgetting to put on her microphone. One day she didn't have her microphone on and Friedman looked over at me and said, 'Yeah, if she wanted to be the number-one person, would you trust your mortgage to someone who forgets to put their microphone on?'

"There was a lot of that from Bryant too, a lot of rolling of the eyes," he went on. "Clearly they had cast their lot with Gumbel being the success of the show. There was a long period of time when Jane was not regarded as a major player in all this and in fact was regarded as a liability."

It was an oddly collective phenomenon—sort of the way little boys act when they are together, which can be entirely different from the way they act when they are alone. Although it did not emanate directly from Steve, he did little to stop it. His only concern was that everyone did his job and did it well.

The television industry had always shut out women at the highest levels. There was only a handful of women executives at all three networks—only one female senior vice president, Betty Hudson, at NBC. Men had always run the business. Barbara Walters had made the first great strides on the *Today* show, starting as a writer and working relentlessly until she finally made it onto the air, not only because of her innate ability, but by sheer will and determination as well. In 1976 she became the first female network news co-anchor on ABC, with Harry Reasoner. Her departure from *Today* was, ironically, the beginning of the show's decline. Steve always said every woman in television should give Barbara Walters 10 percent of their paychecks.

Still, what was happening at *Today* was not solely a male-female phenomenon. It was more a division between "us and them," a division which revolved around the tight inner circle of Spin and Marty, Chicken, Steve, and George Paul.

Scott Goldstein suffered the same kind of treatment when he joined the New York staff shortly after the debut of the Mod Squad. Although Goldstein had established himself as a highly creative and talented producer, he did not share the same macho, streetwise mentality as the rest of the guys. Steve brought Scott Goldstein in because, in typical form, he recognized Goldstein's talent after working with him in L.A. But Marty, Cliff, and Bryant did not relate to Goldstein's kinder and gentler style. Any way you looked at it, the cute, curly-headed, bespectacled Goldstein was not your run-of-the-mill Marlboro Man, in spite of his talent. Neither was Michael Pressman, a second sensitive and extremely capable producer Steve hired who rubbed the men of the inner circle the wrong way.

"They made fun of the sweet," said Janet Pearce, another producer Friedman hired in his reshaping of the staff, who had been at NBC for many years. Her analysis of their behavior was simple. "If you were nice, you were a wimp," she said.

Steve had asked Scott repeatedly to come to New York to work with him after he was promoted to executive producer. Since Scott's true desire at the time was to work on a show in entertainment rather than news—a show like *Hill Street Blues* perhaps—he held out for a long time, telling Friedman he preferred to stay in L.A. When Friedman offered him the job as supervising producer of *Today*, he finally agreed to take it.

Friedman says he knew from the first day that the troika with Chris Wallace and Jane and Bryant was not going to work. Later, when Reuven Frank, who replaced Bill Small as president of NBC News in the middle of the Mod Squad embroglio, asked Friedman why he had agreed to it, he told Frank, "I didn't know Bill Small was going to be fired."

At the time, Friedman had said to Scott, "I need you here. I want you to produce the show. Everybody here is a bunch of idiots." (He was referring to the old-line NBC employees and executives he had already encountered.) "They're stupid, they don't know what they're doing." He explained to Scott that the Mod Squad was not going to work because Bryant's only job for the first half hour was to introduce Willard. While it worked on paper, it did not work on the air. "I have three people doing two point three jobs," he said.

Scott's first impression when he arrived in New York was that his legs itched, now that he had to wear jackets and ties and wool pants instead of the jeans he was used to wearing in L.A. He did not mind the bats and the ball throwing at first. "When that stuff's good-natured and fun, its great," Scott told me. "You'd rather walk into an office and get hit by a baseball than get hit by the bullshit of the corporate offices around there."

The fun did not last long, even for him. "There was a distancing process," he recalled. "I never felt that there was a team involved."

It was obvious to everyone that there was a strong bond building between Marty Ryan and Bryant. "It was almost a protective bonding,"

Scott Goldstein says. "There was an unspoken bond between Gumbel and Ryan that when Steve would do things that would make Gumbel bristle, the impression I got was that 'one day this guy will be out of here' and that they would be running things. It was a secretive relationship. They would talk amongst themselves a lot behind closed doors." The fact that Scott was producer of the show had little relevance.

Once, when Scott had wanted to book a guest that Bryant did not want, Scott had complied with Bryant's objection. When Scott went on vacation, someone else booked the guest, unaware that Bryant and Scott had even discussed the matter. When Scott returned from his vacation, he found a note from Bryant on his desk lashing out at him: "How dare you," Bryant had written. "Do you think you are running this show? Well, you're *not* running this show . . ."

"It was really written with an acid tongue," Scott recalls. "It was the most vituperative, awful thing Bryant had ever said to me. But I had never booked the guest. Somebody else booked the guest while I was gone. I went into his office and explained it to him, but it was like being hammered. It was a meanness that is hard to describe."

Things got worse as the ratings sank. The pressure rose and the anxiety level rose with it. Bryant was proving to be as skilled in interviewing on any subject in any field, from politics to entertainment, as he had been in sports. The renowned publisher Alfred Knopf had been leery about giving Bryant an interview with one of his prized authors, John Updike. After the eighty-year-old Knopf had reluctantly agreed, he admitted that Gumbel's Updike interview was the best that had ever been done.

Bryant worked fifteen-hour days, coming in at five in the morning and staying well into the night. It was no secret that he resented the fact that Jane's hours did not match his. From her perspective, she was included less and less in the daily scheme of things—she was not invited to meetings, nor was she "uninvited." She was basically ignored. Since her opinion was rarely requested, she withdrew and usually left soon after the show and did much of her work from home.

The more she was excluded, the less need she had to be there. After all, she believed she should have been the rightful successor to Brokaw, instead of having to share the duties with two others who had less experience or seniority.

If Friedman knew it from the first day, it was clear to NBC by May that the Mod Squad was not working. A research study was put in motion to gauge viewer attitudes towards the anchors and the format. Friedman made a public declaration: "If we haven't moved ahead of, or become even with *GMA* by October, we should change our format."

In June, as the NBC study was progressing, *GMA* had a 27 share, *Today*'s share was 23 (four points lower than the year before), and CBS had a 14.

In spite of *Today*'s troubles, the competition for viewers in the morning continued to explode, becoming more intense every day. By July, each network had launched an early morning newscast to precede *Today*, *GMA*, and *The CBS Morning News*. The hope was to attract new viewers and hold them over for the next show.

NBC decided that Jane and Bryant should host *Early Today*, which turned out to be a bad idea. They became even more tired and cranky, having to move up their already dreadful on-the-air starting time to 6:00 A.M. The attempt to use Jane and Bryant proved fruitless and Friedman feared it was hurting them on *Today*, that their fatigue and irritation was not only showing, but taking a negative toll as well. After much negotiating, Connie Chung, who was a successful local anchor in L.A. at the time, was hired for the job and Bryant and Jane were off the hook. The speculation in the press was rampant—people were saying that Chung, a favorite of Grant Tinker's, was being brought in to take over *Today*.

The ratings continued to slide. On July 19, *Today* was trounced by *GMA* for the twenty-third straight week. To make matters even more excruciating, *Today* was only .4 of a point ahead of third-place CBS, and *GMA* was ahead of *Today* by more than one whole rating point. "We've bottomed out," Friedman noted grimly. "It's all uphill from here."

———

The announcement was made in August. The conclusions were based on the outcome of the research study conducted by NBC: "We're going to build more and more of the show around Bryant," Friedman told *The New York Times*. "We've been easing him into that role and now we want to make him a star."

It would be the end of the equally divided duties between Bryant, Jane, and Chris. As of September 27, Chris Wallace would become White House correspondent, John Palmer, who had been White House correspondent for NBC, would be brought to New York to read the news, and Jane would clearly take a second place to Bryant, which did not make her happy. She could not even claim discrimination, because the man who got the job she felt was rightfully hers was black.

Friedman believed that Jane was simply not up to the task the job required. He did not feel that Jane could carry the show. "I believe in active and reactive people," he later explained. "The reason they worked in the end was because Bryant is active and Jane is reactive. If you have two Janes, nothing happens. I felt that to run the show you gotta be an active person, and that because Jane was a reactive person, she wasn't right at that time. I told Jane I wasn't making her second banana—it was one and one-A.

"I also didn't know at that time how Jane's head was because she did the *Today* show the *right* way. She'd leave early and go to bed early and really wasn't all-consumed by it. That's why she lasted thirteen years."

In making this decision, he was also taking some risks with Bryant, whose biggest liability at the time was that, in spite of the fact that he had proved his ability to handle nearly every interview comfortably by now, and that he could perform well even in the face of fast-breaking news, many viewers continued to regard him as a sportscaster who was out of his depth when interviewing world leaders.

Friedman believes that Gumbel tried too hard at first. "He tried to show people how smart he was. On television you have to be willing to ask dumb questions to get good answers."

And he had other, lesser problems: Critics complained he had a high-pitched voice and a tendency to gain weight in a medium that put a premium on being slim. Even more troublesome was the fact that he would sometimes interrupt a discussion with the words "time out" or "jump ball." Despite the negatives, Steve had made up his mind to put Chicken in charge and he would stand by that decision, even though in the months to come, the pressure to replace Chicken Gumbo would grow to be enormous.

Six

CLOSE ENCOUNTERS OF THE WORST KIND

Things did not improve—for either the *Today* show or "the Fucking Talent Department." If it had not been for an idea I got just in the nick of time, I probably would have been fired.

It started with my lists—I had miles and miles of them—and the problem of not being able to find a good enough reason to convince big stars to do the show, when the ratings were so much better at GMA and Hartman was the most sought-after host. When I was not being yelled at by Steve, scorned by Marty and Bryant, or turned down by what seemed like every publicist and agent in town, I pondered how to solve it.

Then one day it came to me. Forget Bryant and Jane for the moment. Why not get the stars themselves to interview the stars? They could even pick whomever they wanted to interview. We could do it as a special series, on a regular basis. I even had the perfect name for it. We would call it "Close Encounters."

Luckily for me, Steve liked the idea. Whether I could get it to work or not was another story completely. It would be impossible for a viewer to imagine just how much goes into getting one guest for the show: the number of phone calls that have to be made; the complexity of all the arrangements, arranging for airline tickets or other transportation, and hotel reservations; pre-interviewing the guest and writing the interview; informing whoever is going to *do* the interview why it was booked in the first place; getting the limo to pick up the guest at the right time from the right place; hoping the guest will be there when he or she is supposed to; and last, but not least, praying that the interview itself will go all right. With "Close Encounters," all of these problems were multiplied by two.

I started out with an A-list of the celebrities I would most like to have—among them Goldie Hawn, Carol Burnett, Alan Alda, Dolly Parton, Tim Hutton, Paul McCartney, Steven Spielberg, Sean Connery, Roger Moore, Candice Bergen, Katharine Hepburn, and so on. When I tried the idea out on publicists for the first few times, I got a surprisingly good reception. Things did not go exactly as I had planned, but I had not ever tried to put together a concoction quite like this before, so I did not know what to expect.

I made phone call after phone call, explaining my idea. One thing I knew was that if I just got *one*, it would be easier to get more. The whole thing was very complicated. First someone had to want to do it. Then they had to pick whom they wanted to interview. Then I had to try to get the other person to say yes. If it ever got that far, I had to find a time and place when two famous, busy people could get together, and that was no easy task. Every time I came near to getting two people who wanted to do a "Close Encounter" together, some little glitch would keep it from happening—like the fact that each was committed to something when the other was not, for the next two years or so. One thing that became clear right away was that the only feasible way to make this work would be to tape the interviews. At least that would give us the most leeway in terms of both time and place.

I had a lot riding on this and I was more frazzled than ever. So was Marianne, since most of my time was going into this project, which meant she had to cover more of the frustrating day-to-day stuff. And the idea did not thrill Bryant. Why should it, after all? If it worked and I got big stars to do the show, they would not be interviewed by him anyway.

Finally I got one that sounded perfect. Gloria Steinem wanted to interview George Burns of all people! And Burns had agreed to do it. What an odd combination—exactly what I had hoped for.

It took weeks to get a date when both George and Gloria were available. Since Burns was in Los Angeles, we agreed to fly Gloria to the Coast to do the interview there. It was the only time in all the years I worked at the *Today* show when I got to fly first class: We had to give Gloria a first-class ticket, and I was the producer of the series and was to fly out there with her. It was the only opportunity I would have to sit down with her to talk about her interview and explain what we had to do the next day.

I had never met Gloria Steinem until we hooked up at the airport. When I did, I liked her. She still looked like a woman of the sixties, with her long straight blond hair, her big aviator glasses, and the pale lipstick she always wore, which made her lips disappear. We got along right away and talked continuously the whole five hours to L.A. The thing I remember most is that, as she picked at her airplane food, she told me she had been fat as a kid, and that she had to struggle with her weight. She was the kind of person I would have thought had always been lanky and thin.

The interview went surprisingly well, considering the fact that I had no idea what I was doing. I had never really produced anything like this before, but Steve had told me what to do while we were shooting the interview: "Always make sure there's a tight shot favoring the guest," he had told me—the guest in this case being George. "Then make sure you get Gloria reacting, or George looking at Gloria. Alternate between over-the-shoulder shots of the guest and over-the-shoulder shots of the interviewer. The important thing is to capture the *relationship* between the two people."

Luckily, I had Coby Atlas to help me in Los Angeles. She was an experienced and excellent producer. Besides that, the L.A. camera crew was exemplary. But still, who knew what would happen when the two of them got together? As it turned out, everything went well, and the minute I actually saw them both in the same room together—we had gotten a suite at the Beverly Wilshire Hotel—I breathed a sigh of relief.

Gloria was shy and nervous. When she spoke, you could hardly hear her. George took care of that right away. He was such a pro, and so relaxed and funny, and genuinely happy to meet Gloria Steinem, that Gloria loosened up.

"What are you doing tonight?" he asked her, before the interview began.

"That may be up to you," she replied.

Steinem asked him about his marriage to Gracie and about his life with her. "You had a very modern marriage," Steinem said to Burns.

"I was never a great lover," he replied. "I never remember in thirty-eight years after kissing Gracie, where she applauded." He ended the interview saying, "You know, if it wasn't for Gracie, you wouldn't be interviewing me right now."

And if it was not for George Burns, I would not have gotten my first much-needed "Close Encounter," let alone my second. As I had suspected, having one solid "yes," helped me with the rest. It was always that way with celebrities—they wanted to know who else was doing something before they would agree. George Burns was not a bad pacesetter.

When PMK, the big public-relations firm, which handled a lot of *really* big clients, heard about George and Gloria, they offered me Margot Kidder, better known at the time as Lois Lane in the movie *Superman*. Although she was not on my A-list, it paid for me to say yes. For one thing, it would give me a better chance at getting more of their clients. As it turned out, Kidder wanted to interview the well-known author John Irving, who wrote *The World According to Garp* and *The Hotel New Hampshire*. This would be, I thought, an interview that was not only different, but compelling.

The arrangements were more complicated than ever. Irving was traveling around the country promoting his latest book, and would be in L.A., where Kidder lived, for two days during his publicity tour. He proposed that she accompany him to a reading he was giving on his first night in L.A., and that they have dinner afterward so that they could get to know each other before they did the interview. He would pick Kidder up in a limousine at her home in Malibu canyon. The interview would be the following morning at nine, which Kidder's publicist had not been thrilled about because it was so early. I went in the limousine with Irving to pick up Kidder that first night. When I realized how well they were getting along, it occurred to me that Kidder might have been interested in Irving for more than just the interview. I got a ride home separately from the reading and do not know what happened after that. I only hoped that both of them would show up the next day for the interview. I had the slightest suspicion that my "Close Encounters" might end up getting even closer than I had intended.

When the Steinem-Burns interview ran, it got good play in the press. *Nothing* made Friedman happier than publicity, such as this from the *New York Post*, which appeared under the headline STARS TO QUIZ STARS ON TODAY SHOW:

> NBC's *Today* show has come up with a new idea in its battle to overtake ABC's *Good Morning America* and stay ahead of CBS's improving *Morning News* in the 7 to 9 A.M. ratings.
>
> The idea is to have celebrities interview celebrities . . . the interviews will run about seven minutes each, though the more newsworthy ones among them may be stretched out over two mornings. Not all the encounters are yet in place. For example, Burt Reynolds has committed himself to the project but the "somebody big" who'll be asking him the questions is still to be chosen. One definite interviewer will be TV producer Norman Lear, but his subject is still to

be nailed down. Also among the expected participants as an interviewer will be Joan Kennedy; her interviewee is yet to be determined. Other scheduled interviewers include actors Richard Chamberlain and Michael Caine, model Lauren Hutton, and Mary Tyler Moore.

Which just goes to show you, you can't believe everything you read. Besides Gloria and George and Margot and John, none of the things that the *Post* mentioned actually ever happened. On the other hand, some others did—others that I never expected.

I had lined up Eileen Brennan to interview Ruth Gordon. Everything was set, and, as usual, it had not been easy. The night before the interview was supposed to take place, I heard the terrible news. Brennan had been critically injured when she was hit by a car as she was crossing a street with Goldie Hawn after they had had dinner together at a Los Angeles restaurant. After absorbing the initial shock of this tragedy—which momentarily forced a keener perspective on life—I turned back to the matter at hand.

Ruth Gordon was set and ready to be interviewed. I thought I would have to give the whole thing up, until I mentioned it to Carol Burnett's publicist, Rick Ingersoll, when we were talking about whom Carol might want to interview.

"She loves Ruth Gordon," Ingersoll said effusively. "Let me see if I can get her to do it."

Burnett, one of the nicest and most dignified celebrities I have met, agreed. It was one of the best "Close Encounters" we got. Besides that, Burnett and Gordon had a wonderful time together.

The one I'll never forget, even though it never actually took place, was to be with Katharine Hepburn. Martina Navratilova had been on my list. Her agent had called me to say that the one person she would like to interview was Katharine Hepburn. So, who wouldn't? I had thought. It was an interesting idea, and Martina had indicated that Hepburn might be a fan of hers. I figured I had nothing to lose by asking her, so I wrote her a letter explaining that Martina had asked to interview her, and after that, I didn't think much more about it.

One morning a few weeks later, I was in my office, with Marianne sitting at her desk just outside the door, when the phone rang.

"*Today!*" she said, in one of her "stay away from me, I'm in a bad mood" voices.

"May I speak to Judy Kessler?" requested the voice on the other end of the line.

I could hear Marianne pause and think for a split second as she listened more carefully.

"Who's calling?" she asked.

"Katharine Hepburn," said the voice, doing a perfect imitation of Hepburn's deep, drawn-out, slightly shaky voice.

"Right. And I'm Greta Garbo," I heard Marianne say, in her "don't give me any shit" voice.

Next I heard a rather long pause. I was still looking at the back of Marianne's head, which I could see through the open door to my office. When she turned around, her cheeks were so red they were glowing like burning coals, and her wide-open eyes had expanded to the size of giant saucers. She dropped the receiver and walked into my office in shock, looking as though something terrible had just occurred. She was pointing frantically at my phone, jabbing her finger in the air, signaling for me to pick it up right away, as her red lips frantically mouthed the words "*Katharine Hepburn is on the phone!!!*" Her voice had abandoned her. I stared into her black saucer-eyes and slowly picked up the receiver.

"Hello?" I said, not knowing what to think.

"Miss Kessler," said the unmistakable voice, "this is Katharine Hepburn."

I swallowed. Then I babbled. "Oh, of course, Miss Hepburn, how nice of you to call," I said. "Thank you so much for calling. Uh, uhm, well. Did you get my letter about 'Close Encounters'?" (No, she just decided to call me out of the blue.)

"I can't"—pronounced *cahnt*—"do that"—pronounced *thaht*—said

Hepburn, drawing each word out like a piece of well-chewed gum (but at least she sounded apologetic).

"Of course, I understand," I babbled on, calming down ever so slightly.

"But do tell her for me," added Hepburn, "that she can come for tea—no cameras."

I thanked her and promised I would relay the message.

Through the door I saw Marianne collapsed with her head down on her desk.

Five minutes later the phone rang again. Composed now, Marianne answered, and advised me that it was Katharine Hepburn's secretary. I picked up the phone.

"I'm calling to tell you Miss Hepburn isn't interested," she said flatly.

"I know," I replied. "She just called me herself to tell me."

For me, that was the culmination of "Close Encounters," even though in the end I managed to get Rich Little with Jimmy Stewart, Marlo Thomas with Pete Rose, and Art Buchwald with Gene Kelly—which was so bad it turned out to be unusable. Buchwald is hilarious on paper, but on camera he was a disaster, and Kelly was far more preoccupied with his problematic hairpiece than he was with the "Close Encounter." After that, I ran into a dead end and could not seem to get any more.

Things were continuing to go badly—the ratings were worse than ever—and the pressure on us from Steve Friedman had not decreased. He made it clear to me that I had better start focusing more on day-to-day celebrity bookings and that we had better get some *big* ones soon. There is a well-known saying among those in the business of booking talent which goes, "You're only as good as your last booking." And nothing could have been more true.

One of the important things I had been working on—and that I had been promised, to my great relief—was coming up in May. Elizabeth Taylor and Richard Burton were going to star on Broadway together in the play *Private Lives*, due to open on Sunday, May 8, 1983. The publicist for the play, Fred Nathan, had promised me *Today* would get Liz Taylor for this. *Today* had a slight advantage because we had always been good to the theater, and our audience was older, more affluent, more educated, and thus, more likely to buy theater tickets than *Good Morning America*'s, even if theirs was younger, more female, and generally more appealing to advertisers demographically.

Not to take any chances, I called Taylor's publicist, a woman by the name of Chen Sam, to cover all my bases. We had a good history together. Taylor had been on the show several times by now since I had been at *Today*, and she was especially fond of Gene Shalit. Chen told me she was sure it would work, although it was being booked through Fred. We were set. I thought I had it locked up.

In the meantime, unbeknownst to me, Ellin Sanger was relentlessly chipping away at my stronghold. She had already pleaded with Fred Nathan. She had a new technique, I had heard; she would carry on and cry on the phone and tell people that if she did not get the guest, she would most certainly be fired. She would not take no for an answer.

Nathan told Ellin that he could not guarantee anything, that there were too many people involved in this production, and that she ought probably to go to someone higher up in the chain. "I always believed there is more than one way to skin a cat," Ellin told me years later. "I tried to find the other skin."

She found it. While I was sitting at 30 Rock, convinced that I had Liz Taylor booked—having been promised by both Chen Sam and Fred Nathan—Ellin was having dinner at a fancy Manhattan restaurant with Zev Bufman, the producer of *Private Lives*.

The phone call came several weeks later, at the break of dawn. Marianne was sound asleep in her apartment.

"Hello," she answered in a sleepy voice.

"Turn on your fucking television set, Haggerty!" Friedman spat out the words the way he had a tendency to do when he was furious. She was wide awake after the first sentence. "And call Kessler and tell her to turn on *her* fucking television." That was it. He hung up.

Shaken, Marianne called me at home with trepidation. I, too, was sound asleep, cuddled up happily with my husband. By that time, I did not always watch the show any more if I did not have to.

My phone rang. Marianne was cool.

"Gee," she said, "Steve just called and was swearing at me and screaming at me . . ."

"Why?" I asked.

"Elizabeth Taylor's on *GMA*."

About two weeks later, on May 21, NBC announced in *The New York Times* that it was about to conduct an extensive research study, as they had done a year ago, to determine why *Today* had slipped steadily in the ratings over the last year. Among the factors being tested was the popularity of the show's anchors, Bryant Gumbel and Jane Pauley.

One of the things that prompted this, besides the miserable ratings, was the fact that for the first time in history—the same week that Elizabeth Taylor had appeared on *GMA*—*The CBS Morning News* with Diane Sawyer and Bill Kurtis, had tied *Today* for second place. Each program had gotten an 18-share average, while *GMA* had a 27. It was the sixty-seventh week in a row—well over a year with no letup—that *GMA* had been first in the ratings. To make matters even more intolerable, CBS had actually beaten *Today* in the first hour of the show that week, with a 20 share, to *Today*'s 19.

NBC had reason to be nervous. In its heyday in the mid-seventies, *Today* earned an estimated $20 million a year, more than a quarter of the network's profits. Now financial experts were predicting profits of around $10 million, cautioning that if the ratings continued to decline, so would the profits continue to erode. Not only had the ratings declined steadily since Gumbel had replaced Brokaw, but with its new fast-paced format, along with the presence of the popular former Chicago anchor, Bill Kurtis, and the well-known Diane Sawyer, *The CBS Morning News* appeared to be moving up as fast as *Today* was going down.

Reuven Frank, the president of NBC News, had attended the annual meeting of the NBC affiliates early in May. What he had heard there most from the affiliates were complaints about *Today*'s performance. Most of the criticism, he admitted, had focused on the show's two hosts.

"They think if the ratings are down it has to be the anchors," Frank said at the time. "I don't know if that is true." He added that a number of affiliates complained to him about Bryant Gumbel's background as a sportscaster, which Frank himself believed was unfair. "A lot of people have started in sports and moved on to news," he said.

Besides that problem, Frank allowed that the upcoming study would address the question of whether viewers were bothered by the fact Gumbel was black. It was what he called a "sensitive" question. "I don't believe anybody ignores that possibility," he told *The New York Times*. "It was tested before and it didn't show anything."

As if that were not enough, the rumors that Connie Chung would replace Jane and Bryant persisted. Finally Friedman exploded. "There are no plans to fire either Pauley or Gumbel," he told the New York *Daily News*. "I'm sick and tired of hearing that *Today* is going down the tubes. The ratings are down, but CBS has gained only two share points in five calendar quarters. Connie is not being brought in to replace Pauley and Gumbel. She is just a valuable addition."

Friedman had his own explanation for all this trouble. "The morning shows are becoming the same," he said. "There is no overwhelming reason to turn the other two off, or less charitably, to turn us on. What we have to do is be different."

Mariette Hartley had, by now, decided to do just that. She had snagged herself a role in a new TV sitcom called *Goodnight, Beantown* with Bill Bixby, in which she played a slightly daffy female personality with no journalism background who was hired to boost the ratings of a struggling news program with her own brand of "happy talk," much to the dismay of the presiding Dan Rather–like anchorman, played by Bixby. Sound familiar? As it turned out, the series did not last much longer than Hartley's stint on *Today*.

The headline in the New York *Daily News* on June 26, 1983, read: PAULEY'S MORNING SLICKNESS ABOUT BABY. Liz Smith had done it again. On June 12, she had informed everyone, including Jane's immediate family, that Jane was pregnant. Now, two weeks later, even though both Jane and NBC were denying it, Smith was still insisting it was true. It was. Before long the news could be contained no longer. Even Jane acknowledged the fact that not only was she pregnant, she was pregnant with twins.

"I was thrilled and in shock," Jane said, when she found out she was having twins. "At that point I wasn't prepared to be the parent of one, much less two, but I've never been tempted to give one back."

The effect that Jane's pregnancy would have on the *Today* show, with all of its host trouble seemingly at its peak, was unclear. Historically, so far at least, pregnancies on the set had not been bad for morning show ratings. When Joan Lunden had been pregnant in 1980, *GMA's* ratings had gone up considerably.

After no time at all, people were saying that Jane's pregnancy had affected her positively on camera, that she was looser and more fun—cracking jokes with her male cohorts and reacting more personally in interviews. Even Jane admitted she had changed. "My life outside *Today* is so much richer that I'm willing to take more risks on the air. I've been told by several NBC executives that I'm doing my best work ever."

When Jane's pregnancy was announced, Friedman said he believed that her prior miscarriage had made her a more mature person: "It was a terrible thing, but it made her more compassionate. Before that she had this perfect life, with no problems."

Jane stated publicly that she was not about to exploit her pregnancy on TV. "You won't see me bringing my babies on the air," she said. "The only reason I'm talking about the babies at all is that they've been with me on the show since I became pregnant. After a while I had to acknowledge this pumpkin tummy."

Still, Jane's pregnancy was not without its on-the-air drama. When she was three months pregnant, she was interviewing a health expert on *Today* about toxoplasmosis, a disease carried by cats that can infect pregnant women and that can result in retarded infants. Suddenly, in the middle of the interview, she froze. It had struck her in that instant that she had been ill a few weeks earlier. Garry and Jane had two cats. Could she herself be a victim? It was a moment of agony, but it was not prolonged. Right after the show, she took her cats, and herself, for testing, and was more than relieved to learn that everything was fine.

She did, in fact, suffer from morning sickness, which, with her particular job, took on a slightly different significance than it did for most other women. There were times, she said later, when she had had close calls. "I would often race for the bathroom after an interview. Tom Wolfe and Nora Ephron don't know how close I came to throwing up on them."

She was already thinking about her post-twin work schedule, but she wasn't worried about it at all. "My work schedule allows me to come and go during the day, and my husband will be at home with the children," she figured. Garry had begun a sabbatical from *Doonesbury* the previous January. He was, according to his wife, as eager to learn about parenting as she was. Both of them were paying close attention to what *Today*'s doctor, Art Ulene, had told them. "I have only two words of advice for you," he had said. "Get help."

Those of us in the Talent Department needed help worse than Garry and Jane. The Everly Brothers had decided to reunite after being apart for ten years, and we were fighting a desperate battle to try to get them. Steve really wanted them on the show. *GMA* wanted them just as badly.

The job was made even more difficult by the fact that the concert was to be given at Royal Albert Hall in London. So the people who were handling it were all over the place—some in the United States, and others in England. I could not afford to be outdone again, so I tried to cover every conceivable base. With phone calls and letters and all the wheeling and dealing I could muster up, I had managed to get a firm agreement from their managers that they would do the show. They would do it live from London immediately following the concert, which would be perfect—it would fall during the first hour of *Today,* and live was always better than taped.

As the concert drew nearer, I got nervous, so I called every day to confirm the arrangements. While I did this, Marianne checked every other conceivable contact we knew about, to make sure there were no surprises in store. Yes, we were told, over and over, the Everly Brothers were doing the *Today* show.

The day before the concert, I got a call from the Everly Brothers' manager. He did not know what had happened, he said, but the Everly Brothers would not be doing *Today* after all. He had received orders from "higher up" that they had to do *GMA.* But from whom?

"You can't do that!" I told the manager. "We're all set up. We had a commitment from you. *This will ruin my career!*"

I couldn't believe I had actually uttered those words. I was getting to be as bad as Ellin Sanger. "You have to tell me who ordered this! Who do I talk to about this?" I demanded. Powerless, and figuring I would get nowhere, he gave me numbers to call in London. The trouble was, by this time it was almost tomorrow in London—it was only hours from the day of the concert. They were to do *GMA* immediately after the concert, live, which would be during the first hour of the show in New York. What I finally learned was that someone from *GMA* had snuck into the Everly Brothers' hotel suite in London, and somehow convinced them to promise that they would switch and do *GMA.*

It was getting too late to do any more from the office, so I decided to go home and make calls to London from home, to try anything I could to get them back on the show. When I arrived home, distraught, my husband, Harold, shook his head. He just didn't understand how a booking could be so important, how getting the Everly Brothers or not could affect anyone's life. When I stopped to think about it, neither could I. Still, I had a job to do.

While Harold slept peacefully, I called London frantically—hotels, offices, any people I had numbers for. I even tried desperately to get through to the Everly Brothers themselves in their hotel. I thought of saying it was their mother calling, but I did not even know if their mother was alive. Anyway, I got nowhere. Finally, when the last angry person hung up on me, I gave up, exhausted, allowing myself to wonder why on earth I was doing this. I figured, I'm not getting any pleasure out of this job, so let Steve fire me if he wants. And I went to bed.

I got up in the morning to go to the studio to face Steve now that I had failed miserably. When I walked into the control room, my stomach was churning as the monitors stared back at me—one showed *GMA*, one showed *CBS Morning News*, and one showed *Today*. I stood there, ready to be fired as soon as the Everly Brothers appeared on the *GMA* monitor. Marty and Steve didn't even acknowledge my presence. I watched the monitors with resignation, like a child waiting to be punished. Suddenly, before my eyes, on the *Today* monitor— yes! it was true! It *was* the *Today* show monitor—there was our London correspondent, Ike Seamans, with—yes! There they were!—Don and Phil Everly inside of Royal Albert Hall.

I could not believe my eyes. To this day, I do not know what happened that night, or how the Everly Brothers got there. It reminded me of a joke I once heard, in which a screenwriter had terrible writer's block and his career would be finished if he did not turn in the script he was working on by the next day. But he could not write, and he fell asleep resigned to his fate. When he woke up in the morning, there was a beautiful leather-bound script awaiting him. He had no idea where it had come from.

When he turned in the script his agent was ecstatic. The agent sold the script for more money than ever. This happened time and time again. Finally, one night, the screenwriter got up to see what was going on. Sitting at his typewriter, propped up on a phone book, was a little gnome, typing away like crazy. He asked the gnome who he was and why he had done this for him, and the gnome replied, cheerfully, "I'm a screenwriting gnome. No need to thank me, that's my job." The gnome just kept doing the work and the writer kept making the money and getting the credit.

Several scripts later, in the middle of the night, the screenwriter's guilt overcame him, and he got up, went downstairs, and said to the gnome, "I want to have a talk with you. You have saved my career. I want to pay you back. Just tell me *anything* I can do for you, anything you want. A car? A house?"

The humble gnome replied, "Aw, that's all right, really. This is my job. It's what I do." But the writer insisted, so the gnome thought again, and after a minute, he said shyly, "Well, if you *really* want to do something for me, maybe just a little teensy credit down at the very bottom, in the corner of the screen . . ."

And the screenwriter replied, "Fuck you."

It must have been a booking gnome who got the Everly Brothers for me. Steve never said a word.

The next few months were uneventful, except for the fact that Nancy Reagan appeared as a cohost on *GMA* with David Hartman for an entire two-hour show which was devoted to drug abuse. She joined Hartman in interviewing teenagers, parents, and drug-treatment counselors. This got a lot of publicity, which irked Friedman immensely.

Besides that, he thought it was wrong. "I personally think it is too close to the 1984 elections and the primary season to devote two hours to Nancy Reagan and the fight on drugs," he complained, which did not deter them from doing it.

Shortly after Nancy's appearance, in October, Jane left on her maternity leave. Three people would be filling in for her while she was gone: Carol Marin and Mary Nissenson from Chicago, and last, but not least, Connie Chung.

But Jane did not seem worried at all. Her mind was on other things. She was looking forward to a break and she was looking forward to her babies. Not knowing whether they were boys or girls,

Garry and Jane had painted one of the three bedrooms in their apartment yellow.

"I'll be home sleeping late, watching TV, and twiddling my thumbs," she told her interested audience, from whom she had already received hundreds of gifts. "I know it's going to kill me to leave the babies at home when I come back to work in late February, but in this business I don't feel I have the luxury of taking a year off."

For four weeks in October, the month Jane left, the ratings fell to an all-time low—*Today* actually came in third behind *CBS Morning News*. It was the lowpoint for *Today*, the worst day Scott Goldstein can remember of the four years he was there. "I'll never forget the day the ratings came out that we were number three," he recalls. "The bottom . . . this was like the wildest nightmare, and clearly Gumbel was going to be made the fall guy for this—this was an experiment, he's a sports guy. That was the big issue for a lot of the 'suits.' The *Today* show, this bastion of journalism, had this sports guy running it."

Then, on December 5, while Jane was home sleeping late and twiddling her thumbs, and Marianne and I were scrambling madly, as usual, for guests, something unexpected—by us, at least—happened: Elizabeth Taylor checked into the Betty Ford Center in Rancho Mirage, California, to be treated for chemical dependency, which she said stemmed from prescription drugs she had been given over the years for her various medical problems.

This may have been no more than an insignificant bit of news for most Americans. For me, it turned out to have job-threatening implications. Friedman wanted Taylor the minute she got out of the Betty Ford Center—no matter what. He had lost Taylor once this year already, and he did not want to lose her again. I could not imagine that she would do any show after she got out. It had always been hard for me to insinuate myself into the lives of celebrities when it involved a personal trauma. When I had been at *People*, I had refused to do "Split" stories, when that section, which dealt with people's divorces, had sprung into existence. To me, this was even worse.

But Friedman did not see it that way. The minute the news came over the wire he called me into his office. He was in a rotten mood, and he was convinced somebody was going to get Taylor when she completed her treatment.

He had only a few words to say to me: "You better get her when she gets out. I don't want to lose her again. Or else."

S e v e n

ET²

Once again, my life was being directly affected—no, turned upside down—by another unlikely celebrity. How could I have ever suspected, when I saw her in *National Velvet,* that Elizabeth Taylor, of all people, would ever have anything to do with *my* life? I couldn't have. Now, in the last month of 1983, it looked as though she might possibly ruin it.

This time, I really had the feeling that Friedman meant it, that he would fire me if I did not get Elizabeth Taylor. Truthfully, I was not sure how long I could keep this up anyway, but I could not afford to lose my job until I myself decided to leave. Which meant I *had* to get Elizabeth Taylor. I had no idea how to do it, under what I felt were such delicate and private circumstances.

Even in the press release that had come out when she had been admitted to the Betty Ford Center, Taylor had expressed her concern for the privacy of other patients at the desert treatment center, as well as for her own, saying she hoped the press would understand. If I were Ellin Sanger, I thought to myself, I would check myself into the Betty

Ford Center, pay whatever it took to get the room next to hers, and tackle Taylor when she least expected it, begging her to do my show. Just thinking about it sounded absurd. Considering the way things were going in the morning right now, anything was possible. And I knew *GMA* would stop at nothing.

I decided that the only thing I could do was to write a letter—a letter from my heart—to Taylor, in care of her publicist, Chen Sam, explaining how sorry I was to even ask this of her at this time, but that if she decided to do anything at all, it had to be the *Today* show. She held my fate in her hands. In the letter, I explained to Taylor that Chen Sam was also aware of the mess I had gotten into the last time she did *GMA*. Steve had not only threatened to fire me after the Zev Bufman fiasco, but he had also called Chen Sam, ranting and raving at her that it was her fault that we did not get Taylor, and that it was also her fault that I was about to be fired. Chen Sam had been not only flabbergasted at Friedman's outburst—the first one of these to which she had been treated—but extremely upset as well. It seemed only fair, I said in the letter to Taylor as delicately as I could, that this time it was our turn.

I sent the letter to Chen by messenger. All I could do now was wait and watch the papers. The press release said Taylor would be at the Betty Ford Center for four to six weeks. Beyond that, I had no idea when she would be out. I still could not believe she would do any television anytime soon. I called Chen Sam every day to see what was going on, but after a while she began avoiding my calls. When Taylor was finally released, I could not reach anyone, and I naïvely assumed that I was safe, that I had probably been right that Taylor was not going to do anything public about the experience.

At 8:00 A.M. on December 30, 1983, Steve's telephone in the control room rang. When he picked it up, Garry Trudeau was on the line to tell Steve that Jane had given birth to a boy and a girl, Ross and Rachel.

Connie Chung, who was substituting for the new mother that week, announced the birth on the air at 8:45. Shortly afterwards, Jane received champagne and roses from the staff of *Today*—pink roses for Rachel and white ones for Ross. *GMA* sent flowers too, accompanied by two little tiny *Good Morning America* T-shirts.

A few weeks later, just after the first of the year, Steve called me into his office again. This time he had a look on his face that combined the worst elements of rage and disgust. On his desk was a copy of a letter which he threw in the air towards me. In spite of the sheer animal force with which he threw it, the onion skin paper fluttered back onto his desk.

I picked it up. It was addressed to me, although I had not yet received the original letter. This copy had been sent to him. My stomach turned as I read it.

January 4, 1984

Dear Miss Kessler,

Thank you for your letter asking me to appear on the *Today* show. I am sorry to be so late getting back to you. I have just returned to my home in California. I am sorry for the difficulties you have had because of me. Chen Sam has explained the problems to me and for this reason I am writing you directly. My good friend Betty Ford asked me while I was in treatment to appear with her on *Good Morning America*. I am not doing any interviews as such. This is not a five-part series. I wanted to do her a favor as she has been very good to me. I am sure we will be working together in the very near future. My best wishes for a good 1984.

Sincerely,
Elizabeth Taylor

cc: Steve Friedman

Steve and I stared at each other. Then he said slowly, quietly at first, his voice gradually rising as he spoke in his inimitable manner, "If I look up next week and see Potato Face interviewing Elizabeth Taylor, *you* are fucking *fired!*"

"I'll do the best I can," I said, and turned around and went back to my office, wondering what else I could possibly do. I could not even check myself into the Betty Ford Center anymore—Taylor had already left. My mind started racing.

Then it came to me. Betty Ford! Tony Orlando! It was all coming together. If Betty Ford was the one who convinced Taylor to do *GMA*, that is who I needed to get to. Betty Ford was a good friend of David Hartman—I had known that before. Hartman must have called Betty and asked her for this favor. But what about Tony Orlando? I thought. Tony was a good friend of Betty's, too. She had sat at his table with her daughter, Susan, and me at Tony's comeback performance in Las Vegas. And Tony had, after all, credited me with saving his life. Didn't that mean he would undoubtedly do me a little favor if I asked him? Maybe, I thought. It was all falling into place.

I found out Taylor was to appear on *GMA* in exactly one week, which meant I had less than that to try to get her to change her mind. At least, I thought, maybe I could convince Taylor and Ford to do the *Today* show the same day they did *GMA*. In this case of such extenuating circumstances, that would be better than nothing.

I decided I would start with the normal channels first, to try to reach Betty and have a conversation with her. I knew she was nice and I thought if I explained my situation to her she would understand. Her agent was Norman Brokaw (unfortunately, no relation to Tom), at the William Morris Agency in L.A. It was only 3:00 P.M. in the west, so I picked up the phone and dialed his number. I got his secretary, Rita.

I told her who I was and said, "I have a long, complicated story, but I have to talk with Norman because there is no need to go through it twice."

"I'm sorry," she said. "You can't reach Norman. You can talk to me."

"Well," I said, "it *is* a long, complicated story, but I really need some help." I started to tell her the history of my relationship with Taylor from the beginning, and finally I got to Betty Ford, which was why I was calling Norman.

"We have nothing to do with Elizabeth Taylor," she said.

"I know that," I said. "But I need Betty's help." Now I read her the letter from Taylor.

She waivered for a minute and then said dismissively, "I'll see what I can do and I'll call you back."

Okay, I thought. It was time for Tony Orlando. I hadn't actually talked to him since he had been on *Today* right after I had gotten there, which had almost been four years ago. But I still had the number for Yellow Ribbon Productions in L.A., so I dialed it.

He was not there. I left a message that I was a friend and that I needed a favor. Could he please call me back as soon as possible? The minute I hung up, my phone rang. It was Rita.

"It's impossible," she told me. "There's nothing we can do. I spoke to Betty Ford's secretary. She says there's no way anything can be done."

I decided to take a lesson from Ellin Sanger and not take "no" for an answer. So I asked Rita for Betty's secretary's number. I wanted to talk with her myself. My instinct told me that Rita was becoming a little more sympathetic.

"Okay," she said, hesitating. "Her name is Ann Cullen." And she gave me the number in Rancho Mirage, California.

"I know you just spoke to Rita," I said to Ann Cullen when I called, "but I really need your help on this. Couldn't I just ask Betty myself—explain the situation to her—I was hoping that she could get Elizabeth—I was just . . ." There was nothing but silence on the other end of the line. I realized this was not going to work.

"It's all arranged," said Cullen sharply. "They're paying for her whole trip." (Of course GMA was flying Betty in to New York.)

"We would, too," I said meekly.

"We couldn't possibly change anything now. I'm sorry." The phone went dead.

Just as I was about to walk out the door, my phone rang again. It was Tony Orlando.

"What's up?" he asked.

I explained everything again.

"You know," he said, "you're still like part of my family. You know I'll do anything I can to help you."

He suggested calling Norman Brokaw first. I told him I had already done that, to no avail. Then I managed to get the words out. "Would you mind calling Betty *for* me, Tony?"

"Well," he told me. "I'll do something even better. I'll call Bob Barrett. He's better than reaching Betty herself." Barrett was apparently her number-one man, the guy who made all of the arrangements. "Barrett will be back tomorrow," Tony told me. Then he gave me his own home number, and said, "Call me tomorrow at home and I'll call Barrett."

I hung up again and sat there for a moment, thinking. This all sounded very complicated and I had little control. Suddenly I decided that the thing I should do was to go to L.A. myself in the morning, talk to Tony from there, and try to find Elizabeth Taylor. I had received my copy of her letter by now. On the back of the envelope was a return address: 250 South Robertson Boulevard. I was familiar enough with L.A. to know that this was not a residential neighborhood, but I assumed it was Taylor's office, and that if I went there someone could tell me how to find her. At least I could personally drop off another letter to her and be sure that she would get it.

I got the 9:30 A.M. flight to L.A. the next morning and when I arrived, I rented a car and headed for 250 South Robertson Boulevard with my heartwrenching letter to Taylor. I knew how to get to Robertson Boulevard, although I did not know exactly where 250 South Robertson was. I crept slowly up the street, looking at the addresses. I was going so slowly people were honking like crazy. At least no one shot at me.

Finally I pulled over and got out of the car with my letter. I knew I was close. But when I saw it I could not believe it—a tiny hole-in-the-wall place with a tacky sign that said BEVERLY HILLS MAIL ANSWER-ING SERVICE. Did I feel stupid.

Inside were hundreds of little post-office boxes and a would-be actress with frizzy hair sitting at a little wooden desk, chewing gum and reading a magazine.

"Yeah?" she said, looking up, unhappy that I had interrupted her.

"I want to leave a letter for Elizabeth Taylor," I said. (I came 3,000 miles; I might as well, I thought.)

She took the letter and plopped it into a box and went back to her magazine.

"Can I call tomorrow to see if it's been picked up?"

"Sure," she said, chewing, not even looking up.

I turned around and left.

When I got to my hotel, I called Tony Orlando at home to remind him to call Bob Barrett. Tony was not home, so I left a message on his machine. I called again the next day. I did not hear from Tony and I found out that Liz was vacationing in Puerto Vallarta, Mexico, so I flew back to New York, discouraged. When I got there I left another message for Tony at his home. I never heard from him again.

The day that "Potato Face" interviewed Elizabeth Taylor, along with Betty Ford, on *GMA*, Friedman did not say a word. He did not fire me. Nothing happened at all. I knew it was just a matter of time and I wondered what was going to happen—what the next disaster would be. I found out soon enough.

Johnny Carson's wife, Joanna Carson, had tried to get on the show before, when she was promoting a line of women's clothes. Steve did not have any interest in her at the time, mainly because she was not very interesting. It had just been announced that she was divorcing Johnny Carson. Obviously that changed the whole picture. The divorce spawned a barrage of publicity, which quickly catapulted Joanna Carson to the top of Steve's "Most Wanted" list. He let me know how much he wanted her on the show.

This was unfortunate for several reasons: We had recently turned her down when she had wanted to be on our show, and she was also divorcing a man who was among the most popular talents on our network, NBC. I was more than certain that Johnny Carson would not be pleased if his wife appeared on the *Today* show discussing their divorce. I could not imagine why she would want to discuss her divorce on TV. Of course, Steve did not want any excuses. When I called her publicist, I was flatly turned down, and NBC was not about to help me get to her. I had come to yet another dead end.

In the meantime, my husband, Harold, had just agreed to go to L.A. for a month to help the publisher of *California* magazine rethink and redesign the magazine. It was the middle of winter, freezing cold in New York, and I had not been having an easy time at work. It was eighty degrees and sunny in L.A., so I flew out with Harold for a weekend of tennis and sun.

When I got home, New York felt depressing and dank. I took a taxi home to our apartment, not looking forward to going to work the next day. It was after 11:00 P.M., and I called Harold the minute I walked in the door. We were in the middle of our conversation when the operator came on the line.

"I have an emergency call," she said. "Please clear the line immediately." Both Harold and I were scared. We hung up and I told him I would call right back. It was Steve Friedman on the line.

"I was just watching *Lace*," he said, starting out quietly as usual. "They just promoed fucking Joanna Carson on *GMA* tomorrow!!!"

He hung up.

As it turned out, I did not stay around at *Today* to suffer the consequences of Joanna Carson. Harold was offered the job as editor of *California* magazine, which would be a challenge for him and a good change for both of us. We were growing tired of New York anyway, so we decided to be adventurous, take our chances and go. I was offered a job at *Entertainment Tonight* as senior segment producer. Everyone I knew who had worked there or knew anyone else who had worked there advised me not to take it. They all said it was a tough place to work and that *everybody* there got fired sooner or later. Well, I thought, my kind of place!

I thought it would be better to start out in L.A. doing something other than looking for work. So I took it. I would leave the *Today* show and begin at *ET*, as it was called, in March.

Just before I left, at the end of February, Jane returned from her maternity leave. The ratings reflected how happy the viewers were to have her back—a respectable 4.8 after her first week, up 20 percent from the week before. It was the biggest audience *Today* had had since April 1982. Unfortunately, *GMA* did even better, with a whopping 6.3 rating, its highest since February 1983. Things, however, did not go as well for CBS. *CBS Morning News* had begun to erode, and it finished a distant third with a 3.5, the worst rating it had had since the previous August.

It looked as though, maybe, after all this time, now that Jane was back in her new incarnation as the mother of twins, things might finally be looking up for *Today*.

Part II

THE RISE

(1984–1988)

Eight

BORN AGAIN

It began with the posttwin transformation of Jane Pauley. She was looser, happier, more at ease, more in control. Motherhood was having an undeniably positive effect.

"She somehow decided when she came back that she was gonna let people in," observed Friedman. "Not personally, but she was gonna let people know how she felt about them. After the babies, people were interested in Jane. They watched the show and the show was good." Although Jane refused to involve her twins in the *Today* show in any way, Friedman joked—on the serious side—that he would make them regulars if he could.

Even Bryant was effusive about Jane, publicly at least. "She's the best woman on the air in the morning," he said. "She's bright, cheerful, and understands her role. Our relationship is better than it's ever been.

"It's tough when you're the cohost, but clearly not the person in charge," said Gumbel. "It's a difficult position. You must establish your importance and dignity, but not at the expense of the person you're sitting next to."

He went on to explain the relationship further. "We never had an adversary relationship. But it was difficult to jell immediately. It took some time to know each other and trust each other." After Jane became a mother, it certainly looked as though it had jelled.

At the same time, Gumbel admitted, with a touch of apparent resentment, "A year and a half ago, when the *Morning News* reached ratings parity with *Today* for a short time, it was difficult to be upbeat about anything. *Variety* wrote I was fired, and nobody at NBC jumped to my defense."

At CBS, they perceived themselves to be victims of the change in Jane. Ed Joyce, the president of CBS News, and his predecessor, Van Gordon Sauter, pinpointed the decline of CBS and the surge of *Today* to Pauley's comeback. "Pauley surprised us," said Sauter. "She returned a different persona."

If motherhood was the catalyst, the Republican convention in Dallas that August brought out the best of the new Jane. Whatever doubts Friedman had harbored about her until then dissipated as the Republicans renominated Ronald Reagan and George Bush.

"I never wanted to fire Jane," Friedman told me later, even though he admitted he had been urged to do so when he first became executive producer. "I thought she had command of the screen, which is hard to teach. She just needed to put it together—which she did, starting at the convention in Dallas. When I saw her there in the summer of 1984, I knew she was gonna be a major television star. It had to come from her. From August, she just got better every day. She became the person there that was gonna keep Bryant and Willard in line."

As Jane took control of her role more and more, the ratings of the *Morning News* continued to fall. To make matters worse for CBS, Diane Sawyer departed the show in August to become a correspondent on *60 Minutes*, which left them in need of a cohost. With the born-again relationship between Bryant and Jane—a new on-air familiarity between them which was clearly winning points with the morning

BORN AGAIN

audience—CBS opted for a new strategy. Although several qualified newswomen were considered for Sawyer's job—among them Jane Wallace and Meredith Viera—the network decided to go with former Miss America and sports announcer Phyllis George, who had not one iota of journalistic experience, but was, according to Ed Joyce, "a successful role model for millions of Americans." Not only was she pretty, but she was married to former Kentucky governor John Y. Brown, and she liked to talk about her family on the air. This, according to *Morning News* executive producer Jon Katz, would provide the kind of warmth that had been missing with Diane Sawyer.

Not everyone agreed with this reasoning. "I am heartbroken," said Richard Salant, who had been president of CBS News for sixteen years, ending in 1979. "Quite a few people at CBS share the view that it's the last straw on the question of where the hell we are being made to go these days." Salant would prove correct. Within the year, the hiring of Phyllis George would turn out to be a big mistake.

The confluence of Pauley's return, George's arrival, and Gumbel's brilliant performance on *Today* when it was broadcast from Moscow for a week in September finally began to turn the tide of morning television in 1984.

The trip to Moscow grew from a plan by NBC News to spend a week in Russia looking at U.S.-Soviet relations. It was a week in which Bryant interviewed everyone from members of a Soviet family to Georgi M. Korniyenko, a first deputy foreign minister; from members of the Soviet military to Marshal Sergei F. Akhromeyev, the new Soviet chief of staff; a week in which Bryant's question to Korniyenko asking if a meeting between President Reagan and Foreign Minister Andrei Gromyko would be valuable actually resulted in the announcement on the *Today* show that such a meeting would take place. More than anything, it was *the* week that Bryant Gumbel was finally able to shed his identity as a sportscaster and establish his credibility as a full-fledged journalist.

It was a turning point for Bryant Gumbel and a turning point for *Today*. Among other things, it marked the beginning of a series of trips

143

masterminded by Friedman that would take the *Today* show on the road and, ultimately, be responsible in large part for putting the show back solidly in first place—for a while, at least.

While this was happening, the increasingly hysterical, fevered pitch of the competition between the morning shows spun wildly out of control.

October 31, 1984. Shortly before 9 A.M., Indira Gandhi opened the door of her private bungalow, came down the steps, and walked onto the winding gravel path which led to her offices in the sprawling compound at 1 Safdarjang Road in New Delhi. It was a beautiful, sunny autumn morning, and the gentle breeze delicately brushed the leaves of the tamarind and margosa trees which towered there.

Two security guards followed discreetly behind Mrs. Gandhi as she headed for her meeting with British actor-director Peter Ustinov, who awaited her with a television crew, ready to conduct an interview she had agreed to give.

As she proceeded down the winding path, Mrs. Gandhi passed two khaki-uniformed security men wearing the traditional beards and turbans that identified them as Sikhs. One of them, Beant Singh, was a favorite of Mrs. Gandhi; she had known him for ten years and trusted him, even though others had doubted the safety of maintaining Sikh guards after Gandhi's controversial decision to have the Indian army root out Sikh extremists at the Golden Temple in Amritsar, the Sikhs' holiest shrine. Of Beant Singh she had said, "When I have Sikhs like this around me, I don't believe I have anything to fear."

On this last day of October (which happened to be Jane Pauley's thirty-fourth birthday), as she approached within a few feet of Beant Singh, he drew a .38 revolver and fired directly into her abdomen. As she fell to the ground, the Sikh guard standing with him pumped all thirty rounds from his Sten automatic weapon into her crumpled body.

Although Gandhi was killed instantly, a team of twelve doctors worked on her body for several hours, trying desperately to perform a miracle. It was not until 1:45 P.M. New Delhi time that an Indian news service sent the bulletin: MRS. GANDHI IS DEAD.

President Reagan was awakened with the news of Indira Gandhi's death soon after midnight. Marianne Haggerty's phone rang only moments later, just as she returned home from a party. It was Allison Davis, the *Today* show writer who was in charge that night, calling to inform Marianne of the assassination, and to tell her that she had to get Henry Kissinger for the show the next morning to talk about Gandhi's death.

The good news was that Marianne had Kissinger's home number in her Rolodex. The bad news was that it was two o'clock in the morning and she woke him up when she called. On top of that, she was the one to break the news to Kissinger that Indira Gandhi was dead.

"Oh my God, what do you mean?" Kissinger had said, half asleep and shocked.

"She's been killed. Indira Gandhi's been shot," Marianne repeated to him. "And it's reported that she died." She read him the wire copy in front of her.

"Oh my God, who *is* this?" Kissinger asked.

"This is Marianne Haggerty of the *Today* show," she told him, "and we'd like you to come . . ."

"I have to make some calls," Kissinger blurted, before she could even ask him to come on the show. "Call Nancy back." And he hung up.

But before Marianne could call Nancy Kissinger back, she got another phone call, this time from Steve.

"Haggerty, I want you to get the Indian ambassador to the United Nations for the show in the morning," Steve had told her. He had the same magnetic hold on Marianne that he had on most of the other staffers: In spite of his gruff manner, his crudeness, and his often bizarre behavior, he had a charisma that made you want to die for him if necessary, to do *whatever* he told you to do. Marianne would stop at nothing to fulfill her latest mission. She had less than five hours to do it.

Like a pro, she somehow managed to get the ambassador's home number, which she shamelessly called, in spite of the fact that it was nearly three o'clock in the morning. The ambassador's wife answered the phone, and Marianne launched into her heartfelt plea for the help of the Indian ambassador.

"I am sorry, no, he cannot do it," said the ambassador's wife after Marianne's moving monologue.

"Please . . . well, listen, I'm just gonna come anyway," said Marianne.

"No, no, he can't do it," said his wife.

But Marianne persisted. She had acquired the maniacal *modus operandi* currently being employed by every booker who was going to get *anywhere* in the morning race for guests, which was by now bordering on insanity: a combination of persistence, determination, and utter desperation.

She called the ambassador's wife back five more times.

"Oh, Marianne, *please* . . ." The ambassador's wife begged her to leave them alone.

Marianne arrived at the residence of the Indian ambassador with an NBC limo just before seven that morning, still wearing the clothes from the party she had been at the night before. With resignation, the ambassador's wife let her into their home—the most lavish mansion Marianne had ever seen. She sat in the living room in a very large chair and waited, nervously. Finally the son of the ambassador appeared.

"My father regrets that he cannot do the interview," said the ambassador's son.

"Oh! No!" said Marianne. "Where is your mother? I have to talk to your mother!"

The son left the room and returned with his mother.

"My husband cannot do it," said the ambassador's wife. "I told you there was only a chance."

Those words set off the built-in alarm that was ticking in Marianne's head. The minute she heard them she was sure she would be fired.

And then the tears came—either from sheer necessity, exhaustion, or the vision she had in her mind of Friedman's face when she would have to tell him she did not get the Indian ambassador. Marianne sobbed hysterically, out of control.

And then the ambassador's son reappeared, distressed.

"Oh, dear, don't cry. Please," said the son.

The ambassador's wife, hearing the commotion, came back into the room. "Please don't cry, Marianne," she said. "I am going to go get my husband. Just don't cry. Please."

Marianne's tears overcame her. They would not stop. Finally, the ambassador himself came in. "Okay, okay, I'll do it, I'll do it. Just stop crying. Please," he said.

The tears began to subside, ever so slowly, as Marianne left the ambassador's residence with him and they piled into the limousine together. The *Today* show was the only show to get the Indian ambassador on the morning following the assassination of Indira Gandhi.

While Marianne was on the phone to the Indian ambassador's wife, over at the GMA offices, Ellin Sanger had been instructed by one of her superiors, Amy Hirsch, to attempt the impossible. Amy wanted Ellin to get—of all people—Mother Teresa, for the show in the morning. After all, they were kindred spirits.

Even Ellin knew this was a long shot, but she would never admit anything was impossible. So, at three o'clock in the morning, she called the Missionaries of Charity Convent in Harlem, which was where she had learned Mother Teresa was, and left a message requesting an interview with Mother Teresa live the next morning on GMA.

At around four Ellin Sanger's phone rang. It was Sister Priscilla from the Missionaries of Charity Convent. "Ms. Sanger," she said, "Mother Teresa would like me to express to you that she graciously regrets that she cannot appear on your broadcast tomorrow morning."

Ellin listened, amazed that she was getting a reply so quickly. "However," Sister Priscilla continued, "she would like to offer you her blessing."

To this day, Ellin remembers clearly what was going through her mind as she listened to Sister Priscilla: "I don't want her friggin' blessing—I want her to appear on the show in the morning."

———

Meanwhile, back in Los Angeles, my quest for Elizabeth Taylor continued, but now I was doing it for *Entertainment Tonight*. Taylor was shooting a television movie called *Malice in Wonderland*, with Jane Alexander, on location at Perino's, a once fancy, old-time Los Angeles restaurant that had closed several years earlier.

I had been dispatched to the scene with a crew, hoping to get an interview with Taylor. But the motivation was not nearly so great as it had been at *Today*.

I could not believe it when one of my first assignments for *Entertainment Tonight* was to try to get an interview with Elizabeth Taylor. I was getting too old for this. I had talked to the publicist for the movie and she had told me to come down and see what happened—she would do what she could, but she could not promise anything. We could take our chances and be there. We went.

I waited with the crew through the afternoon as the scheduled scenes were shot for *Malice in Wonderland*. The publicist kept telling me she did not know if we would get Taylor or not. As the day wore on, I got weary. When they took a break from shooting, I went across the street to get some coffee.

As I returned, I took a shortcut through the parking lot to get back to Perino's. I was walking slowly, with my head down, when I almost ran into the person walking towards me.

"Excuse me," I said, distracted. I looked up, and then I saw the notorious lavender cat's eyes staring back at me. I was face-to-face with Elizabeth Taylor.

"Oh my, Miss Taylor, I'm Judy Kessler," I said to her, startled. "I feel like I know you."

She recognized my name immediately, and then a look of sympathy mixed with apology filled her penetrating eyes, which I could have sworn glistened with the tiniest inkling of tears. And she said to me, "Oh! I am *so* sorry for all the trouble I've caused you."

That night, she gave *Entertainment Tonight* an interview.

———

Steve Friedman had seen the light in Moscow. Travel was the key, the way to get attention for the show and the way to build the audience. He decided he would take a gamble on three big trips that year, and build the *Today* show around them. After signing a new three-year contract, he declared in his inimitable style, "*Today* has turned the whole industry around with Moscow. We even got Ted Koppel out of the studio." (Koppel had done a headline-making series from South Africa after the NBC Moscow trip.) "*The CBS Morning News* will send Bill Kurtis to Israel," Friedman said. "They are reacting to our program."

It was the beginning of a trend that would become another extension of the frenzied competition between the morning shows. Because of the new technology—satellites that enabled television to be broadcast live from virtually anywhere—the show could now move out of the studios in New York and do more broadcasting directly from the field. This had been Friedman's plan, and now everyone was clamoring for travel. Besides CBS's plan to send Kurtis to Israel to broadcast from there for a week during Holy Week, ABC announced it was planning to send David Hartman to Vietnam at the end of April.

As fate would have it, Kurtis's trip was canceled after two Lebanese members of a CBS News film crew were killed by Israeli shellfire shortly before he was to go. That left Holy Week entirely in the hands of the *Today* show. Elaborate plans had been developed to broadcast *Today* live from Rome for the entire week. Friedman called the event unprecedented.

"Nobody has ever done the Colosseum live from the inside," he declared. "We're also still negotiating with the Vatican, and hope to show scenes never before televised. And we've made serious attempts to get the pope on camera."

The trip was initially conceived to cover not only the religious aspects of Holy Week—live from the Vatican in Rome—but every other aspect of life in Rome as well: from fashion and football to terrorism, to Italian politics and the mafia, to the underground econ-omy, to the plot to kill the pope. Interviews were planned with Sophia Loren, designer Valentino, Marcello Mastroianni, and Peter Ustinov, as well as a tour of Naples with Gore Vidal, and a tour of Sicily with Claudia Cardinale.

Nobody thought that *Today* would wind up with the pope. Miracle of miracles, they actually did. It happened, in large part because of the advance work of Timothy Russert, an NBC vice president and a devout Catholic, who wrote a letter to the pope in Polish requesting "an opportunity to pray with you." As it turned out, Russert did everything right. His timing was perfect. His appeal to the pope arrived at a time when the pope himself was acutely aware of the unique power of television. Russert also appealed to Archbishop John Foley, the head of the pontifical commission for social communications, who saw the NBC program as a way for the church to communicate not only the Gospel of Christ, but also what his church was doing. The fact that Foley was from Philadelphia and a former journalist familiar with the American press did not hurt *Today*'s chances.

On Monday, April 1, at 5:45 A.M., in the early light of the Ro-man dawn, during the holiest week of the year, Bryant Gumbel and Jane Pauley, both wearing their microphones, were driven in cars to the Vatican to attend Mass said by the pope at the Pauline Chapel. There they would have an audience with the pope, and the NBC crew would film the pope blessing pictures of the children of Bryant Gumbel and Jane Pauley. The crew captured moving scenes of this event, with the overwhelmed Gumbel, who was raised Roman Cath-olic, and the equally touched Pauley, who was not. Even Garry Trudeau, who accompanied his wife, was awestruck after meeting the pope.

If it was not technically an interview, which the pope has never allowed, it was as close—and as good—as one. *Today* had scored a coup that would not be soon forgotten.

Although that was undoubtedly the highlight of the week, the rest of the week drew attention and raves. Some of the staff of *Today* had gone to Rome more than a month early to plan and prepare different segments. Steve's number-one man, Marty Ryan, who was becoming more attached to Bryant every day, Cliff Kappler, second in command under Ryan, and Karen Curry were the producers, each contributing their own special talents to the success of the week, with the help of some forty staff members.

On Monday, the show opened at the Colosseum in Rome, moving Tuesday and Wednesday to the Spanish Steps, and finally spending Holy Thursday and Good Friday at St. Peter's Square in the Vatican.

Perhaps Willard captured the true spirit of the week, though, when he stood outside in St. Peter's Square and said, "Friends, Romans, Countrymen . . . I come to bury David Hartman, not to praise him."

It was a beautiful week, and an emotional one as well for the *Today* show staff; the ratings were up, and so was the morale—with the exception of one small incident. At the end of the week, a group photo was to be taken of the key people who had been involved in putting the Rome show together. Karen Curry, who had moved to London permanently only a few weeks earlier, had been instrumental in the show's success. She had spent five whole weeks in Rome—more time than anyone else—planning the show, and working on it. The photo was to be taken on a stage that had been built specially for the Rome broadcast, and in order to get onto the platform, several stairs had to be climbed.

On the day of the photo session, Steve Friedman led the way up the stairs. Karen followed behind him. As she was going up the stairs, she heard a voice. It belonged to Bryant Gumbel. She was stunned by what he said: "Oh, come on, Karen, just the guys." He did not want her in the picture. It should not have surprised her. It was normal behavior with "the guys." Cliff, Marty, and Bryant never hid their disgust and their displeasure with her, and not only her—they behaved that way towards many of the female producers on the staff, but that didn't make it any less painful.

Confused and hurt, Karen turned around and walked down the

steps. Then, as she describes it, she did "what any mature woman would do": She walked away and burst into tears.

———

If Steve Friedman had a dream in the tenth month of the thirty-eighth year of his life, it was to beat *GMA* not only in the ratings, but in baseball as well, in the same week.

The sizzling rivalry between the shows had carried itself onto the baseball field. Each show had a team, and the battle on the field was as vicious and mean as it was on the air. The only cardinal rule in terms of baseball was that each team had to have three women playing at any given time. Friedman had two key woman players on whom he relied heavily: Allison Davis, fairly new to the show—the first black writer, male or female, ever to be hired on *Today*, and Marianne Haggerty, an equally gifted baseball player. Both of them were as good at the game as most of the men on the team.

Every Thursday, the Nielsen ratings came out. Friedman studied them with the precision and the eye of a cross between a soothsayer and a bookie. He knew how to predict from the "numbers," as he referred to them, what was likely to happen in the weeks to come. If you understood the numbers, trends were apparent in television ratings. Friedman had known that three years earlier when *GMA* was about to overtake *Today*. Now, as May sweeps approached, in the spring of 1985, he saw that the reverse was about to happen. You never knew for sure, but it looked as if *Today* was on the verge of breaking *GMA*'s three-year hold on first place.

As luck would have it, a baseball game between *Today* and *GMA* had been scheduled for that week. If *Today* won, Steve Friedman might very well fulfill his seemingly unattainable dream.

By chance, Allison Davis stopped by Friedman's office several days before the game. In spite of the fact that she had been at *Today* less than a year, she had already proved her worth, both as a writer and as a baseball player. With Friedman as her boss, she was not sure which of those was more important to her career.

As she entered his office, Friedman pointed at the calendar on his desk, to show her The Day: The day the baseball game was scheduled during the week he predicted *Today* would beat *GMA* in the ratings. It was only a few days away.

Allison looked at the date marked on Friedman's calendar. "Gee, Steve," she said to him. "I can't play. My husband and I are going to Europe."

Steve turned ashen. "What?!" he said.

"I'm sorry," Allison said. "I'm going to Europe. My husband and I are taking a vacation. We got two free tickets on Pan Am."

Steve looked back at Allison with the most serious look she had ever seen on his face.

"Cancel the trip," he said.

Allison laughed. "I'm not canceling the trip," she said.

"Cancel the trip," Friedman repeated. "I'll pay for it."

"I can't cancel the trip," said Allison. "They're free Pan Am tickets. I'm not canceling the trip."

"Cancel the trip," said Friedman. "I'll pay for it. You will not be leaving the show."

Allison stared at him. Suddenly it hit her. "You're serious," she said.

"I'm dead serious," said Steve.

So Allison went home and she said to her husband, "I've got bad news. We're gonna have to postpone the trip for a week."

"Why?" he asked.

"Because I have to play baseball," Allison said.

Her husband started laughing, until he realized she was not kidding, and then he became livid.

"Why are you doing this?" he asked her. "You wouldn't make those sacrifices for me. You wouldn't make those sacrifices for anybody in your family."

It was then that Allison understood why she was doing it. Just after she had begun working on *Today* she received a call from her mother telling her that her father was dying. When Steve heard this news, he took over. He had sent a limo to take Allison to her car, and then he had made arrangements for the limo to stay and get Allison to the airport. After she arrived at the hospital, Steve had called her there several times a day. When her father died a few days later, Steve had sent flowers. The *Today* show had sent flowers. There were to be two wakes for her father: one in Philadelphia where he died and one in Harlem where he was born. On the night of the wake in Harlem, in the middle of a fierce snowstorm, Steve Friedman had shown up. He had been a great comfort to her.

She told this story to her husband with tears streaming from her eyes, and then she said, "If all this man wants me to do is hit a ball, so be it." And she did. Her husband never said another word about the trip. With the help of Marianne Haggerty, whom Steve had recruited in the midst of—and in spite of—a violent attack of stomach cramps, *Today* won the game. They also beat *GMA* in the ratings that week. Friedman's dream had come true.

That was not the end of it. The next baseball game with *GMA* rolled around, and this time not only was Allison three months pregnant, but she had a terrible case of morning sickness. Steve would take no excuses.

"I'll come up for moral support," Allison told him, "but I can't play. Steve, I'm three months pregnant, I'm throwing up, *I'm pregnant!*"

"Okay," said Steve. "Come on. We'll talk about it on the field."

By the time they reached the baseball field, Allison had turned green.

Steve turned to her. "Can you catch?" he asked.

"Steve," she said, "I'm three months pregnant."

"Don't worry, I'll give you some padding," he said.

She went out and caught a couple of balls. Then he said, "Allison, all I want you to do is hit. *Just* get on base."

"Steve," she said. "I'm three months pregnant."

"Please!" he said.

Allison hit a single. By then she was feeling pretty good, but instinctively she put her hand to her stomach. Steve went crazy.

"Get her off the field! Get her off!" he yelled. Then he turned to Marianne. "Haggerty, you run for her!"

He put his arm around Allison. *"All* I wanted was that hit," he told her. He knew that was what he needed to win, and, as usual, he had gotten what he wanted.

——

Scott Goldstein was the one who first got ahold of the story. In 1977, when she was sixteen years old, Cathleen Crowell Webb testified that she had been kidnapped, cut with a broken beer bottle, and raped by a young man whom she identified as Gary Dotson. He was subsequently sentenced to six years in prison.

In March 1985, Webb, now a born-again Christian, told authorities that her accusation had been false. That is when Scott had first learned of the story and gotten her for *Today*. Appearing on the show, Webb had insisted that she made up the story out of fear that she was pregnant by a boyfriend. In April, the judge who had presided over the original trial rejected Webb's recantation and refused to throw out Dotson's conviction. In May, after a three-day hearing, Illinois governor James Thompson commuted Dotson's sentence, although he refused to pardon Dotson, which would have cleared his record of the charges. Dotson was in the process of appealing for a new trial.

When the news of the appeal came down, *Today* went into high gear. By this time they had an "in," not only because Webb had already appeared on the show, but because *Today* had also arranged an earlier appearance together of the mothers of Dotson and Webb. Phil Griffin, the writer assigned to the case, called Dotson's lawyer to propose a meeting between Dotson and Webb together on the *Today* show. The lawyer said he would ask them. He got them to agree.

It was a coup for *Today* to get them first, and no one really cared what happened *after* the two appeared on the show. The value in this case was getting them first. If Dotson and Webb wanted to do *GMA* and *CBS* after that, it was fine—it would only add more hype to what promised to be a full-blown media event.

The hard part for *Today* would be to keep the rest of the media away until after the appearance. Phil Griffin arranged to fly Cathy into New

York on Monday, May 13. Since Gary had just been released from jail on Sunday, he told Phil he would not be able to come to New York until Tuesday. This left Phil with the problem of "hiding" Cathy for twenty-four hours until Dotson arrived. It had been agreed that Gary Dotson and Cathleen Webb would meet for the first time in a hotel room on Tuesday night, after he arrived, along with their lawyers and Webb's husband.

Webb flew into New York from Chicago on American Airlines and Griffin was at La Guardia to pick her up. The problem was, everyone else was there too. The airport was packed with media—every local station and the networks as well. As Webb came out of the airplane, Griffin saw a camera crew trailing behind her. He got her to his car and they began driving—he had to lose the people following them. Webb's husband and her lawyer were in the car with them. They drove around for hours—to Shea Stadium, all through Manhattan, through Chinatown, until they seemed to have freed themselves from the cameras. When they were finally safe, Griffin took them to the expensive hotel on Manhattan's Upper East Side that he had booked for them, where they would have to stay until Dotson arrived the next evening.

Today chartered a plane for Dotson and flew him into the much more obscure Teterboro airport on Tuesday. This time, there was no problem—nobody knew either where or when he was coming. Griffin brought him to the fancy hotel where Webb was, and notified Cathy that Dotson was there. Then the lawyer had asked Griffin to leave. That night, purportedly for the first time, Cathleen Webb met the man she had accused of raping her eight years before.

The next morning, at 7:09, Dotson and Webb appeared on *Today*. They sat stiffly elbow to elbow on a couch together, facing Jane Pauley, and told Jane about their dramatic meeting at the hotel the night before. Webb had told Dotson that she "could not apologize enough," she told Pauley, adding, "He's not a rapist. He doesn't have the character of a rapist."

Dotson, who was painfully inarticulate during the interview, insisted he was not angry, that he bore more ill will against the system that imprisoned him than against his false accuser. "I hold no bitterness towards her," he told Jane.

Having said that, Webb and Dotson were whisked away in separate limos, first for an appearance on *GMA* and finally to appear on *CBS Morning News* in an interview with Phyllis George—an interview which would ultimately lead to her demise as the show's co-anchor.

Effervescent and chirpy as ever, George ended her interview by calling on Dotson and Webb to shake hands. Finding themselves caught in an unbearably awkward situation, they shook hands limply, but then George took it one step further: "How about a hug?" she prodded.

Astonished, Webb and Dotson declined. George's suggestion was even more inappropriate in light of the fact that Illinois officials were continuing to assert that Dotson was guilty.

George later explained to *Washington Post* critic Tom Shales that she had not meant to offend anyone and that, in any event, the entire Dotson-Webb affair seemed to have become a "charade." The now infamous invitation to hug could not be easily erased from the minds of those who had witnessed it. Less than four months later, on September 4—not even a year after she had gotten the job—Phyllis George would resign from *CBS Morning News*.

Bill Kurtis had left the show two months before that to return to his local anchor position in Chicago, and had been replaced by Bob Schieffer. As the gap between *Today* and *GMA* disappeared, it had been increasingly rumored that Friedman's weekly staff-meeting prediction about David Hartman was coming true: Hartman's status at *GMA* was weakening greatly. Hartman did not respond kindly to the speculation. Although *GMA* still held the lead, *Today* had actually beaten them twice in the ratings that spring—in April, the week of the momentous baseball game, and the following week as well. At the time, Shales wrote in *The Washington Post*, "The usual industry sources claim Hartman staged one of his typical tantrums upon learning of the calamitous mishap," to which a former *GMA* staffer replied, "They were bound to be slitting their throats over there, if David Hartman wasn't doing it for them."

Hartman took exception to the accusation—he wasn't even in town that week, he said—and he insisted that he was as well entrenched as ever in his job at *GMA*. "I've got the best job in television," he said, "and I'll be dragged kicking and screaming from it."

But Friedman would not let up. He calculatingly increased the pressure. He knew the turning point—the day when *Today* would regain its number-one spot after this long, hard haul—was near. "They want us to die," he declared. "I'm telling you, it's war, and we're out there to kill them."

Nine

COME FLY WITH US

Working at *Entertainment Tonight* was nothing like working at *Today*. The pressure was not nearly as great as it had been at *Today*—Steve Friedman, along with Ellin Sanger and the rest of the competition, were conspicuously absent. Besides that, there was no one to beat. Without a war, the dynamics changed completely. All I did was produce one celebrity interview after another, each almost indecipherable from the next. Compared with the *Today* show, *ET* was one-dimensional.

Even as the *Today* show had gotten more dependent on, and desperate for, celebrities for ratings, the core of the show remained news. It was, after all, still a news show, and the news was what held it together. Although *Entertainment Tonight* purported to be entertainment news, there was not much news in entertainment besides the questions of which celebrities were doing what, where, to whom, and why.

The irony was that in the years to come, news coverage—in both print and television—would become more like *Entertainment To-night*. Gradually, as unimaginable as it might seem, even tabloid journalism would begin to have a profound and startling effect on everything including the network news. Television was fast becoming a bottom-line business, and if sensationalism brought ratings while it sacrificed journalistic integrity, so be it. The large corporations that would soon take over the networks—Cap Cities at ABC and General Electric at NBC—sometimes seemed to care more about the business than the journalism.

Still, in the spring of 1985, the *Today* show revolved around news events. If they, in turn, were sensational, then all the better. That is why the hijacking of TWA flight 847 bound from Athens to Rome shortly after 3:00 P.M. on June 14, 1985, became the quintessential news event—the culmination of the booking battle in the war between the morning shows. It brought out, if not the worst, certainly the basest instincts of everyone involved.

It was a perfect media setup. The terrorists who hijacked the plane, members of the Islamic Jihad terrorist organization, knew how to use the airwaves. The drama of the bloodcurdling seventeen-day event unfolded on TV screens around the world for everyone to see: The hijackers forced the pilot of the plane, Captain John Testrake, to land in Beirut, where he was interviewed and photographed by a reporter from Agence France-Presse and an ABC cameraman in the cockpit of the plane with a gun to his head, a startling and terrifying image that was broadcast around the world (instantly making him one of the most sought-after morning-show guests in history).

Each day brought a new set of variables, tantalizing the morning shows as they tried to calculate how to capitalize on the hijacking, and ultimately how to get their hands on the passengers who had become hostages, if they were indeed ever released alive. The terrorists wanted the release of hundreds of Shi'ite prisoners in Israel. It soon became clear that the man who controlled them, a Lebanese Muslim by the name of Nabih Berri, held the key to ending the hijacking. (With that, Berri zoomed to the top of the morning show's "most-wanted" guest list along with Captain Testrake.)

After the first landing in Beirut, where nineteen women and children were released (immediately becoming highly valued prospective morning-show guests), the plane was forced to fly to Algiers, and then back to Beirut again, where one hostage passenger was shot, his body thrown out on the tarmac.

Next, the hijackers demanded that Testrake fly back to Algiers, where the plane landed on Saturday, June 15, nearly twenty-four hours after the hijacking had begun. This time sixty-four more hostages were released (upping the ante for the morning shows considerably), leaving forty male American passengers and crewmen aboard the plane.

It soon emerged that one of the crew, a stewardess named Uli Derickson, had been instrumental in keeping the terrorists at bay, and she became a heroine of sorts (taking her place at the top of the list along with Testrake and Nabih Berri).

The following day, Sunday, June 16, the plane went back to Beirut, where the remaining passengers were taken off the plane, split into small groups and hidden throughout the city—a ploy on the part of the terrorists to thwart a rescue mission. The tension among the press increased each day as the stakes became higher.

During the week that followed, the terrorists allowed five hostages to give a press conference, where one man, Allyn Conwell, an oil executive from Texas who had been working in the Middle East, asked Reagan to refrain from a rescue mission. He caused a stir when he also stated that he sympathized with the hijackers' position; at the same time, he became the spokesman for the hostages. (This, of course, catapulted Conwell to the top of the morning-show wish list.)

On June 26, Nabih Berri released another hostage, Jimmy Dell Palmer, who needed medical attention for a life-threatening heart ailment (and he thereby joined the ranks of the most desired guests).

Four days later, on June 30, after more than two weeks of high-intensity political wrangling, the White House announced that the hostages had been freed and were on their way to Damascus, where they would board a plane to Frankfurt, West Germany, on their way back home to the U.S. (at which point all thirty-nine of them instantly became fair game for the morning-show predators).

The first thing Steve Friedman did when he heard about the hijacking on Friday afternoon, June 14, was to assign *Today* staff members to each of the hostages' families. For the next two weeks, someone on the *Today* show staff was in touch with each family daily, cultivating friendships, trying to be of comfort, but more than anything, doing whatever they could to get them to get their loved ones to do the *Today* show if and when they were released.

He immediately assigned Karen Curry, who had moved to London three months earlier, and her new outspoken assistant, Amy Krivitzky, to cover the crisis from their vantage point in Europe.

Although she was barely five feet tall and looked like a teenager, Amy was a quantity to be reckoned with. She had the classic drive of an overachiever—she would do anything (except kill, she told me later) in order to achieve her goal. She had worked her way up at the *Today* show in New York, where she had begun at the reception desk answering the phones, until the day a viewer who wanted Willard to greet his one-hundred-year-old grandmother called in at 5:00 P.M. on the eve of the grandmother's birthday with the request. The office manager had overheard Amy chastise the caller for waiting until the last minute. "Well, you certainly had time, mister!" she had spouted, referring irreverently to the fact the grandmother was, after all, nearly one hundred years old. After that, Amy was taken off the phones and assigned the job of production assistant.

When she thought she could go no further in New York, Amy Krivitzky decided to leave for Europe, where she became a free-lance producer for NBC and wound up with the more desirable job as Karen Curry's assistant in London. Now the two of them were assigned to the TWA hostage crisis.

On Saturday, the morning after the hijacking, Karen and Amy left for Paris. The word was out that the hostages who had been released by the terrorists in Algiers would be flying directly to Paris. Karen had already learned which hotel in Paris they were headed for, so they got on the first available flight from London to Paris and sped to the hotel with their singular mission: to find whatever hostages they could get their hands on and get them on the *Today* show, live.

When they got to the hotel they split up—they could cover more territory that way. Amy ran into trouble immediately—she was stopped by a hotel security guard. "You can't come through! You're a journalist!" he yelled, blocking her from moving another inch. She understood French, but she ignored him. She was determined that nothing was going to stop her—until she looked up and found herself staring into the face of a fierce, snarling attack dog, who looked like he was ready to kill her. She screamed at the top of her lungs. Miraculously, just a canine incisor away from her demise, like a scene directly out of *Superman*, a soundman she knew from London appeared out of nowhere, scooped her up, and saved her life.

Undaunted, she crept around to the back of the hotel and found a way to sneak in, surreptitiously making her way to the hotel elevator. When she stepped into the elevator, she couldn't believe her good fortune. She had hit the jackpot—the elevator was filled with hostages.

She kept her cool. "Where are you all going?" she asked them.

"We're going up to the room for a reception," one of the weary hostages replied.

All Amy knew was that she had to get into the reception room. She followed them as though she were one of them, and this time she got past security. "I'm here to see . . ." She thought for a moment. ". . . My uncle Joe was on the plane." The words spilled out of her mouth.

"Oh, sweetie, come here," said one of the hostages in the room, motioning her over. "Sit down on the bed. Where is your uncle Joe?"

A few feet away, another security guard eyed her suspiciously. After several minutes he came over. "Who are you looking for?" he asked, staring at her jewelry. She was only wearing a watch and a ring, but the hostages had been stripped of all of their jewelry by the terrorists. It struck her then that she was the only person in the room with a watch on. That was it for Amy—the guard ejected her from the room—but not before she managed to get a list of names of some of the hostages. Now at least she could begin to try to find out which rooms they were in.

While this was going on, Karen had been downstairs in the lobby on the phone, talking with the *Today* show office in New York, where wire reports were coming in each moment adding new names to the list of passengers who had been aboard TWA flight 847. After she got kicked out of the reception, Amy went down to the lobby, and as Karen got the names from the passenger list, she gave them to Amy, who set out immediately to try to track them down.

When Karen had all the information, she joined Amy in the hostage search. They covered every inch of the hotel like private detectives, two zealots possessed by a mission that had to be accomplished at all costs. It would be an understatement to say that Karen and Amy were relentless: They went to the coffee shop, calling out hostages' names; they called their rooms; they trailed the representatives from TWA, begging them to help; they wrote notes ("We know you've been through a terrible ordeal, but . . . would you do the *Today* show?") and left them on toilet seats, on scraps of paper, anything they could find.

Back in New York, an aggressive researcher by the name of Cheryl Wells had become astonishingly adept with the hostages' families, and she was making headway on the domestic front, getting any information she could from them; convincing them she really wanted to help, that the *Today* show wanted to help them in any way they could; talking with them for hours, coddling them, and then delicately extracting details only they could provide—the names of other family members, which room their loved one was staying in at the hotel in Paris, and even personal messages they might like Karen or Amy to deliver.

Bit by bit, Cheryl passed her information along to Amy and Karen, bringing them one step closer to their prey. With Cheryl's information, they were able to add specific touches to their notes: "We've spoken to your family and your mother is fine . . ." "Your brother, Bob, says hello . . ." The hostages were anxious for any information they could get.

It still was not easy getting a hostage to do a live shot for the show the next day. In fact, it proved to be impossible. It was turning into a circus; CBS and ABC were equally desperate. In the end, nobody got a live shot from Paris, because the hostages departed before airtime on Monday morning. The astounding saga continued.

In no time, the word came down from NBC to do whatever was necessary to get the hostages for NBC's air. The next day when the remaining hostages were taken off the plane, split into groups, and hidden throughout Beirut, Amy Krivitzky was sent to Cyprus. Since the U.S. had no diplomatic presence in Beirut, Cyprus was the key point, the best place to monitor what was going on in Beirut, and the first place planned for touchdown if and when the remaining hostages were released.

While Amy laid wait in Cyprus, Jimmy Dell Palmer, the man with the potentially fatal heart ailment, was released by Nabih Berri. Exhausted, Amy had been lying in the sun in her bikini, trying to rest for a moment, when the news of Palmer's release had blasted over her walkie-talkie. By this time, it already seemed that all the world's press had descended upon Cyprus. As Amy heard the earthshaking announcement, it certainly appeared to her that all of Cyprus was heading for the airport. She didn't even waste the time to change her clothes—she just threw her T-shirt over her bikini and made a beeline for the airport.

Ironically, the *Today* show was on the air when Jimmy Dell Palmer and his fragile heart touched down in Cyprus. The press was there in droves. Amy was in charge of the *Today* show crew, since Karen had gone to Athens to try to get Allyn Conwell's wife when they had learned she was on the island of Corfu, near Athens.

The airport was overflowing with reporters and television crews. Amy was undoubtedly the shortest person awaiting Palmer's arrival. She was stuck all the way in the back, barely able to get a glimpse of what was going on, which did not make her happy. She strained to see over the crowd, and pushed her way forward, clutching in her hand a tiny broadcast microphone and an earpiece the NBC soundman had given her, which was a direct link between NBC and whoever wore it. All three American networks were wired and prepared to go live.

The tension was unbearable—the air was charged with so many conflicting emotions, most notably sorrow and greed. Everybody felt sorry for Palmer the man, but Palmer the guest was an invaluable object that everybody wanted to get his hands on.

When the plane finally landed, Palmer appeared. The crowd fell stunningly silent. Jimmy Dell Palmer stood there, dazed, staring at the people who were gawking back at him.

The instant she got a look at Jimmy Dell Palmer, something—a mysteriously powerful, indefinable force—overtook Amy Krivitzky. She simply could not fight it—it was so much bigger than she was. In the thick, tense silence, unaware of what she was doing, she lifted her hand, clutching the tiny earpiece. Her arm grew, until it felt like it was ten feet long, and short little Amy Krivitzky, clad only in her T-shirt and her skimpy bikini, reached all the way up to Palmer with the earpiece and uttered these words: "Stick this in your ear."

She did not know where the words had come from, but they slipped out of her mouth as though they had a life of their own—and they were broadcast live, through the tiny NBC microphone she held gingerly in her hand, for millions of people to hear.

But that was not the end of it. Something even more astounding happened next. Palmer, still reeling from his ordeal, reached down and took the earpiece and put it in his ear. When the shocked crowd realized what Amy had done, things deteriorated even further. Someone from ABC ripped the NBC earpiece out of Palmer's ear and replaced it with an ABC earpiece. When that happened, someone else from CBS ripped out the ABC earpiece and stuck a CBS earpiece into Palmer's ear. And Palmer, the man who had been released as a hostage because of a grave heart condition, stood there, nearly trampled.

In the end, nobody got Jimmy Dell Palmer. In all the scuffle, the lines went down, because everyone was stepping on everyone else's cables. Nobody was able to broadcast anything. When the State Department got wind of what had happened to Palmer, they hid him away from the press until his flight left Cyprus.

Back in New York, at GMA, Ellin Sanger had been working on the hostage case like Woodward and Bernstein rolled into one. While Nabih Berri was deep in the throes of negotiating the release of the hostages, she had tracked down a person in a group called Save Lebanon and with that, she had struck gold. The man had sent her to another contact, who told her he could put her directly in touch with Nabih Berri. She never saw the second man and never knew who he was—she only spoke with him by phone. All he told her was that she should call the number he gave her at a certain time and that Nabih Berri would be there.

Never doubting her abilities for a second, she arrived at the GMA control room at 3:00 A.M. on the appointed day to begin calling the number she had been given. The only place she could call from was the audio booth in the control room, a soundproof booth that was constructed in such a way that the noise from the control room was blocked out, as was any noise coming from within the booth.

Ellin called the mysterious number in Lebanon for four hours. It began to seem like a futile exercise. Each time she got through, someone would answer the phone, she would ask for Nabih Berri, and then they would hang up. She kept dialing with resolve anyway. Finally, at 7:00 A.M., just as GMA went on the air, Nabih Berri himself picked up the phone. Ellin almost imploded—she could not believe her ears! She was talking directly to her first *live* terrorist. She had Nabih Berri, the man who was the key to the TWA hostage crisis, on the phone with her from the control room at GMA—*while her show was on the air!* All she had to do now was let someone outside of the sound booth know.

The short, stocky Sanger began to pound madly on the Plexiglas window of the audio booth, desperately trying to get someone, *anyone,* to look at her. Since she could not risk letting Berri get away, she could not leave the booth. She banged and pounded and waved. She gesticulated wildly. No one saw or heard her from the insulated sound booth. She pounded harder, making bizarre faces, while she kept up a running conversation with Nabih Berri. She started to go crazy, like an animal in a cage, when finally, at last, someone looked up and noticed her.

But this was Ellin Sanger, and Ellin was prone to unpredictable behavior, to say the least, so this was nothing new. "Throw her a piece of meat!" said the guy who had spotted her, and he turned back to what he had been doing before he looked up. Luckily someone else saw her and this time paid attention. Within moments, David Hartman was on the air with Nabih Berri by phone, live on GMA.

When it came time for the news break, Ellin had to keep Berri on the phone so they could get him back on the air. She had to keep the conversation going. "How's the weather in Beirut?" she asked Berri. "Are you tired? What's new?"

She could not believe she was asking him these mundane questions, and she was not paying attention to his answers, just trying to keep him talking, until the words she heard Berri utter caught her by surprise. "Miss Ellin," he was asking her, "would you like to talk to a hostage?"

Her heart leapt into her throat. "Which one?" she replied, riveted, struggling to contain herself.

"Which one you want?" he asked her nonchalantly.

At that moment, Ellin looked up on the monitor in the control room and saw that Pierre Salinger, an ABC correspondent, was standing in Cyprus with the wife of Allyn Conwell, ready to go on the air with her for an interview.

Ellin's head was spinning. "I want Allyn Conwell," she told Berri. "No problem," said Berri obligingly. Just like that, Ellin Sanger got Allyn Conwell, and ABC was able to link Conwell together by phone with his wife—while he was still a hostage—for all of GMA's viewers to see. As Ellin Sanger watched the monitor from the sound booth, she heard Mrs. Conwell pleading, "Would you please release my husband, Mr. Nabih Berri?" Across town, over at the *Today* show control room, Steve Friedman was on the brink of throwing another shoe through the monitor.

Amy had gone crazy when she learned that ABC had chartered a jet and flown Mrs. Conwell in from Corfu to Cyprus for the interview. She and Karen had been foiled! Losing Mrs. Conwell was a major defeat, and Amy was not about to let it go at that. She got the ABC producer to promise she could have Mrs. Conwell after the ABC interview was over—that would at least mean the *Today* show could have her on the air the same day.

When the interview was over, the ABC producer sped off with Mrs. Conwell in tow and shepherded her into the ladies' room. Aghast, Amy chased after them. It was clear that ABC had no intention of keeping their promise, and now they were trying to hide poor Mrs. Conwell in the bathroom. There she was, her husband still a hostage, and they had shoved her into a stall in the ladies' room of the hotel where the interview had taken place.

This, after all, was war, and Amy Krivitzky was not about to be outdone. Barely able to keep herself from crawling right into the stall with Mrs. Conwell, she slipped a note under the door begging her to do the *Today* show. She pleaded with her through the stall's partition. There was no time to spare—the seconds were ticking away. Mrs. Conwell burst into tears. And *Today* never got Mrs. Conwell that day.

Twelve days had passed since the hijacking had occurred. With each passing day, the intensity of the war for the hostages grew. The fact that the *Today* show was now beating GMA regularly in the ratings only fueled Friedman's fire. He did not want to lose this one. And neither did the network. Now it was made clear by the highest echelon at NBC that they wanted to "own" the hostages.

So the pressure was cranked up as high as it could go. Every second of this mad drama had been monitored by the press, which had been fed by the White House, which had been fed, in turn, by Nabih Berri. Now, finally, on June 28, two full weeks after the plane had been hijacked, word was out that the end was near. When it came, the press was firmly led to believe that the hostages would be released in Damascus and then flown to Frankfurt, Germany.

Friedman pulled out all the stops. He wanted everything—every one of them. He wanted to lock them up, literally, which is almost what his loyal troops did.

Amy flew to Frankfurt and Karen went to Damascus. Another *Today* producer, Merle Rubine, who had been working on the hijacking in London and Paris, also went to Frankfurt. Allison Davis, who had finally gotten her European vacation with her husband, was tracked down and summoned to Frankfurt. And last, but not least, Cheryl Wells, who had by this time established close ties with several of the hostage families, arranged transportation for members of two of the families—four people in all—to Frankfurt, courtesy of NBC, and she personally escorted them there.

In fact, the chaos had just begun. In Frankfurt, things got really messy. An NBC office was set up at the hotel where the incoming hostages were scheduled to stay. When Cheryl Wells arrived with the four family members, Allison Davis met all of them at the gate. "Look, Allison," Cheryl said to her, before they even took a step. "These people are very tired. All they want is a room. They don't want any press. They just want to be left alone."

Allison was more than happy to comply. It had obviously not been NBC's intention to fly these people all the way from the U.S. to Frankfurt, Germany, so they could appear on other television shows. But there was still some dangerous downtime for the family members NBC had flown in, since they had arrived on a Saturday and could not appear on the *Today* show until Monday.

Allison insists that she pulled the hostages' family members aside at the gate and told them, "There are a million press people at the hotel.

They have discovered you were on the plane. They've been hounding our little office here. Would you like to speak to them?" (She did not, she says, want anyone to say that NBC had hogged the story.) According to her, the family members replied, "Absolutely not. We are exhausted. All we want is our rooms."

When they got to the hotel, their rooms were not ready. They were told there would be a three-hour wait, so Allison offered them her room. She told them they could rest there until their own rooms were ready. At least she had two double beds. Then she left for the NBC office, and that was when the trouble began.

The word had gotten out very quickly that NBC had flown some hostages' relatives in. As Allison Davis stepped into the hotel elevator on her way to the office, she was cornered by a producer from CBS. "Are you Allison Davis?" she asked.

"Yes, who are you?" Allison replied.

"You are harboring hostage families!" screamed the producer.

"Excuse me?" Allison replied.

"I want to know where your room is," the producer blurted, "because you are harboring hostage families and that's not fair!"

"What are you talking about?" said Allison. "I know where these families are, but they asked me not to disturb them and they asked me not to reveal where they were. If they had told me they wanted to talk to you, I wouldn't care. They can talk to whoever they want to—it's a free country. They're gonna be on our show on Monday and that is all I care about."

Incensed, the CBS woman had hesitantly left, but soon after that things got worse. There was one run-in after another. All of the other networks blatantly accused NBC of harboring hostages. A reporter from *The New York Times* was especially irked with the situation, and he began to harass Allison, accusing her of illegally harboring hostages, and the next day the story made it to the front page of *The New York Times*.

Allison contends that after that, she called all the people from the *Today* show together and insisted that they behave according to the rules. "We're going to go by the book on this one," she told them. "Do what you can for the hostages' families, but don't tell them they're restricted. Don't tell them they can't do another show. Don't tell them any of that."

These instructions were impossible for Amy Krivitzky to grasp. After she arrived in Frankfurt, she had only one mission: to get Allyn Conwell's wife and keep her until Conwell was released. NBC chartered a plane to bring Mrs. Conwell from Corfu to Frankfurt. She was escorted on the flight by a free-lance reporter Amy had hired, a former colleague of hers by the name of Jonathan Mann, who personally delivered Mrs. Conwell into Amy's hands in Frankfurt. Amy knew exactly how much Steve Friedman wanted Allyn Conwell. She repeated her instructions to herself like a mantra. "Don't lose the wife," she chanted in her head. "If we have the wife, then we'll get the guy when he's released."

She had already booked a room in a hole-in-the-wall in Frankfurt, well away from the fancy Sheraton Hotel in which most of the members of the press were staying. Then she kept Mrs. Conwell hidden. She would not let her out of the room. She sent out for food; she fed her and took care of her; she would not even let her answer the phone, shielding her completely from the other networks. Even when the State Department called, Amy, telling them she was a friend of the family, would only say that she would get their message to Mrs. Conwell. She insists that Mrs. Conwell did not mind the way she was being treated—ironically the same way as her husband who was being held by terrorists. "She was emotionally exhausted," Amy says emphatically. "Mrs. Conwell just wanted to be taken care of."

On the day of the release of the hostages, June 30, 1985, the families were told by the State Department to be at the U.S. military airbase near the Frankfurt Airport at three o'clock in the morning. Amy arranged for an NBC driver to take Mrs. Conwell to the gate, but that did not make her any less terrified of losing her. People from all the networks had been harassing her incessantly, calling her and saying things like, "You can't keep people there. You can't hide people away like that." ("We weren't harboring hostages," Amy explains. "We were harboring the hostages' families.")

As an added measure of protection, Amy asked one of the senior NBC executives who had come to Frankfurt if she could send her free-lance reporter, Jonathan, with Conwell's wife, and say he was a family friend. "All right," the executive replied. "He's free-lance. I don't know what you're doing, you crazy girl. We never had this conversation." With that, Amy planted her reporter at the arrival gate in the middle of the night, with Mrs. Conwell.

George Bush, who was vice president at the time, was at the gate to meet the hostages when they alit from the plane. So was Amy Krivitzky's former colleague, the free-lance reporter Jonathan Mann. Amy was back at the hole-in-the-wall hotel, nervously watching the whole thing on television. She saw Allyn Conwell step off the plane. She saw the other hostages coming off the plane, and then what she saw next, she could not believe: The reporter she had planted there, who was dressed like a hostage and had not shaved for several days, was on TV right before her eyes, shaking hands with Vice President Bush, pretending he was one of the hostages!

Amy was certain that Jonathan Mann was going to get arrested. But he managed to meet Allyn Conwell, and that did not hurt at all. Her job was not done yet, though. She had booked the Conwells a room in the hole-in-the-wall hotel to keep them away from the rest of the crowd, which was exactly what Amy says the Conwells said they wanted.

Shortly after the happily reunited couple arrived at the hotel, Amy knocked at the door of their room with a bouquet of flowers to say welcome back. In spite of everything that had happened, the Conwells were gracious and Amy Krivitzky finally attained her lofty goal. Allyn Conwell appeared on the *Today* show on Monday.

When it was over, the *Today* show had won the hostage contest in Frankfurt hands down, but not without a price. Amy herself had become one of the most despised enemies of the other networks. "Whenever they would see me, they would say, 'You . . . little shit.'

It was really abusive. I had really bad nightmares. I went away for a few days in Germany after it was all over," she says.

There, she had some time for a bit of introspection. She knew what had been driving her: "If I'm given a job and my job is to get this person, I will do what I have to in order to do it. I would do anything in my means to get that job done. I didn't do it because I really believed I was helping any of them. I didn't do it because I thought I was doing something for mankind or even for Mrs. Conwell. I just wanted to do the best I possibly could and I wouldn't stop until I tried everything."

What she never could understand, though, was why no one ever said no to her. "If the woman had told me 'Lady, you are giving me a headache, go away,' I would have," she insists. "She never told me to stop. I always wondered why none of these people ever told me to go away—'Please stop.'

"I remember we poked one of the hostages' eyes with our walkie-talkie and still he talked to me. His best friend had been killed by the terrorists and he still talked to me. It makes me sick that everyone talked to me. I never understood it. I was always waiting for them to say 'Please, lady, go away.' "

Even when it was over in Frankfurt, it was not over for the morning shows, and the rivalry did not diminish. On the day the hostages returned to the States, via New York, Adrienne Wheeler (who had once been Tom Brokaw's assistant on *Today*) was in her kitchen making dinner. It was Sunday afternoon and Adrienne was right in the middle of one of her favorite recipes when her phone rang. It was Cliff Kappler and Merle Rubine together, telling her to get to the airport. They had just received word that the hostages' plane was going to be arriving at JFK.

"Okay. Fine," said Adrienne, and her mind immediately started churning. The hostages had become a consuming passion for much of the *Today* staff, and Adrienne immediately began to work out a plan—

how she was going to beat the other networks to the hostages she wanted at the airport.

Merle had informed her that Cheryl Wells had been told by one of the hostages' wives that he would do the *Today* show on Monday. They still had to lock him up, and Adrienne did not know how they were going to find him.

Cheryl Wells, who had just returned from Frankfurt, was going to accompany Adrienne. Cheryl had already talked with the hostage's wife, who had said she thought her husband would do it, but that he would need a new outfit of clothes if he were going to appear on TV.

Adrienne left her half-made dinner, got in her car and went to Stern's clothing store, which luckily was open on Sunday. There, having learned the hostage's size from Cheryl, who had gotten it from his wife, she bought him a pair of Calvin Klein pants and a Ralph Lauren shirt and then she had the clothes put on a hanger. Her strategy was forming. Soon she knew exactly what she would do. She would pretend to be his sister-in-law, bringing him a change of clothes. (She knew she could not pose as his sister, because he was white, and she was black.)

Cheryl and Adrienne proceeded to the airport in the NBC limo. When they arrived, Adrienne announced her plan to Cheryl. "Okay, I know what to do," she told her. "I'm just gonna go up there and get him."

Cheryl watched as Adrienne talked her way past one of the airline officials. While Adrienne got closer to the gate, Cheryl functioned like a blocker on a football team, keeping the competition occupied each time one of them made their way toward the gate.

Although there was a planeful of ex-hostages coming in, the particular hostage that Adrienne was after was especially desirable because he met the main requirement for the show: he was a "good talker." Cheryl already knew this about him from Frankfurt, but so did everyone else, and all of the networks were after him.

When Adrienne encountered the next official, she began to act very emotional. Tears welled up in her eyes. "I want to see my brother-in-law," she told him. Then, becoming more excited, she said, "I have a change of clothes for him," and she held up the clothes on the hanger.

When she looked up, she saw that the hostages were getting directly onto a bus that had been waiting there for them. Seeing no other alternative, she climbed onto the bus with the hostages. As the bus pulled away, Adrienne looked out the window. There was Cheryl at the curb, waving her good-bye. Then Cheryl got back into the NBC limo and followed the hostages' bus—the one carrying Adrienne Wheeler.

The bus arrived at the hotel, where the hostages were to gather, according to plan, in the hospitality room. All Adrienne knew was that the man she was looking for would be wearing a red shirt. She had not been able to identify him on the bus she was on, and that was the only information she had, so she went directly to the hospitality room. The minute she walked in, she saw a man in a red shirt sitting on the couch.

Everyone in the room was watching her as she walked over to the man in the red shirt. She sat down next to him on the couch, and then she flung her arms around him and embraced him emotionally. "Thank God, you're okay," she said, the tears overflowing again. He looked at her as if she were crazy—he had never seen her before in his life.

"Listen," Adrienne whispered in his ear. "Please don't give me away. I'm Adrienne Wheeler from the *Today* show." She continued hugging him, squeezing him as tightly as she could. He continued looking at her like she was a lunatic.

"Look!" Adrienne said cheerfully. "I got you a change of clothes!" She had won him over. The man, who had just acquired a black sister-in-law and a new designer outfit, appeared on the *Today* show the next morning.

The TWA hostage story would not end for the morning shows for several months. Two highly valuable guests were still up for grabs: Captain John Testrake, the pilot of the hijacked plane, and Uli Derickson, the heroic stewardess.

Marianne Haggerty had been on the case of Testrake and Derickson since the day their names first surfaced on the wires. Steve had given her this mission. He really wanted Testrake and Derickson, and no one was more vulnerable to Friedman's wishes and commands than Marianne. "We would get firsts because of Steve," she says. "Because people didn't want to say to him, 'I can't,' or 'I'm not going to,' because if you didn't deliver, that was it."

From the moment she had been assigned to the case, she had been calling the public-relations man at TWA. She had called him every day for months, harassing him unrelentingly. She would call him and then she would cry on the phone and she would plead with him. "Please," she begged, "don't you ever let them do any other show . . . If you do, I'm dead."

After a few months, when Uli Derickson was ready to talk, the TWA man put Marianne in touch with her, and Marianne skillfully convinced Derickson to do the *Today* show. She also made it painfully clear to her that she could not do anything else. She made her understand the way the morning shows operated, the extent of the competition, and the fact that she could only do one show. Uli liked Marianne and she agreed.

On the day of the interview, Marianne arrived in an NBC limo to pick up Uli Derickson, who was accompanied by the public-relations man from TWA. Marianne had scored a coup by getting Uli, and the word that she had gotten her was out. Before the interview, Tom Brokaw came to the *Today* show greenroom and said to Marianne, "How in the world did you get her?"

"By virtue of the fact that I was afraid not to," Marianne replied.

"Well, I'd like to do a little thing with her when you're done," said Tom. Then he turned to Uli and said, "I'm Tom Brokaw, and I'd like to do a story with you when you're done here."

"I'm sorry," replied Uli Derickson. "I promised Marianne that I would only do one thing and I am here to do that."

Brokaw and his producer, M. L. Flynn, who was standing with him in the greenroom, could not believe their ears. "You don't understand, Tom Brokaw is our network," said Flynn. "He is our anchor, this is very prestigious. Tom is here this morning and he never comes out personally to get a guest . . ."

Uli turned to Marianne. "Marianne," she said, "could you explain to her that I am only doing one thing. I promised you, and I'm not going to do anything else."

Marianne was not nearly as lucky in the battle for Captain Testrake. Ellin Sanger had been dogging him from the beginning, and she had caught up with him the day he returned from Frankfurt. Testrake had also been interviewed by Hartman, along with Allyn Conwell, the day Ellin had gotten Nabih Berri by phone. For all intents and purposes, Ellin had Testrake locked up.

There was nothing Marianne could do about that, but she had every intention of getting Testrake for the second hour of *Today*, after the *GMA* interview was over.

The morning of the Testrake interview, Ellin picked up Captain Testrake and the public-relations man from TWA in an ABC limo. Ellin noticed that they were being followed. They arrived at ABC and did the interview. Ellin had already decided that when it was over she would take Testrake and his wife to Windows on the World, a restaurant atop the 107-story World Trade Center in Manhattan, for breakfast. She figured that as a pilot, Testrake would be comfortable as high up in the air as she could get him.

On the way to the restaurant, Ellin noticed that they were still being followed by the same car that had been tailing them earlier. As they alit from their limo in front of the World Trade Center and entered the rotunda, Marianne Haggerty appeared. The man from TWA was exasperated to see her again. "Not you!" he cried. "I'm going to have you arrested!"

"You have to be kidding!" said Marianne. "You can't arrest me. I'm on public property!"

"If you follow me one more time, I am going to have you arrested!" he shouted back. "I don't want to see your face again—you are screaming at me in the lobby!" He looked as though he was going to burst into tears. They were yelling so loudly their words echoed throughout the building.

"You can't do anything to me!" said Marianne. "I'm following you in a car! There's nothing you can do to me!" All she could think of throughout this mad encounter was having to tell Steve that she did not get Testrake.

They had finally come to the end of the road. The TWA public-relations man, weary and defeated, turned to Marianne. "Miss Haggerty," he told her. "I just want you to know I'm retiring, and you're a very big part of that decision."

For the morning shows at least, the TWA hostage crisis was over.

Ten

THE LIGHT AT THE END OF THE TUNNEL

During the worst moments of the TWA hijacking, the world seemed so immense. The hostages were being held captive in a faraway land by members of a terrorist group that most of them had never heard of. Conversely, back in L.A., the world seemed to be getting smaller each day. Rona Barrett surfaced at *Entertainment Tonight*, and I, of all people, was assigned to be her producer.

This was problematic. Rona had been hired to do a "Hollywood News" segment on *ET*. I knew when I was given the job as her producer that Rona's style was different from mine, that I did not want to do the kinds of pieces she wanted to do. Ironically, Rock Hudson's death from AIDS at precisely the time of Rona's debut on *Entertainment Tonight* cemented our incompatibility. Highly charged for her opening show, Rona joined the circus surrounding Hudson's death by doing a story that focused on whether any of Hudson's costars over the years, from Doris Day to Linda Evans, were in danger of contracting the disease from having kissed him.

From that moment, I knew I would not last long as Rona Barrett's producer.

I finally left *Entertainment Tonight* because of yet another highly publicized death thousands of miles away. On December 31, 1985, the famous primatologist Dian Fossey was brutally murdered in her cabin at her research camp in Rwanda, in Central Africa. My husband was assigned by *Life* magazine to cover the story of Fossey's murder in Rwanda. I could not pass up the chance to go with him. It was the impetus I needed to act on my decision to leave *Entertainment Tonight*.

I told my boss at *ET*, Jack Reilly, that I would be leaving my job in a few weeks. It would take us that long to get the visas we needed, and I was obligated to give adequate notice. To this day, I am convinced that it was the best decision of my life. Uncovering the Fossey story with Harold turned out to be the most intriguing experience I have ever had.

———

The year I left *Entertainment Tonight*, 1986, was the same year *Today* finally and unequivocally regained first place in the morning race for the first time in more than three years.

For the second time in three years, Jane Pauley was pregnant—which she later admitted was as much of a surprise to her as it was to everyone else. Friedman was especially chagrined. His show had finally clawed its way back to the top. This meant that now, too soon, he would lose Jane once more, when she took her maternity leave at a terribly inopportune moment. That could really cost him, more than just first place. *Today* and GMA were now one full rating point apart, and that one-point lead was worth an additional $10 million in revenues for NBC. It was a lead they did not want to lose.

Jane pleaded total innocence. "If Friedman was shocked, I was shocked more," she insisted. "Believe me, this is not the way I planned to spend the year. I planned to have two children. This third baby decided to come on its own. I want to go on the record that the baby [she already knew it was a boy], is welcome. And I'll find room for it."

Jane would have a very full schedule from the time her pregnancy was announced on January 1 until she went on maternity leave, which she planned to do immediately following the wedding of Prince Andrew and Sarah Ferguson in London on July 23. Friedman had every intention of keeping her as busy and as visible as possible until then. He planned to continue his highly successful travel strategy: *Today* would go to Rio de Janeiro and Buenos Aires in February, and in May it would be broadcast live from the S.S. *Norway*, a mammoth cruise ship, while it sailed from Wilmington, North Carolina, to Miami and various points in between.

Friedman had his whole "family" in place now, exactly the way he wanted it: Bryant and Jane were on a magical roll as the anchors; John Palmer was an appealing newsman; Gene Shalit was zany and popular; Willard added the final essential touch of folksiness, and Friedman knew that people were obviously responding to that. He recognized Willard's value. "Scott is a very important factor on the show," he explained. "He appeals to people who might not warm up right away to Bryant and Jane: the older generation—people in smaller towns. What Willard does is give you something to smile about. When you realize he is real, you fall in love with the guy."

A close-knit, attractive family was essential to morning television. It fed the intimacy between viewer and talent that was so uniquely integral to the morning-show ratings. Friedman finally had in his *Today* show "family" exactly what he needed: "I had the streetwise tough kid in Bryant; everybody's sweetheart in Jane; the wacky uncle in Willard; the wacky cousin in Gene Shalit; and the man every mother wanted their daughter to marry in John Palmer," he said.

Everything was going so well. The trips continued to be a gold mine for the ratings, and South America was no different. It was a smashing success, except for two minor but unpleasant incidents— one on the air, and the other off. The core of the "Boys Club" had gone off to Rio: Steve, Marty, Cliff, and Bryant. Scott Goldstein stayed in New York.

Everything proceeded smoothly for the first few days—Jane appeared on the set in Rio with Bryant, wearing sunglasses, and the hot, enticing equatorial sun beamed down on both of their happy faces—until the gods, or the wind currents, intervened on the third day when a fierce storm hit. Scott Goldstein was at his post in the control room in New York when the disaster struck. The chance that such a thing could happen was infinitely small, but that did not keep it from happening: The satellite went down in the storm, which meant there was absolutely no transmission from Rio, right in the middle of the *Today* show—there was nothing at all on the air, which was a producer's ultimate nightmare. It was up to Scott Goldstein to figure out what to fill the dead air with from New York. And, of course, all this was happening live.

It was a total debacle. Scott could not believe what was happening. The only words he could think of were *Oh shit*. He alone was in charge of the control room, and, under the circumstances, that was an unfortunate thing to be in charge of. There was literally not a second to lose. Scott started to scream orders amid the confusion that had erupted. The prevailing wisdom said that should such a thing ever happen, you should go to a commercial or to a backup tape. Scott went to a commercial, because there *were* no backup tapes, a direct ramification of Steve Friedman's go-for-broke style. As he had done all his life, Friedman played to win, and it was his philosophy that if you could fall back on something you would, and *that* would drain the immediacy from the moment. That was one thing that did not happen during the Rio show.

To say there was total chaos in the control room would be a gross understatement. As Scott screamed at the top of his lungs from New York, Marty and Steve screamed back from Rio. It was one of those moments that never leaves you. "I saw my life flash before my eyes in the middle of it," recalls Scott. "John Palmer, who was at the news desk, was vamping, and we reran parts of interviews that we had shown earlier that day. We made it up as we went along."

Under the circumstances, Scott did all that he could do, but it did not begin to stem the crisis. The hysteria continued for what seemed like forever. Nobody knew exactly how to fix it, so everyone just kept screaming back and forth between Rio and Rockefeller Center.

In the end, they all learned at least one lesson: From that time on, in spite of Friedman's play-to-win theory, they made it a point to prerecord interviews from abroad and send them in advance, so that if the satellite ever went down again, they would not be caught without something to run on tape.

Another negative thing happened during the trip to South America—yet another blatant incident of cruelty on the part of Marty, Cliff, and Bryant directed at Karen Curry. During one of the days *Today* broadcast from Argentina, all of the producers, including Karen, were supposed to go to a location together. Karen was driving a separate car, when the boys decided to take off on a high-speed chase in an attempt to get rid of her. They succeeded: She never got to where they were going. They were repeatedly hurtful and mean. When the control room was built for the broadcast of the show from the Argentina location, they purposely neglected to put a seat in for her.

In spite of their behavior, the ratings for the week in South America not only marked the *Today* show's tenth straight victory, but the largest television audience ever for *Today*—or any other morning program. (*Today* had a 6.9 rating and a 27 share, which translated into nearly eight million viewers, while *GMA* had a 5.3 rating and a 21 share, and CBS stayed in last place with a 3.3 rating and a 13 share.)

Friedman could finally say legitimately for all the world to hear, "There's no doubt about it now. We're number one. There's no tie; no tenth-of-a-rating-point lead. This is really it."

With *Today* now in this strong position, NBC was reaping an estimated $68 million in ads from the show. The price of a thirty-second ad on *Today* was up to $13,000.

While all this was happening, I was as far removed from the price of an ad as anyone could be. While Bryant and Jane were basking contentedly in the South American sun, I was slipping and sliding my way in dreadfully gooey mud, surrounded by mosquitoes and stinging nettles, at an altitude of well over ten thousand feet, up to the top of Mt. Visoke in Rwanda, to the camp where Dian Fossey had been murdered.

About the time Karen Curry was being ditched by Marty and Cliff and Bryant, I was sitting with Harold in a tin cabin at the camp, drying my wet, mud-caked socks by the fire and talking with Wayne McGuire, the man the Rwandans would accuse within days of our visit of murdering Dian Fossey.

As Harold and I chased around Africa interviewing the people who had been instrumental in Fossey's life, an amazing story began to emerge. I was not a filmmaker, but I could instantly see, as anyone could have, that the tale of Fossey's life—and death—had every element of great fiction, and more: sex, passion, love, hate, violence, politics, mystery, intrigue, and in the end, finally, murder. It truly was astounding.

The day after we returned from Africa, I had a meeting with Brandon Tartikoff. We had met when I produced one of Rona Barrett's in-depth interviews with him only days before I left my job at *Entertainment Tonight*. Since I had almost literally just stepped off the plane, the Fossey story was intensely on my mind and that is what we ended up talking about. Brandon introduced me to Steve White, who at the time was the head of TV-movie production at NBC. White thought that a friend of his, Judy Polone, at Phoenix Entertainment, might be interested in buying the rights to Harold's *Life* piece for a television movie. Ironically, Judy Polone had been the executive producer of *Malice in Wonderland*, the TV movie Elizabeth Taylor was starring in when I had run into her in the parking lot of Pereino's and she had ended up doing an interview for *Entertainment Tonight*.

The events that followed proved to be my initiation into the bizarre world of movie production. By the time it was all over, I learned more than I ever wanted to know.

Judy Polone did buy the rights to the *Life* piece. In the deal that was made, the movie would be based on Harold's *Life* magazine article, which was entitled "The Dark Romance of Dian Fossey." I was to be a coproducer. As it turned out, another producer, Peter Guber, who was then at Warner Bros. along with his partner, Jon Peters, subsequently bought the rights to the *Life* piece from Judy Polone to make it into a feature film instead of a television movie.

A storm of moviemaking jockeying and activity followed. Universal was attempting to make a similar movie because they owned the rights to the book Fossey herself had written about her work with the gorillas. The project became a war of its own. Each studio took out full-page ads in the Hollywood trade papers almost daily, announcing the director they had hired one day, the writer they had hired the next. Warner Bros. and Universal were each trying desperately to get the upper hand, because it would not pay for both of them to make what would essentially be the same film. In the end, they agreed to merge and produce the movie together—a rare occurrence in Hollywood. The last time two studios had produced a movie together had been with *The Towering Inferno*. Now they had decided the film we were involved in would be called *Gorillas in the Mist*.

When the *Today* show broadcast live from the S.S. *Norway* in May, the golden travel formula continued to work. The trip attracted not only ratings, but publicity as well. It started in Wilmington, North Carolina, where Mickey Spillane, the mystery writer, gave a guided tour, and Senator Lowell Weicker and the astronaut Scott Carpenter discussed the need for ocean research.

In Savannah, Georgia, the star of *Night Court*, Harry Anderson, came aboard, and so did singer Gladys Knight—her gospel roots were there. The secretary of the navy, John Lehman, joined the show in Jacksonville, Florida, and the last day of the trip was spent in Miami.

In spite of all that Scott Goldstein had done for *Today*—producing many of the successful road shows, working closely with the show's writers, and getting his hands on some of the best stories to hit the air—things had not improved for him. Although he was one of the producers of the S.S. *Norway* trip, he was also one of the few people not invited aboard the ship.

"It was another way of saying, 'Fuck you, Scott,' " said a staffer on the trip.

"Some people could say that. Some people *did* say that," replied Scott Goldstein. "All I know is they sent me by land. It was a boat show and I wasn't even allowed on the boat." By then it did not matter to him anymore. From the beginning, Scott had only planned to stay in New York for three years, and his legs had been itching since he arrived. Now he was into his fourth year. He had established a close relationship with Steven Bochco, the producer of *Hill Street Blues* and *L.A. Law*, and what he wanted more than anything was to return to L.A. to work for Bochco. It was on the last day of the S.S. *Norway* trip that Scott Goldstein learned that Bochco wanted to hire him as a producer of *L.A. Law*.

The S.S. *Norway* trip brought the competition between *Today* and *GMA* to new heights—or depths. *GMA* was so exasperated with Fried-man's travel ploys that they decided to take to the water themselves to try to one-up him, and with that, the following story appeared in the *Hollywood Reporter*:

ABC's *Good Morning America* is taking the morning news ratings battle to the high seas. The show announced it will make network television history by broadcasting segments live from the *Queen Elizabeth 2* while it is sailing in the mid-Atlantic Ocean July 1-3. The GMA broadcast follows last month's *Today* show broadcasts from the S.S. *Norway*, but differs, according to a spokeswoman for GMA, because the *Norway* was stationary or docked when *Today* aired its programming.

The trip on the *QE2* did not do much good. In motion or not, on sea or on land, the *Today* show maintained its solid first-place lead. There was only one possible hitch: On July 24, 1986, Jane Pauley would abandon *Today* once more, and she would not be back until October 13, the day of her tenth anniversary on the show.

Eleven

THE SUN ALSO RISES

The effects of *Today*'s return to first place were greater than anyone could have anticipated—and, surprisingly, they were not all good. Being number one again was deeply satisfying for everyone on the show who had fought so hard in the frenzied battle. Still, things were far from perfect. The "inner circle" had become more entrenched with time. The ambience that grew out of its presence hurt the morale of those who were not in it. Being first in the ratings made certain things easier for everyone in terms of doing their jobs, especially when it came to booking the toughest guests. But the prevailing atmosphere inside the show was one thing that certainly had not improved with the ratings.

There were a variety of activities in and out of the office—from baseball pools to golf pools, even the *real* baseball games—that promoted an increasingly separatist and disturbing atmosphere. The "guys" and the few select women they thought were okay, the women they allowed to play along with them—those women, that is, who chose to do so—were "in" while the rest of the staff was condescendingly "out."

Along with the newfound success of the show, Bryant Gumbel seemed to be feeling his oats, especially when it came to sharing his feelings openly with the press. After all, he had worked very hard—and almost nonstop—for four years in the face of huge obstacles and he had been instrumental in getting the show back into first place. Now he was reveling in his success. In the end, his honesty with the press may not have been the best way to celebrate, because he began to unveil a side of himself that would later cause him some trouble. If Bryant lacked anything at that moment, perhaps it was the foresight to anticipate the damage that the honesty on which he so prided himself could do. One of Gumbel's most striking qualities was his overwhelming sense of invulnerability.

This particular attitude began to create some tension on the executive floor of 30 Rock by the summer of 1986: NBC's Press Department saw the potential danger of Gumbel's brazen outspokenness. They were concerned that this excessive frankness might wind up hurting both him and the show.

In a candid interview he gave to *New York* magazine in July, in which he spoke his mind about various people he had interviewed for *Today*, he announced, for instance, that it was beyond him why Elizabeth Taylor was held in such high esteem by so many Americans when she had been divorced so many times, while the publisher of *Penthouse* magazine, Bob Guccione, was perceived as morally decadent just because he printed nude pictures. That did not make Guccione any worse than Taylor, Gumbel averred. After all, Guccione had only been married twice.

He also gave an open assessment of Nancy Reagan, without any attempt to conceal his irritation with her about the way she handled questions about her husband. (The first lady had been displeased with Gumbel when he had arrived late to his taped interview for *Today* with her after a long lunch with a friend at which he had reportedly downed several margaritas.)

When he was asked to defend the charge that he foisted all female guests and issues on Jane, he cited his interview with Mick Jagger's girlfriend, Jerry Hall, noting, "I'm the guy who did—what's Mick Jagger's girlfriend's name?—I'm the guy who did four parts with her. *You* try that sometime. It's like talking to a window."

A few months later, he added fuel to the fire when he gave an interview to *Playboy* while he commented on the attributes of the variety of women who passed by his window during the interview. This time he dealt with questions about himself, admitting that he knew he often ruffled some feathers, but it did not seem to upset him. "I am the way that I am," he said. "I didn't come on this show to make friends. For that, I go to the Y." When it came to his feelings about people in general, he offered this piece of self-analysis: "It's not that I dislike many people. It's just that I don't like many people. There's a difference."

If Bryant Gumbel lacked insight in terms of what was good for him, he was still arguably one of the best interviewers on television. He had worked unstintingly to get where he was, and he had come by his confidence honestly. He had shown to himself—and to millions of others—that he could do virtually anything he wanted to do.

Born in Louisiana, Bryant moved to Chicago as a young boy, where he grew up in an integrated middle-class neighborhood in Hyde Park and attended Catholic schools. He was extremely close to his father, Richard, a probate judge, who influenced him greatly, and he had been devastated when Richard died of a heart attack in 1972. Bryant's older brother, Greg, also affected him profoundly as he grew up. (He also has two sisters, Renée and Rhonda.) "Most people focused on Greg," a childhood friend recalled. "Bryant was a chubby tagalong, hanging around his older friends." Bryant perceived his older brother as the good-looking one, the smart one. "There was competition," recalled the friend. "He always had to prove himself." Even Bryant admitted, "I had to speak up a little louder to be heard."

Jane Pauley once analyzed him this way: "At the heart of Bryant's aggressiveness and his drive," she said, "you can see a struggle to be noticed, to be recognized on his own terms."

Bryant had not always had the keen sense of focus he displayed so clearly in his impressive on-air talent. After he graduated from Bates College in Lewiston, Maine, in 1970 (where he played football, baseball, and club-hockey) with a degree in Russian History, his first job out of college was as a salesman of cardboard boxes. When that proved less than fulfilling, he decided to combine his interests in writing and sports, and talked his way into a writing job on the now-defunct *Black Sports* magazine. He became its editor after only eight months.

Gumbel was invited to audition for a job doing sports on television at KNBC in Los Angeles because of the exposure he got at the magazine. During the audition, he amazed everyone by his flawless performance and his natural ability. He was hired as weekend sportscaster at double the salary he had been making. Within five months he was promoted to the daily five o'clock news; in 1977 he began doing sports for the network. When he re-signed his contract in 1980, it called for him to do three sports segments a week on *Today*.

His professional rise to one of the most coveted jobs in broadcast journalism was direct and straightforward. Bryant Gumbel, the man, is infinitely more complex. An absolute perfectionist, moody and temperamental, he is as hard on himself as on anyone else, but has always had little patience for anyone who falls short of his expectations.

His quest for perfection has been attributed to the fact that his father was his idol, and he died before Bryant got his first job in broadcasting. "My father," he once explained, "was turned down at various law schools because he was black. He didn't bitch and moan about it, he simply went off and got accepted at Georgetown University Law School, worked two jobs to support us, went to school full-time, and graduated with honors."

According to Paul Brubaker, one of his producers during his first years on the *Today* show, Bryant's drive was directly related to his father. "Privately it's his father he wants to please," said Brubaker. "So he worked for more than perfection—it was absolute perfection squared. He was proving himself to someone who could never be satisfied because he's no longer here."

Gumbel's compulsive nature is evident in almost everything he does: For a while on the *Today* show, he went so far as to color code his pens to the people he was interviewing—green for an economist, red for a liberal—until he decided that the system did not work very well. He makes lists compulsively—every city he has been in, every golf course he has played on—which is, according to his wife, June, "just the way he relaxes." His wardrobe is always perfectly coordinated; his ties, his socks, and his underwear always match. Even when he puts his feet up on his desk in the office, he never loosens his tie. David Letterman, his longtime enemy, once alluded to Gumbel's obsessiveness on his show, joking that Gumbel was the kind of guy who would spend a weekend alphabetizing his colognes.

The question of race never had much to do with Gumbel's life—professionally at least. He got his first job, he believes, because he was black. After that, it ceased to be a factor. The biggest complaint he gets from his critics is that, if anything, he's not "black enough."

Jane Pauley has called his attitude towards women "Neanderthal." He married June, a former stewardess, in 1973, and they have two children, Bradley, thirteen, and Jillian, nine. He rarely attempts to hide his interest in other women, something he had not even attempted to conceal during the *Playboy* interview. When the *Playboy* article's author asked him what his wife said about "all of this girl watching," he replied, "Al McGuire [a former NBA basketball star and sportscaster] once said that one of the rules of marriage he always followed was never commenting on another woman in his wife's presence. Not a bad rule."

When he was pressed on the issue by the article's author ("She sees your eyes wander?" he had asked), Gumbel had replied, "I think she'd have to, don't everybody's?"—a philosophy he has never made any effort to conceal.

Everyone, including Bryant, agrees that he is a man's man. He likes big Cuban cigars and all-male clubs, and he admittedly hates "sensitive" movies. "You'll never get me to see *On Golden Pond* or *Julia* or *Tess*," he once said. Nor does he care for Woody Allen, but he loves everything Arnold Schwarzenegger does. "I'm the kind of guy," he told a reporter, "who cries when guys truly hug after a very important touchdown."

Whatever could be said about Bryant Gumbel the man, by the summer of 1986, when *Today* had finally secured its post-Brokaw place at the top, it was Bryant Gumbel the anchor who was credited, in very large part, for the show's stunning comeback. He had braved three tough years on *Today*, in the long, slow climb back up to first place. He had managed to stay in place and persevere against great odds, and now he had indisputably become not only a star, but a major force on network TV.

NBC rewarded him by offering him the job as prime-time anchor of the 1988 Summer Olympics, a job that would ultimately take a decisive toll on the *Today* show. He said yes, on the condition that he would be the sole anchor. Now that he had shaken his image as a sportscaster he did not ever want to go back, but he perceived the Olympics as a news event, he said, and he had learned from his experience on *Today*. He wanted it clearly determined that he would be the focal point in the studio. "It's tough enough to get it on the air without worrying about who's delegating what," he said at the time. "There's going to be news breaking, crises developing. If we're interested in doing the job right, let's make sure we have one central individual we run things through."

Ironically, Bryant Gumbel's success was perfectly synchronized with David Hartman's decline. Shortly after Cap Cities took over ABC in 1985, management there made it clear to the staff at GMA that Hartman, notorious for his egocentricity, would "either be a team player or he would not play at all." Hartman's incipient downfall was also inevitably tied to the sliding ratings at GMA. His demands for editorial control, and his status in general, were less pressing now that the show was in second place. He had lost a good deal of his leverage.

At the same time, David Hartman's loss turned out to be Joan

Lunden's gain. When she re-signed her contract in August, she was named cohost for the first time, becoming the first woman on GMA ever to get that title. She had been earning $700,000 a year to Hartman's $2 million, and now, besides a substantial raise, she was guaranteed an equal share of on-air duties. She, like Gumbel, had weathered a storm of her own.

About the time Joan Lunden signed her new contract, Jane Pauley gave birth to her third child. Thomas Moore Trudeau was born on August 29, and soon after that, Steve Friedman, who had had his fill of Jane's maternity leaves, made a personal request to Garry Trudeau that he "do more cartoons and leave Jane alone."

Like Bryant, Jane had prospered professionally from the *Today* show's impressive turnaround. On the eve of her return to work after her three-month maternity leave—her tenth anniversary on *Today*—*The Washington Post* headline read:

10 YEARS ON THE JOB & THE LADY HAS IT ALL:
FAMILY, FORTUNE, NO. 1.

It certainly seemed to be true. Now, besides her handsome, talented husband, she had three beautiful children, a reported salary of $975,000 a year (to Bryant's $1.5 million), and she had just signed a new five-year contract. No one would ever have suspected then that well before the contract was up, she herself would ask to be let out of it.

"I'm more than satisfied with my role on *Today*, Jane had said, shortly after she signed her new contract. "But now that I have three children, I wonder if my commitment to family will ever compromise my professional ambitions for the future. I've never turned down a *Today* assignment to be with my children, nor would I. But I have a very full plate now, and there are a couple of lessons I've learned from motherhood: I don't have to be perfect, and one way or another, things get taken care of."

Things were hardly as perfect as they appeared to be between Bryant and Jane from the other side of the camera after the red light went on. Like anyone who fell short of his expectations, Bryant's respect for Jane was tenuous at best. He put in fifteen hours a day, while she spent time at home to be close to her family and did much of her work from there. He deeply resented the disparity in the hours they spent at the office. Jane was treated no better by the inner circle, of which he was an integral part, than she had been before.

Bryant himself had an increasing and substantial amount of power on the show. He clearly had the upper hand in deciding what he wanted to do. "The show was not determined until Bryant decided what pieces he wanted," recalled one staffer. "And this was all happening five steps from where her office was, and he was unconscionable. But Jane is a survivor. The classiest thing about her is that it was water off her back. She was able to say, 'You know what, it doesn't affect my life, I'm a success.' What the hell did she care? She just played it right. She always felt, 'This is a great job and I have a great life and I'll take it as long as I can take it.' "

In Jane's mind her priorities were simple. Her family came first, and leaving her children was not a simple proposition. "Of course I feel guilty," she said after she had returned to work. "I've sometimes left home with tears in my eyes. The only thing I have going for me is good intentions. I think my children know that Mother's priority is to be with them first. But I don't think it has to be an either/or situation. Work is very important to me, and it wouldn't be in the best interest of my children for me to stay home seven days a week. That said, I've stripped my life to work and family."

What her critics failed to recognize was that while Jane's attachment to her family may have detracted from her performance in certain ways, at the same time it made her more effective and more appealing. And this crucial aspect of Jane's role on the show, which balanced beautifully the starker persona of Bryant Gumbel, was absolutely essential, even if it was overlooked by some, including Gumbel himself.

The concept of family was somehow inevitably intertwined with morning television, across the board. It was a part of the unique and intimate relationship between the viewers and the hosts. Even David Hartman used the notion of the importance of his family to cushion his less-than-happy departure from *GMA*, when he issued a simple statement only a few days after Jane had returned from her maternity leave. "I want to spend more time with my wife and four kids," the statement had said. It was, for Hartman, a succinct confirmation of the fact that the fifty-one-year-old host of *GMA* would leave the show four months later, in February, after eleven years on what Steve Friedman now referred to as "The David Hartman Show."

The kings and queens and pawns of morning television seemed never to stop moving. In an attempt to be a player in the game most recently dominated by the other two networks, CBS announced that it would unveil a whole new morning show, which would be called *The Morning Program*. In an effort to give viewers an entirely new alternative, the latest CBS concept was drastically different. The *CBS Morning News* had been the most news-oriented of the three morning shows. *The Morning Program* would no longer even be produced by the News Division, but would fall under the auspices of the Entertainment Division. Regular features would include everything from personal ads (in which singles would promote themselves in thirty-second video clips) to stand-up comedy routines, and there would be a live, applauding studio audience. To host the show they chose none other than Mariette Hartley, along with Rolland Smith, a local New York anchor.

It was every bit as bad as it sounded it would be. Steve Friedman described it as "The Colgate Comedy Hour comes to morning television." *Time* magazine said it had "something to embarrass everyone," and the show managed to bring CBS's ratings to an all-time low of a 10 percent share of the morning audience. Hartley fared no better than before. Critics repeatedly noted that she "babbled constantly," was "inexcusably cheerful," and that her awkward one-liners were "particularly grating." *The Morning Program* would be off the air within a few short months.

Now that *Today* was running smoothly in first place, NBC turned more of its attention to its early-morning show, which by now had been renamed *NBC News at Sunrise*. Connie Chung had been absent from the show increasingly, working on specials and a variety of other things. During that time, Bob Jamieson, a well-respected NBC correspondent, had unofficially become the anchor of *Sunrise*. He also filled in for John Palmer, doing the news on *Today* when Palmer was away.

The executives at NBC would not commit to giving Jamieson the *Sunrise* job. The early-morning audience, as opposed to that of *Today*, was primarily male, composed of a significant percentage of businessmen. It seemed to make more sense to have an attractive woman anchoring the show at that hour. It did not take them long to find one—at WMAQ in Chicago, which was the same station from which Jane Pauley had come to the *Today* show. Her name was Deborah Norville, and she was an attractive—some would say stunning—tall, blond, twenty-nine-year-old southern woman, whom *Playboy* described as having the "best newscaster lips on TV."

Whether it was because of her lips or other more noble attributes, Norville became an instant success on *Sunrise*. Within months after she began, *Sunrise* widened its lead over the other two early-morning shows significantly. Although no one knew it at the time, Deborah Norville's very presence at the network would soon have a profound effect not only on *NBC News at Sunrise*, but on the *Today* show and ultimately all of NBC News as well.

The executives at NBC were taken with Norville, and so was Bryant Gumbel. Soon after she was hired at *Sunrise*, Norville began substituting for Jane Pauley when she was gone. To the chagrin of Bob Jamieson, she was also tapped to substitute for John Palmer when he was away. It was not long before Jamieson was pushed out of the *Today* show completely. As Deborah Norville filled in more and more on *Today*, Bryant Gumbel was heard more and more frequently referring to Jane Pauley as "frumpy," an attitude with repercussions that would ultimately affect not only Jane Pauley's life, but many others' as well.

Now that *Today* was flying high, Steve Friedman estimated that the *Today* show, which cost between $35 and $40 million to produce, was taking in between $150 and $200 million a year in advertising revenues for the network and affiliates combined. He knew for a fact that since he had arrived at the show, network billings had tripled—from roughly $30 million to $90 million—and he was convinced that he was, to a large degree, responsible for these magnificent figures. When his contract came up for renewal in June 1987, he believed he should be compensated in kind for his work.

Besides that, he was tired—tired of getting up every day for seven years at four in the morning and tired of the fight. Friedman thrived on adversity and now that *Today* was comfortably ensconced in first place, the uncontested winner, his motivation was waning. He wanted a piece of the action.

So he went to Larry Grossman, the president of NBC News, and told him how he felt. "We have to decide if I'm going or staying," he told Grossman, who was not one of Friedman's biggest fans. "I won't stay unless I have some kind of arrangement that makes me financially not just a worker, but somebody who can share in the profits."

Friedman had made up his mind, and in typical style—he had never been long on patience—he was not about to bend. "We've got to work this out, Larry," he told Grossman. " 'Cause I'm not just gonna sit around here waitin' for this to happen. And you gotta do it quick."

Friedman's enthusiasm for Grossman had diminished over the months they had worked together and the feeling was totally mutual. Grossman was less than captivated by what Friedman had told him he thought he deserved, and he worked out the only plan he was willing to set forth. On a pleasant Friday afternoon in early June, he called Friedman to read him the details. The proposal did not even come close. It met none of Friedman's demands. After the phone call, it was more than obvious to Friedman that Grossman had no intention of giving him what he wanted. "I told him that it was unacceptable," says

Friedman. "I wanted to tell him that I'll pick up my marbles and go someplace else, but I wanted to have until Monday so that I could tell Bryant and Jane and some other people before the announcement was made."

Grossman would not even give him the weekend. "No," he told Friedman. "We're going to make the announcement now."

Friedman contends that Grossman wanted the announcement of his departure buried in the weekend press to keep the play down in the papers. "He wouldn't give me what I wanted," Friedman says. "And I felt I had no alternative but to leave, and he thought I was bluffing. I wasn't bitter, though. It made it easier for me to leave."

With that, Friedman's seven-year run as executive producer of the *Today* show ended. Although he had rarely appeared on the show during that time, the week of his departure the crew got a shot of Friedman in the office he had occupied for nearly seven years. He appeared on *Today* appropriately—if only for a moment—swinging a baseball bat.

After Friedman left, he was, perhaps, more inwardly reflective than was customary for him. "If I had it to do over again," he said, "I would have been a nicer guy." Then, acknowledging his enemies, he added, "I once told Jack Perkins, our West Coast correspondent, that I wished that just once when somebody died that everybody hated, people wouldn't say nice things, that they'd say what a bastard he was. And Perkins said to me, 'You won't live to see it, but it will happen.' "

Part III

THE FALL

(1988–1991)

T w e l v e

THE CASE OF
THE LEAKING MEMO

With Steve Friedman's precipitous departure, things at the *Today* show changed significantly and almost instantly, but not solely because he was gone. Marty Ryan had been named executive producer to replace Steve. Although some of those empowered with the decision felt that Ryan lacked creativity, he was a skilled producer, he knew the way the show worked—and nobody could say it was not working well— and he was a pal of Bryant Gumbel's. Besides that, there was no other obvious replacement for Friedman, and Friedman had left so quickly that there was little time or apparent necessity to ponder the issue much further.

Within days after Marty Ryan took over, there was a strike of NABET, the union to which the show's writers belonged, and it threw things into a mess. The show's writers were all out on strike, and with a two-hour live show to do five days a week, this was a serious problem. The strike did not warm the hearts of the new NBC management team, either. The General Electric people had now taken over: Robert

Wright was now in Grant Tinker's old job as president of NBC. He was a strong-willed, curious man with thinning blond hair who looked older than his forty-two years. He had once run the Plastics Division of GE. In spite of his engaging smile, he was known to be a tough bargainer. Jack Welch, another hardboiled executive, a stern-looking man of fifty-three, balding, with reddish brown hair—who some thought bore a resemblance to Wright—was now the chief executive officer of the company. Wright and Welch were hardly sympathetic to strikes, and in the end, the NABET strike gave them the opportunity to pare down what they had already considered to be the overly plump *Today* show staff, because it allowed them to see that the show got on the air every day with little noticeable difference, in spite of the strike.

When Marty Ryan had been named executive producer, he had called Coby Atlas, the head of the West Coast bureau, who was in London at the time doing a piece with *Today*'s music correspondent, Rona Elliot. Could she, he asked Coby, return to L.A. via New York, so that he could talk with her about taking the job as supervising producer at *Today*, under himself and Cliff Kappler, whom he had asked to be senior producer?

Coby was flattered. She was a hardworking, highly intelligent, extremely skilled woman who had first come to *Today* in 1981 with Rona Barrett as her producer. When Rona left, Steve and Marty had recognized Coby's value and asked her to stay on in spite of the fact that she would be getting much less money than she had been earning with Rona.

Coby had agreed to stay. She was a unique personality—a self-assured, very bright, independent thinker, who always marched to the beat of her own drummer and rarely got thrown off track. She commanded respect in an almost saintly way—it was difficult for anyone to argue with her—and she was absolutely uncompromising. She would not accept what she thought was wrong and was outspokenly honest about what she believed. She was unfailingly devoted to her work and always did more than her share.

Coby had told Marty she would be happy to come to New York and talk with him about the job. Her only concern (besides the money he was offering her, which was not enough) was that both Jane and Bryant felt comfortable with Marty's decision and that they openly agreed that they wanted her. She did not want to wind up in the kind of situation her predecessor, Scott Goldstein, had encountered. She told Marty she wanted to hear personally from both of them that they were sure they wanted her, before she came.

Both Bryant and Jane met with Coby in New York and encouraged her to come. She accepted the job, becoming the highest-ranking female on the *Today* show staff. By mutual agreement, however, she would not be able to begin in New York until things settled down. Besides the strike, the Iran-contra hearings were in progress. Since the proceedings were being televised, the show had to be updated for the West Coast daily, a problem that occurred in morning television when newsmaking events continued after the original show was over live in the East.

The show was taped live, Eastern Standard Time, and run in its entirety on tape for the later time zones, but when things happened live during Pacific or Central time, it was necessary to include them in a new, updated version of the show. Because of the strike, there were only two people left in the L.A. bureau who could make the necessary changes for the Iran-contra hearings. One of them was Coby Atlas, and she simply could not be spared right away.

So Marty began his tenure as executive producer of *Today* with one strike against him, so to speak, and from that time, the inner dynamics of the show began to change subtly but certainly. With Steve—who had indisputably been a major creative and editorial force—out of the picture, Bryant's role in the editorial process grew. As Hartman had done at *GMA*, Gumbel sought and assumed more and more power and became increasingly opinionated about what was right and what was wrong with *Today*, and what the show should and should not contain.

In spite of the strike, there was business to be done, and the meager non-NABET staff had to do it themselves. Amy Krivitzky, of TWA hostage fame, was flown in from London. Most of the producers on the show had done writers' jobs before, and everybody did what he had to. Surprisingly—and unhappily for the union—most of the work got done with little obvious distress to the viewers, and the ratings sailed.

The most important thing on the agenda was a long-planned trip to China, in September 1987, just months after Friedman had left, and right in the middle of the strike. It turned out well in spite of the extenuating circumstances. The worst thing that happened in China was that Jane got a frightful case of "Montezuma's revenge" in the middle of the show, with the Great Wall of China looming behind her, and had to disappear during a piece Boyd Matson was doing. When the piece was over, Jane had not yet reappeared. Boyd gracefully covered for her and threw the show to a commercial. By the time the commercial was over, Jane was back in her chair, where she belonged.

The strike lasted until the end of October. By the time it was over, it had taken a great toll on morale. People were afraid of losing their jobs. There was a growing sense of tension and uneasiness among the *Today* show staff, and the increasingly unsettled mood set the stage for the turmoil that lay ahead.

While this was going on in Rockefeller Center, my education in Hollywood continued. I learned that the film business was truly magical, but not in the way I had perceived it. Every promise made had the uncanny ability to disappear. Numbers, as in grosses, net profits, percentages, and bottom lines, could be made to change miraculously before your very eyes. The element of creativity was astounding, but it was by no means confined to the art of filmmaking.

Harold and I witnessed this firsthand with "our" film, *Gorillas in the Mist*. What we were promised, in terms of money (in spite of a signed contract) and content (in spite of our own naïve trust in what we were told) had nothing to do with the end reality. Still, the film got made, which was a feat in itself, and we were none the worse for it. Certainly we were wiser.

It was shortly before the release of *Gorillas in the Mist* that our lives would undergo such a profound and shocking change that my perspective of everything that had gone before would be altered immeasurably and permanently. Never again would such issues as who got Elizabeth Taylor, and who did not, have any significance for me. The frenzy, the insanity of the amount of energy invested in these kinds of pursuits, suddenly became clearly absurd.

In January 1988, Harold became ill with what appeared at first to be a minor problem. Within months we were devastated when we learned the unfathomable truth: My husband had a brain tumor. His chances of surviving it were zero.

May 1988. The train chugged purposefully through the European countryside, the rhythm of its wheels bringing an odd sense of levity to the passengers inside. The magical aura was inescapable. This was the famous Orient Express.

Excitement pervaded the train as the sound of the wheels punctuated the air, not allowing anyone to forget for an instant where they were. Night had fallen and the passengers were content, pleasantly tired after a long day, as they dressed for the formal dinner and made their way to the bar car of the train. An abundance of fine wine flowed freely throughout the car. As the Montrachet and Pouilly Fuissé warmed their spirits and the train lulled them gently, the group that had gathered aboard the train felt a stronger bond than ever before. Odd things happen to people when they are stuck on a train together for any period of time, and these people were nearing the end of their five-day trip aboard the Orient Express.

At that moment, everything seemed perfect. The dinner was superb, and afterward everyone settled back in the comfortable space of the bar car with more wine, brandy, and an occasional cigar, to absorb the finishing touch of the evening, the pleasant strains of a piano. The sweet music mingled seductively with the chugging of the train as it made its way through the Austrian Alps in the wee hours of the morning.

It was then that someone handed the microphone to the well-liked, usually reserved blonde in the group. She reached out and took it, and as she brought it towards her lips, everyone fell silent. You could have heard a pin drop inside the bar car. As the piano player began to play, the pretty, wholesome blonde opened up and sang the most awesome rendition of "It's Now or Never," one of her favorite Elvis Presley songs, that anyone had ever heard. Then she segued into an even more astounding version of "Love Me Tender," and finally broke into a knock-down, tear-jerking version of "Edelweiss," so appropriate to the Austrian terrain through which the train was chugging as she sang.

They were all mesmerized, stunned. Her husky voice had a gospel quality—it was unbelievable. Who would have ever thought? After all, this was the thirty-eight-year-old woman who had been cohost of the *Today* show for twelve whole years now—some of the people on the train had worked with her for that long—and nobody had any idea that she could sing like this.

Bryant Gumbel, in his tux, the collar of his shirt now unbuttoned, stared at her in disbelief. He was as taken as everyone else. She had not told many people of her secret desire to be a rock-and-roll singer, but then, that was hardly surprising.

Her sister was sitting next to her in the bar car—she had accompanied Jane on the Orient Express trip and Garry had been left behind. It would turn out to be one of the most exciting remote broadcasts *Today* had ever done, and maybe her sister's presence was what made Jane feel more at ease, less shy than she usually was. Marty and Willard, Michael Pressman, several writers, and production assistants all stood there motionless, glued to the mellifluous sound of her voice, each more captivated than the next. The *Today* staff had never felt more like a family, a close-knit, loving, happy family, than they did at that very moment.

Nevertheless, after Jane surrendered the mike, she returned to her tiny sleeping compartment with her sister, Ann. It was then that reality began to set in again. She felt suddenly self-conscious about the brief concert she had just given. "Ann, I feel so foolish," she told her sister. "I feel like I've gone to bed with fifty people."

"Don't worry," Ann reassured her. "If it's any consolation, you're going to wake up with your sister."

———

The intimate, familial feelings that had been so intense in the bar car that night were not destined to last for long. Like any other all-American family, this one was not without its problems. By the end of the summer, before he left to prepare for his eighteen-day stint as host of over eighty prime-time hours of the Olympics in Seoul, Korea, Bryant was still embroiled in negotiations for his new contract, which had not yet been ironed out. Tensions were high, and at one point, NBC president Robert Wright, true to his reputation as a tough bargainer, was ready to throw in the towel, to cut off the negotiations with Gumbel completely. He ultimately had a change of heart, but while this was going on, Gumbel was keenly aware that his future was in limbo, which added even more angst to the psyche of a man who was already under a substantial amount of pressure. The undertaking in Seoul was enormous, and it was resting, for the most part, on Bryant Gumbel's shoulders.

To exacerbate these difficulties, Gumbel's problems with the press had not improved. If anything, they had intensified. On the eve of his trip to Seoul, *Sports Illustrated* published a piece about him entitled "The Mourning Anchor," a vituperative article which some believe was a turning point in the way Gumbel was perceived by the public. The author's premise was that Gumbel, a raging egomaniac, revered his dead father on the one hand, while being inexcusably mean to his mother and sisters on the other.

Gumbel also overspoke himself again in an article in *Us* magazine, in which he referred to what seemed like an endless array of people as "assholes" and admitted that he had problems with the whole concept of monogamy.

From the moment he arrived in Seoul, even before the Olympic coverage began, things did not go well. Bryant was, understandably, overwhelmed by the stressful circumstances that were dominating his life. Marty Ryan was concerned as much about Bryant as he was about the *Today* show. Coby Atlas was worried about him too, and she would eventually come to fear that Bryant might actually break down. He seemed to be distancing himself, drifting farther and farther away. He was clearly going through a difficult time. He seemed to be angry about everything.

He was increasingly resentful of the continuing disparity between his schedule and Jane's. Jane continued to come in late in the morning by his standards—at 6:00 or 6:30—and she would leave soon after the show, usually around 9:15, while Bryant would arrive much earlier in the morning and stay until 5:30 at night.

Even though the *Today* show was holding its place solidly as number one, Marty Ryan sensed that there were potential problems. He believed if they wanted to hold on to their lead, they had better get at the problems early on, before they got to be too big. He decided to address himself to those things he could do something about. Bryant had a great deal of input in the show. While he was in Seoul for the Olympics, five thousand miles away from New York, and since *Today* could be seen on Armed Forces TV in Seoul, Marty thought it would be a good opportunity for Bryant to watch the show and critique it with an objective eye. So he communicated this to him via the NBC central computer system, asking him to do just that: to evaluate *Today*'s contributors and staff members, how the segments played, and the way the segments were done.

Bryant dutifully complied, writing back to Marty on the computer four single-spaced pages containing his complete and total assessment of the show. As was his nature, he tended to hyperbolize about everything and everyone. As one producer told me, "You know him well enough to know that if you ask him, 'Is it raining out, Bryant?' you'd say, 'Yeah, it's raining out,' I'd say, 'Yeah, it's raining a little bit,' and he'd say, 'It's fucking pouring out,' with a tone in his voice. That's the way he is and that's the way the memo was."

Gumbel let all of his opinions out, in the most unequivocal terms, although he prefaced his memo to Marty by saying, "I hope you understand this note will be for your eyes ONLY. In trying to be honest and helpful, I don't want to gain more enemies than I've already got." Little did he imagine what would occur in a matter of months.

He started with the area of "consumer news," and observed, among other things, that "Horowitz is a walking cliché, but unless you have research to indicate otherwise, I've got to believe he's known and effective. The same I fear can't be said for Betty [Furness]. I like her and some of her stuff is good . . . but lots of it isn't and she's VERY local."

Next he dealt with "medical" issues and *Today*'s Dr. Art Ulene: "I think on the whole we're being well served by Ulene," he wrote, "but his 'Health Week,' 'Women's Month,' 'Children's Year' shit is both boring and repetitive. (I know they're sponsored, but more often than not they suck. I'd like to see us keep Art, but nuke his series.)"

In the "music" category he was pleased with correspondent Rona Elliot, whom he called "solid." But, he observed, "we should avoid putting on too many folks no one ever heard of, as we sometimes do. Our viewers may care about Whitney Houston and Elton John; but I doubt they give a shit about Icehouse or Simply Red. That's not to say we shouldn't do folks who aren't big names; but we should make sure they're different or have a new angle involved before we put on a newcomer."

Gene Shalit didn't fare as well as Rona Elliot. "This one's difficult," wrote Gumbel, "because I like Gene and more than anyone I guess think he's very important to the show. But his reviews are often late and his interviews aren't very good. I suspect we can live with a few of the latter but we should limit them much more than we have to date."

Gumbel's comments about the way "sports" was handled on *Today* were not surprising. "Although it doesn't bother me," he told Marty, "I do find it odd that we do medicine, science, economics, etc. with regularity . . . but not sports. Give that some thought."

He was less than enthused with some of the show's contributors:

"You and I have discussed these enuf [*sic*], so you know my feelings about whose [*sic*] good and whose not. Among the main cuttables: Christy Ferrer, Betty Rollin (has she EVER produced a person you really wanted to know?) and Bob Berkowitz . . . (is he still with us?)"

It was clear that when it came to the Talent Department he was no more enthused about my successor, a woman by the name of Jeffrey Culbreth, who had been Gene Shalit's assistant before she got my former job, than he had been about me, and it was obvious that he still harbored the same negative feelings about the area of talent, which he stressed was "vitally important to the show": "Here too I think we've talked of this so much I doubt I can say anything you don't already know," he told Ryan, describing the Talent Department as inept and calling my successor a "lazy broad."

He went on to say that he thought the *Today* show could use a person to do "Hollywood News." When it came to books, and the superb job done by the woman in charge, Emily Boxer, he had no complaints. In the category of "news," he had his own thoughts: "This continues to be one of our weakest links for a lot of reasons . . . the department does us no favors . . . it's not terribly well written . . . John [Palmer] doesn't make it a lot better and it looks like every other newscast anywhere and everywhere."

Without a doubt, Gumbel's hardest-hit target, and the one that would ultimately bring him the most grief, was Willard Scott:

> This one's a big problem but something has got to be done. Each and every day he holds the show hostage to his assortment of whims, wishes, birthdays and bad taste. We can't do business like that and you know it. If you're looking for a pleasant way around this one there is none . . . and if you can't bring yourself to do what's unpleasant then maybe you need to ask yourself what kind of job you're doing. This guy is killing us and no one's even trying to rein him in. Some suggestions: nuke Morrison Cruise [Willard's assistant] . . . if Willard had no one giving him that shit every

day, he'd be too lazy to organize it himself . . . if you keep
Morrison you should demand to see a listing of the crap he
wants to put on by noon of the previous day . . . that way
you'd have a chance to limit the stuff he's got and nuke the
stuff that's stupid or too commercial . . . you should also
limit him to one birthday per weather report: However it's
done Marty you have GOT to exhibit some control over this
guy. He's got your show by the balls and is doing what he
damn well pleases . . . you don't limit him or edit him, and
so he drags us all down. In addition to any or all of the
above, I'd like to see us take a further step and eliminate
him from the first half hour altogether. That half hour is
hard and all he does is take up 3 valuable minutes (when
we're lucky). Palmer could easily give the weather headlines
and get us quickly into the top stories of the day. We'll lose
no one by eliminating him in the 1st half hour, we already
do that with Shalit. Yes, Willard will be pissed . . . so what
. . . what's he going to do, walk away? He's got a contract
that pays him more than anyone in their rite [sic] mind
should . . . he can't leave this job and couldn't get a better
one. Until or unless you bring this guy into line, you're
going to continue to have major problems that render anything said in this note useless.

Besides these assessments, he offered some suggestions on how to
keep the show "fresh." His ideas included making the news capsules at
the beginning of each half hour anchored by John Palmer "more active
. . . fewer tapes, more live reports," and he suggested more background and educational reports on politics. He also wanted a segment
that addressed the public's "huge ongoing appetite for video cassettes."
And finally, he didn't even spare Marty Ryan: "You're my last topic
. . . but my primary concern," he wrote, accusing Ryan of "a lack of
guidance and a lack of willingness to stand on folks and make sure they
do what's necessary." He went on:

Nice guys may not finish last, but it's hard for them to stay in first. Somehow or other, you're going to have to find it within yourself to do some unpleasant things . . . to crack down on Willard . . . to tell Betty what to do . . . to let Gene know what you want and when . . . to make sure writers do what they're told . . . none of those things is pleasant, but they've got to be done . . . you can't be a great executive producer and a great guy to boot. You've got to look hard at yourself and either do what's necessary or admit you're not up to it . . . you can't have it both ways. I'll be glad to give you all the support you need . . . and I'll even be happy to play the heavy whenever . . . but for the good of yourself and your show, you've got to show people that you've got the balls to make some hard choices . . . I'm not sure they think you can. Anywho . . . I've rambled on enuf [*sic*] . . . I hope you've read all this in the spirit in which it was given . . . yours seemed a serious request so I took it as such. I just hope this all remains confidential because it's meant only to help you . . . not hurt others.

Marty read the memo with interest and agreed with much of what Bryant said. They had many subsequent discussions about it after Bryant returned from Seoul. The one person Bryant had refrained from commenting on in his memo to Marty was Jane, since Marty had specifically asked him not to do so. He already knew exactly how Bryant felt about Jane, as did virtually everyone else, since Bryant made little effort to keep his feelings a secret. As far as Bryant and Marty were concerned, the memo's purpose had been fulfilled.

Fate, however, sometimes throws you a curve, and that is precisely what happened to Bryant Gumbel and Marty Ryan five months later when NBC decided to change from one computer software system to another. Virtually all of NBC had been fully computerized since the middle of 1985, and like many places, the operations of the company—including every show, *Today* among them—relied heavily on computers. The oversized book with the plastic pages that Steve wrote in with his grease pencil during the early years had now been replaced by a computer grid in which every segment booked could be seen by every person with a computer. People communicated now largely by computer. It was hardly necessary to talk with a person face-to-face. All you had to do was write a message and send it directly over the computer—a practice which Gumbel employed regularly to vent his wrath about whatever was bothering him.

In February 1989, it was decided that the company would switch from the current system, BASYS, to one which was thought to be more effective, called SISCOM. Everyone with a computer at NBC was notified well in advance. Employees were told that on a given day that month it would be necessary for them to transfer all of their files from one system to the other. In order to do this, each person would have to take each of his files, one by one, put them into a central area, duplicate them, and from there put them one by one into the new system. It was a small inconvenience, but it was the only way the switchover could be made.

The tiny hitch in this matter was that while the files were being duplicated in the transitional no-man's-land, all of them would be, by necessity, unlocked. Michael Pressman, among others, noticed this flaw as he transferred his files. "The mistake they made," he explained, "was that no-man's-land was not protected. Many of us noticed, as we were sending our files and then going into the new system to retrieve them, we had to sift through everyone else's files—not read them, but sift through them—until we found our own, which is what everybody was doing. If you wanted to, while you were sifting through, you could have opened up any files you saw. Everyone's files were in there—Jane Pauley's, Tom Brokaw's, Bryant's. Anyone who was on the system could have read any file in that no-man's-land and all of NBC was doing it, not just the *Today* show."

Coby Atlas also remembers that day well. There was, she says, always a group of people at NBC—people referred to as "trollers"— who spent a good deal of their time sifting through other people's files trying to break their codes. On this particular day, the code breaking was not necessary, since all the files were already unlocked.

"People were trolling that afternoon," she recalls. "Suddenly the word spread throughout the *Today* show offices: 'All the files are open and you can read Bryant's files!' I was walking down the hall and I stopped at the first computer I passed. It belonged to one of the sweetest men on the staff. Like everyone else, he went into Bryant's files and he was screaming at me, 'You've got to see this!' I leaned over and said, 'Oh my God.' It was like you're not supposed to read other people's mail. I walked away. I didn't read the whole thing and I didn't think much more about it."

Thinking about it proved to be inevitable. Within hours, hard copies of Bryant's memo to Marty, in its entirety, were circulating throughout all of the NBC offices at 30 Rock.

The next day, Emily Boxer, the producer in charge of booking all of the authors on *Today*—which was by its very nature one of the most powerful positions on the show because of the weight *Today* carried in the publishing industry—was contacted by *Harper's* magazine. They had received a copy of Gumbel's memo and wanted to know if it was authentic. "It sounds ridiculous to me," Emily had told the publicity person at *Harper's* who had called her, but not knowing exactly what to do, she went directly to Bryant.

Bryant, in effect, told Emily to lie. "He said that it was true," recalls Emily. "But he said, 'Tell her it's not true.' He asked me if I wanted to read it, and I said no, if I was going to lie I was going to lie telling the truth, that I'd never seen it. So I called the magazine back and said, 'Not true, ridiculous.' "

Shortly after the *Harper's* incident, Kevin Goldman, a reporter for *New York Newsday*, a respected New York newspaper, was contacted by someone who advised him of the existence of the memo and its contents. In order to obtain the memo, Goldman was sent to what he calls a "drop-off point," a location in Manhattan that was well removed from 30 Rock. It was Friday morning, February 24, 1989, when Goldman met his source as he had been instructed to do. Since he was not convinced the document was real, he set out to see what he could find.

Goldman felt that there were four key people who could confirm the validity of the memo: Bryant Gumbel; Marty Ryan; the new president of NBC News, Michael Gartner; and Gartner's deputy, Joe Angotti. He spoke to Marty on Friday. "I have this memo . . ." he told Marty and he described some of the more inflammatory statements that it contained.

"That memo was written in August, so what?" replied Marty. To Goldman, that statement alone was confirmation enough.

On Sunday morning, Goldman called Marty at home and had another lengthy conversation with him. He also reached Michael Gartner, who had been chosen by Bob Wright and Jack Welch to replace Larry Grossman, whom they had decided to get rid of almost as soon as they took over. They had hired the forty-nine-year-old Gartner in 1988, primarily at the suggestion of Tom Brokaw. On paper, Gartner had looked like exactly the right man for the job. He had a long and distinguished journalistic career—albeit on newspapers—he had a good degree of visibility in the column he wrote every three weeks for *The Wall Street Journal*, and he also possessed an element of flair that had been sorely lacking in Grossman: He wore bright bow ties and suspenders, and he was known for his acerbic wit. He would prove, however, to be less than skillful in his dealings with those he worked with in general. But the qualification that would finally stand out as the one that was most conspicuously absent from Michael Gartner's résumé was the fact that he had virtually no experience in television journalism, which would quickly prove to be a disadvantage in the crisis the News Division was about to face.

That Sunday morning, when Goldman contacted him, Gartner told Goldman that he had not seen the memo. When Goldman replied that he could be in his apartment to show it to him in ten minutes, Gartner told him flatly that he was not interested. Several hours later, Gartner called Goldman back and read him a statement, which said, in essence, that the memo was "ancient history," having been written in Seoul when Bryant was doing the Olympics, and that it had apparently been stolen out of Gumbel's computer file by an NBC employee. Period.

By this time, the NBC Press Department had gotten involved. They had learned that Goldman had gotten ahold of the memo when Goldman had initially attempted to find Marty Ryan to confirm it. Everyone in the Press Department desperately wished that Goldman had not found him. "The reporter would have had a harder time getting it published if Marty hadn't confirmed it," said an NBC executive. "By his comments and the way he handled himself, Marty let the reporter know he had something that was real."

"What NBC News really wanted," countered a *Today* executive, "was for Marty Ryan to lie. And Marty Ryan didn't do that."

The Press Department snapped into action immediately in an attempt to diffuse the effect of Ryan's candor, but it was already too late. Someone tried to convince Goldman not to run the memo, pointing out to him how hurtful it could be to the individuals involved, to which Goldman only replied, "I didn't write this memo."

"Our act involves a pan and a broom," said an executive in the Press Department. "In this particular case we knew it was boiling and about to boil over."

To make things even more difficult, Bryant had left for California for a long-planned vacation the previous Friday. By the time things began to percolate, he was difficult to reach.

Several key people at NBC immediately gathered in what became a sort of "mini–task force" to devise a plan about how to deal with the impending crisis. It consisted of Gartner; Betty Hudson, senior vice president in the Press Department; Tim Russert, another NBC vice president; Peggy Hubble, Hudson's assistant; and several outside consultants. They finally reached Bryant in California, and Gartner spoke with him on the phone.

Gartner informed Gumbel of the impending publication of the memo and proceeded to impart to him the collective advice of the task force. "We need to develop a statement for you," Gartner told Gumbel, "that says, 'Look, this memo, which was a private communication between me and my boss, is many months old, most of the issues I address have long since been taken care of, and everything is swell,' and maybe some appropriate remark about whoever would steal and distribute this kind of communication. The other thing we think you should do is call everybody you mentioned in this and tell them what the genesis of the document was and that it is six months old and you be the one who gets to them first, so they hear it from you, so that when the press comes around to Willard, for instance, his response might logically be, 'Bryant and I have talked about it.' "

This conversation, slithering along the telephone lines between New York and L.A., was Michael Gartner's first major crisis at NBC News—the first one, at least, in which the "talent" was instrumental, and it would soon become painfully obvious that Gartner had no experience whatsoever dealing with talent. Such a phenomenon simply does not exist on a newspaper. Now he was faced with a crisis involving one of the most important programs at NBC News, and nearly all of its talent: Bryant Gumbel, Willard Scott, Gene Shalit—everyone, in fact, but Jane Pauley, who was the only person to be spared from the memo. (Many people contend, however, that Pauley was only omitted because Gumbel had dealt with her exhaustively in a separate communication to his agent, Ed Hookstratten.)

"This episode was Gartner's first full-force exposure to a true talent man," said an executive, referring to Gartner's ineffective conversation with Gumbel. "This was major—Willard and the whole cast and all the forces at work here, and here you have a guy used to being the editor of a paper. Here, he gives Bryant this well-formulated plan, and Bryant simply says, 'No, thank you.' Bryant seemed to genuinely believe this was not going to be a big deal. He thought it would blow over in twenty-four hours, and Gartner put down the phone and said, 'Now what? He says it isn't gonna be as big a problem as we think.' "

In fact, Bryant refused to do anything. He made what Willard Scott calls "a feeble attempt" to reach him, and left a message on his answering machine: "We have an imminent crisis," it said. "Try to call me." Willard could not reach him.

"An attempt was made," says Willard, "but a feeble attempt. He didn't quite apologize, not in the classic sense. He sounded like East-ern Airlines advising passengers, 'We regret the inconvenience.' At no point did I suspect any sincere regrets."

Satisfied that he had a legitimate story with the validity of the memo now absolutely confirmed, Goldman wrote the piece for *New York Newsday*, which ran in the paper on Tuesday, February 28. That morning, Gartner circulated his own memo to "all network news bureaus and staff," to emphasize: "1. The memo is ancient history— five months old. It was written, I'm told, when Bryant was in Seoul doing the Olympics. 2. The memo apparently was stolen out of Gum-bel's computer file and then was given by an NBC employee to Kevin Goldman of *Newsday* . . .

"The troubling aspect of all this is that someone at NBC would take this memo—a piece of private correspondence—and then give it to a reporter. That, quite simply, is theft. It won't be tolerated. Anyone who steals will be fired. Period."

He continued: "This morning, I have spoken with Marty and Bryant and Jane and Willard and Gene and John and others, reaffirming my own pleasure with the success of the show and reinforcing my belief in open and candid discussions in an effort to make us ever better. I'm always ready for such discussions with anyone . . . frank, face-to-face discussions are a hell of a lot better for all of us than half-baked, anonymous cheap shots . . ."

He pointed out *Today* had been the number-one morning show for thirty weeks. "It is top-ranked because it has a cast of producers and anchors and correspondents and writers—an entire team—that is un-matched in television. Everyone connected with the show wants to make sure that it continues to excel, so we always are probing, ques-tioning, suggesting, prodding. Bryant's memo was part of that process and was written in response to a request from Marty. It is a continuous, healthy procedure. We encourage dissent, discussion, disagreement."

Gartner's ameliorative memo, and Gumbel's assessment of the im-pact of the leak as "no big deal" notwithstanding, the NBC Press Department had no delusions about the seriousness of the matter. "We knew it was gonna be messy. And it happened in a slow news period when there was not that much else to write about," says a member of the Press Department.

Bryant stayed silent for over a week, and during that time, the furor grew. "The feeding frenzy began," says an executive, "Willard is a dear but nutty person, and very tightly wound. The more he didn't hear from Bryant, the wilder he got. Finally, he was stopping in airports and giving quotes to people. It kept escalating and every day there was more in the paper, topped off by a four-page spread in *People* magazine with Willard just flipping out."

The headline in *People* magazine read, WILLARD SCOTT BLOWS HIS TOP. The author of the article demonstrated the extent of the potential damage of the incident when he wrote, "The memo shows a shocking lack of sensitivity, portrays Bryant as a man of little compassion, reveals a surprising ignorance of the chemistry that has made the *Today* show the top-rated morning program, and demonstrates a level of hubris unusual even for a TV star."

Willard's wife, Mary, defended him in the *People* article. "I was up all night," she told the reporter, "rehearsing all the beautifully controlled things I was going to say . . ."

" . . . You mean," Willard interrupted, "not use the word prick?"

Mary would not let up. She was fed up with Gumbel and his attacks on her husband—the memo had not been the first. "Every time he attacks Willard," she told *People*, "he looks worse and Willard looks better. He must be a slow learner."

A week later, Gumbel broke his silence about the matter during the first half hour of the *Today* show: "To you who may be one of the many who have recently called or written with expressions of support for many of us on *Today*, please know that Jane, Willard, Gene, John, and I are very grateful. We appreciate your concern and in spite of what you may have heard or read in recent days, we are together and hopefully going to be with you for many years to come," he said.

"Now that may come as sad news for those who have tried to

capitalize on our differences, but rest assured that our *Today* family is intact and still smiling. We'll still be here long after the recent head-lines are forgotten. Enough said."

Hardly. The backlash of the leak of what was now the infamous memo was light-years away from being over.

T h i r t e e n

TROUBLE ON THE COUCH

The worst thing about the publication of the memo was that it shattered the dream—the illusion that the *Today* show cast was one big, loving, happy family. Now that the fatal flaw was exposed, it would be difficult—if not impossible—to repair. Bryant's memo set off a chain reaction that would ultimately take a devastating toll.

Ironically, Bryant was angrier than any of the people he had written about. He felt that NBC had betrayed him by responding to the memo controversy with a press statement and nothing much else, that they had failed miserably to protect him and had just stood idly by while the press had a field day. "I didn't feel there was a proper expression of support from the executive side," he said later. "It started from there and it deteriorated." Gumbel blamed only one person for this: the president of NBC News, Michael Gartner.

By July, Gumbel had virtually stopped speaking to Michael Gartner. This was obviously an untenable situation for NBC News. In order to resolve it, Robert Wright informed Michael Gartner of what he saw as a solution to bridging the perilous gap between the two: He wanted Gartner to hire Dick Ebersol, the creator of *Saturday Night Live*, among other things, and now the president of NBC Sports and a friend of Gumbel's, in the added capacity of vice president in charge of *Today*.

The six-foot two-inch New England–WASPy Ebersol, widely known as the wonderboy of television, was as charming as he was slick. At forty-two, his thinning brown hair was balanced nicely by his Paul Stuart clothes and Dunhill cigars. He lived high on the hog, in an apartment at the posh Trump Plaza on Fifth Avenue in Manhattan and in his country home in Connecticut. He was known to be rather impulsive—he married his first wife, a game-show model, eighteen days after he met her. Now he was married to the actress Susan Saint James, and she seemed to have a settling influence on him. Still, people who knew him called him everything from talented to grasping, ambitious, and devious.

Gartner initially considered accepting Wright's "suggestion" that he make Ebersol senior vice president in charge of *Today*, until he talked with Tom Brokaw and Tim Russert, an NBC News vice president, about it. Brokaw told Gartner he thought the appointment would be a serious mistake, that Ebersol was wrong for the job, that he could jeopardize the integrity of the program. "You can't allow this to happen," he said. Russert agreed that it would be a grave error, as did Gartner's deputy, Joe Angotti and another NBC vice president, Tom Ross. Although Angotti and Ross warned Gartner to tread carefully in disagreeing with Wright, the entire group agreed to support him, to stand behind Gartner in opposition to the appointment of Dick Ebersol as vice president in charge of *Today*.

At that point, Gartner summoned Bryant Gumbel to his office to tell him where he and his colleagues stood on the issue. The previous Sunday, after Wright had told Ebersol he was going to give him the *Today* show, Ebersol had driven to Gumbel's country house and had spent the evening talking with him. Now Gumbel was standing in Gartner's office, surrounded by Gartner, Brokaw, Russert, Angotti, and Ross—and Gartner was telling him how he felt about Ebersol. "I just want you to know where we are here," he told Gumbel. "I've told Bob Wright that if he insists that Dick Ebersol be appointed to this position, then I am going to resign."

Gumbel was completely taken aback. His eyes scanned the room as he tried to gauge where the others stood on this issue. "Well," he said quietly, slightly shaken, "I'm sorry to hear you're taking this position, because I think Ebersol's terrific and he's an old friend and he would be good for the program. And I think the program needs this kind of new approach and new blood. I think it does," he repeated. Still, it was made clear to Bryant Gumbel in that room that day that a very strong core of men with clout from inside the News Division were united against the appointment of Dick Ebersol, and ready to back Michael Gartner in the face of Robert Wright.

A few days later, a strange thing happened. Jack Welch, the chairman of GE, arrived at 30 Rock in the corporate chopper for a lunch meeting with Gartner and Wright. When Gartner returned from the lunch, his colleagues asked him what had happened in the meeting. "Oh, nothing," Gartner replied. "We barely talked about that subject, we talked about Maria Shriver and some other things. . . ."

That was all Gartner would say. "I got the impression," said one of those who had backed Gartner in his opposition to Ebersol, "that he had just kind of left us all out there to twist in the wind. He probably caved in, knowing Wright and Welch and how they work. There's no doubt in my mind that Jack Welch put his finger on Gartner's chest and said, 'You play by *our* rules,' because Gartner was a kind of changed man after that and the subject never came up again. There is no doubt in my mind they scared the shit out of Michael Gartner, they just absolutely scared the shit out of him." And so Dick Ebersol became the vice president in charge of *Today*, a move that would leave an indelible and irreversible mark on the program.

Ebersol and Bryant Gumbel had a lot in common. Sports played a major role in both of their lives, both men were voraciously ambitious, and neither was known for his sensitivity to women. All of these qualities would combine to have a startling effect on the *Today* show from the day Dick Ebersol was put in charge of it.

Except for the fact that Ebersol successfully patched up the relationship between Michael Gartner and Bryant Gumbel, things plunged rapidly downhill. At least one highly placed, well-informed member of NBC News thought the appointment was wrong from the beginning: "It was a bad idea," said the newsman. "It was bad internally because it sent the wrong signals. Dick was always into quick fixes, and his whole career in television had been going in there and doing the glitzy thing. And that's exactly what he did. He didn't realize the institution he was dealing with."

Ebersol had wanted to get his hands on *Today* from the moment another good friend of his, Brandon Tartikoff, whom he has often referred to as his alter ego, suggested to Robert Wright the previous April that he hire Dick Ebersol to be president of NBC Sports. Ebersol had agreed to take the sports job but told Wright at the time that what he really wanted to be in charge of was the *Today* show. Wright agreed in principle with that notion at the time, but didn't commit to acting on it. Now, finally, the *Today* show was officially in Ebersol's hands, and he didn't waste any time getting at it.

If *Today* was not exactly broke when Ebersol took over, he was convinced that it was ailing. Even though the show was still in first place, Ebersol fixated on one disturbing trend. Every research study showed that *Today* was losing crucial ground in the most desirable demographic area of all: women between the ages of eighteen and thirty-four. Ebersol knew this spelled danger. It also gave him something solid to sink his teeth into. His mind was set in motion.

It was Ebersol's theory that each of the major players on the show—Jane, Bryant, Gene, Willard, and John—should attract their own following to the show, and he believed that there were people who watched the show specifically for Jane, for Bryant, for Willard, and even for Gene Shalit. But he did not believe that John Palmer had a constituency of his own.

On top of that, he did not think Palmer was good in his second capacity, which was to fill in as a substitute host for Bryant or even

Jane. So in spite of the fact that John Palmer was one of the most respected newsmen in the business, a man who had covered everything from the White House to international politics for twenty-five years, Ebersol concluded that Palmer needed to be replaced. He coupled this conclusion with the misguided assumption that young women only want to watch young women—that women in the desirable demographic group *Today* was losing wanted to get their news from other women in the same age group—and like a child constructing a castle in the sand, Ebersol continued to build on that assumption.

Then, conveniently, there was the fact that a beautiful, talented blonde, Deborah Norville, was sitting in *NBC News at Sunrise*, the show was a strong number one in its time period, she had substitute hosted for seven weeks on the *Today* show and everyone—especially Robert Wright and John Welch—were crazy about her. Not only was she the bright rising star at NBC News, but she was a young woman who also happened to be beautiful. To add an even more complicated twist, the word was out that CBS was trying to steal her away. The handwriting was on the wall.

It did not take a great deal of soul-searching for Ebersol to decide on Norville. "He knew that Jack Welch, the chairman of GE, was in love with Deborah because he used to watch her on the air and she really played the executive game very well," said a senior *Today* executive. "Wright liked her and Bryant liked her. What's not to like about her? She's an attractive blonde who plays the game."

Another executive at *Today* saw it differently. "They fell in love with Deborah and they thought everybody else would too," she says. "And who was Jane to them? Jane was a boring old shoe. They hardly listened to any woman except Susan Saint James, who was not fond of Jane."

The appointment of Norville to Palmer's job as newsreader on *Today* filled the bill for Ebersol in other ways, as well. "He wanted to please his bosses," explained a *Today* executive. "He didn't like Jane, and he knew Bryant was frustrated by Jane—to be kind—and I think he wanted to kiss up to Bryant."

Ebersol moved quickly, rapidly undercutting what remained of

Marty Ryan's power. In August, only a few weeks after he took over, he put his new plan into Gartner's hands, and quickly received Gartner's blessing. The unsuspecting Palmer, whose contract was conveniently coming up for renewal, was summoned to Michael Gartner's office. He immediately began to sense that something was awry. Gartner greeted him coolly, and then he said, "I like the job you're doing on the *Today* show, you were a terrific White House correspondent, a terrific overseas correspondent . . ." He droned on.

"Wait, wait, wait . . ." said Palmer, becoming suspicious. "Where's the 'but' here? Why don't you give me the 'but'?"

Gartner stared back at him. "But," he said, "we would like someone else to do the news on the *Today* show."

Totally numb now, the genteel Palmer simply shrugged, and reaching for something to say, told Gartner evenly, "Well, it's your candy store." Then, gathering his quiet composure, he asked Gartner, "Well, alright, who's going to be doing—who's going to take my job?"

"Well," Gartner replied. "There's a feeling here that we would like Deborah Norville to come take your job and do the news there."

"Well, why?" Palmer asked.

"No, you did nothing wrong . . ." Gartner waved the very thought from the stale air in his office. "Things just happen like this occasionally in the business and we would like you to stay here. We kind of owe you one for this," he told Palmer through his crooked half smile. "You think about what you would like to do with NBC News."

In the meantime, Palmer was told, he would take Deborah's old job as anchor of *NBC News at Sunrise*. He had never seen Dick Ebersol, except briefly at a party at Robert Wright's house that summer. At the time he had gotten the weird impression that Ebersol was trying to avoid him. Palmer knew this had been Dick Ebersol's decision. During his meeting with Gartner, Gartner had said to him, "I know the news business and Ebersol knows TV, so it's kind of a good marriage between us." It was no secret around the *Today* show that Dick Ebersol was engineering all of the new changes. In fact, he had spoken to every member of the *Today* show cast personally about them—with the glaring exception of John Palmer.

Deborah was named the news anchor of *Today* immediately. She was also named the show's first-ever permanent substitute anchor. For these services, the new, bright, young star of the future was signed to a five-year, $5 million contract—nearly as much as Jane's $1.2 million annual salary after more than twelve years on the job.

Palmer had still never spoken with Ebersol. Whenever he saw him in the hall, Ebersol would take the other hallway, obviously just to avoid him. Since Palmer did not know him, he figured Ebersol either felt bad or the situation was just too awkward. Finally, one day as Palmer was packing up his office to move out to make way for Deborah to move in—he had been relegated to her old office—he heard a knock on his door. Ebersol pushed the door open and stepped in.

"May I talk to you a minute?" he said.

"Sure," replied Palmer. "But I don't have any furniture."

"A packing box is fine," said Ebersol, seating himself on the edge of one of Palmer's sealed boxes. He cleared his throat. "I just want you to know," he said, "that your future is going to be my number-one priority, that you're always going to be on the front burner with me until your situation is resolved, and resolved to your satisfaction."

That was the last time John Palmer saw Dick Ebersol. A while later, Palmer sent Ebersol a memo asking him for help on another matter, and he never heard back from him, or saw him again. He met with Gartner several times and Gartner offered him a job as an anchor of a local station in Miami, a job of considerably less stature than the *Today* job that John Palmer had just lost. Palmer did not take it. He accepted what he felt was a better job as an anchor of a syndicated show, *Instant Recall*, which was canceled after one season. So John Palmer unceremoniously left the network he had been at for twenty-five years.

Jane, who was carefully observing Ebersol's actions, had to handle her feelings judiciously. "When it was first revealed to me that John and Deborah were going to switch, that was a real blow," she said later. "I like him very much and I thought, 'Why John? What did he do to anybody?' But as soon as you say anything, it sounds like a jealous older woman talking about a younger one."

It was not difficult, however, for Jane to surmise the ultimate meaning of Norville's new status. "Jane knew when they signed that contract," said a *Today* writer, "that NBC was declaring that Deborah Norville is the future."

At this point, Ebersol made what would turn out to be his fatal error, the error upon which his castle would crumble. He wanted to have it all: Bryant and Jane and Deborah, too. And he wanted to make it clear to the viewers that Deborah was not just the newsreader, but much more than what John Palmer had been. He figured that he needed somehow to orchestrate that message, which he accomplished, as one observer put it, "with all the grace of a mudslide." He would, he decided, move Deborah out of the news nook and onto the couch with Bryant and Jane at the opening of each half hour, before she read the news.

Perhaps the most blatant flaw in Ebersol's thinking was that Deborah would attract more young female viewers. Coby Atlas saw the paradox right away: "The wonderful double-talk that I used to get that still makes my head spin was that on the one hand they would tell me that what's wrong with the *Today* show is that it doesn't have a women's audience, and on the other hand they would tell me the person that can save this is Deborah," she recalls. "Why? 'Because she's so beautiful,' they said. Women don't care that she's beautiful. Then they tell me that Jane, who is perfectly pleasant and wonderful, has to go to make room for a kind of Madonna–Marilyn Monroe type. If we're trying to get women, then putting on a dazzlingly beautiful woman, no matter how smart and talented, is not a great idea. Now, if they had told me, 'You know what, we lost the women to *GMA*, we're never going to get them back, let's try to get every single guy in America to watch,' then I could have understood it."

The question that begs to be asked is why a show that is watched in large part by women did not have, with the exception of Coby Atlas, who was not asked to participate in the reshaping of the show, a woman in any decision-making capacity—why men, primarily from a rather select "boys' club," men like Bryant who had displayed in the past attitudes toward women that were insensitive at best and offensive at worst, were the ones deciding what women wanted to watch.

By this time, although the often outrageous behavior of what remained of the boys' club had tempered somewhat, Bryant's behavior towards many of the women on the staff had not improved at all. Most people were aware of the way he often referred to Jane, and to other women as well. His behavior towards women was often filled with hostility. Although he was not overtly mean, he was astoundingly insensitive, and at times in the office his behavior was simply childish. He got a kick out of "scaring" women. One staffer described his antics. "He would grab a dead mouse—dead mice were abundant throughout the *Today* show offices because there was a lot of construction going on at 30 Rock—and he would run around waving it in women's faces. He would hide behind an office door on his hands and knees like a dog, barking at women, nipping at their feet, trying to scare them."

This Bryant Gumbel was totally at odds with the persona millions of viewers saw conducting brilliant interviews with some of the most powerful and influential people in the world. But his behavior and his attitude towards women was relevant because Bryant Gumbel was an instrumental force on the *Today* show in the summer of 1989. It was this general mentality, common, for the most part, to the men in charge, that would eventually bring the *Today* show down to one of its lowest points in history.

Deborah Norville took her place on the couch on September 5. The show opened with a "three-shot" of the newly constituted nucleus of the *Today* show family: Bryant and Jane and Deborah. From the beginning, Norville handled the situation with an unfortunate lack of aplomb. She did little to endear herself to the staff, writing a memo upon her arrival announcing how glad she was to be there, which many interpreted as self-promoting and imperious. She often criticized Jane in the presence of other staff members as she watched her on the air, saying things like, "Can you believe what she's wearing?" or "Look at that hair." Her behavior caused one staff member to observe shortly after her arrival, "Obviously, she's hungry. As hungry as a shark that's never had a meal in its life."

From the moment Deborah sat down on the couch that first day, the tenor of the show changed drastically. Tension and hostility wafted through the morning air like smoke from burning bacon. Gumbel's demeanor changed visibly when Deborah was present. He seemed animated and enthused when chatting with her, while he appeared cool and stiff when dealing with Jane.

Literally overnight, the smart, well-heeled, intelligent news show transformed into a raunchy soap opera. "Watching the three of them on screen together is like looking at a broken marriage with the home-wrecker right there on the premises," wrote *The Washington Post* television critic, Tom Shales. "Gumbel seems more comfortable now with Norville than with Pauley, and Norville sometimes has a self-satisfied smirk on her face. Like Eve in *All About Eve*."

This image of a marriage being usurped by the "other woman" live on the air at seven o'clock in the morning was hardly what the *Today* show needed to garner the support of more female viewers.

Ebersol insisted that Jane had been totally apprised of every change he made. However, Coby Atlas says, "Jane would come into my office and talk to me. I realized that she was just fed up with them. Jane had one version of what happened and Dick had another. And they both believed it. Dick would come into my office and swear to me that Jane had signed off on everything. Jane would come into my office and swear to me she had agreed to nothing."

There had obviously been a gross misunderstanding and Pauley did not like what was taking place right before her eyes. "If there was a specific departure from what I was told and what I saw, it was not so much *who* was sitting *where* as *who* was on-camera *when*," she said later. "At some point a decision was made to shoot the cast of the *Today* program as if it were a threesome. What I wasn't told was that there would be a three-shot at the top of the show. No, I was never told that Deborah would be sitting on the couch. *Small* things. *Subtle* things. I think Dick can be forgiven for not anticipating how not just me but the viewers interpreted what they saw. People were wondering what was going on."

The fact that the headlines were screaming things like WATCH OUT JANE PAULEY, DEBORAH NORVILLE IS THE SUPERSTAR OF THE '90S and that Liz Smith wrote a long column declaring that the *Today* show situation was a clear demonstration of the new, attractive younger woman coming in and pushing the older woman out, did not make Jane, who was a mere thirty-eight years old, feel any better. According to an executive in the NBC Press Department, "Jane got up every day and read and became a little more tense and a little more tense and started thinking about what it meant. Her friends began to say to her, 'They're trying to screw you.' And she began to say, 'Wait a minute, maybe I've been sold a bill of goods.' And she went to Ebersol and said, 'Is there something I'm missing here?' "

Whether or not Ebersol had technically informed her of Deborah's impending presence—and the degree of it—quickly became irrelevant. As one female *Today* staffer put it, "Any woman in Ebersol's place would have known that even if Jane had said it was all right with her, that it couldn't possibly be all right with her. Even if she had felt compelled to say it was all right so she would not look like a bitch, it couldn't possibly be all right. The guys did not understand that when Jane said, 'It doesn't bother me,' it bothered her. They wanted her to be the good little girl and take the three-shot while they eased Deborah into her job. They wanted an easy transition where this gorgeous woman drained the blood from Jane and then they would hit her and she would roll over, and there's Deborah."

But Jane did not roll over. What she did do, however, around September 7, was submit her resignation to Dick Ebersol. This, of course, was not what the men in charge had expected from Jane Pauley. "For the first time in my life," Jane told me later, "I acted instead of reacted. I had always been a good soldier, someone who never said no. But now I had to decide what I wanted, make a plan, and carry it through." Jane Pauley was a different person in the fall of 1989 than she had ever been before. "I was confident that I had a career in broadcasting—that I would work again," she said. "I was sending my kids to kindergarten for the first time. Up until that moment, the job worked really well with the flow of family life. But suddenly it was working against it."

And that was not the only thing. Jane, who for more than twelve years on the *Today* show had been the quintessential team player, was watching her very team disintegrate. First it was John Palmer. Soon after that, it became increasingly clear that Marty Ryan's position was rapidly weakening. Very quickly the strength of Jane Pauley's ties to her team were waning, and Deborah's presence had not done much to bolster her spirit of loyalty. In fact, she figured, naïvely as it turned out, that since her successor was essentially in place, and since the viewers already knew her and she appeared to be capable of handling the show, her own departure would not even be very significant. She turned out to be as wrong as she could be.

The possibility that Jane would even consider leaving the *Today* show, not to mention the network, had not had a place in Ebersol's repertoire. It had not even been a possibility. When she told him she wanted to leave, he was shocked. "It appears you are ready with another team," she had told him, "and that suggests the timing is good for NBC, too."

The men running the network could not believe that Jane would walk away from her $1.2 million contract. Nor had they anticipated the public's outcry about what had been done to their "loved one." As events unfolded, Pauley was shocked too—not only at the network's desperate desire to keep her, but also at the overwhelmingly supportive response of her fans.

Nine weeks of intensive negotiations began—endless meetings with Dick Ebersol and Michael Gartner, in which Jane Pauley persisted in her attempts to convince them, without losing her equanimity for a moment, that she really would walk away from her contract and that she was not jockeying for more money. "They thought it was some kind of power play," she said later, "that my contract was not up and that I was pitching for more money. I do remember at one point kind of laughing at the thought of me in a power play! I said, 'Dick, you know if this was a power play I'd be buckling.' "

She insisted that all she wanted was out of her contract, that since she would not be working, she did not expect to be paid. Ebersol and Gartner were beside themselves. They persisted in thinking what Jane wanted was more money. "They were terribly confused," said one network executive. "Because she was telling them the truth and they had no experience with people who tell the truth."

Through all this, Brokaw took on the role of "information broker." He knew Jane well and had a long conversation with her in the midst of the negotiations. Afterwards, he went to Gartner and Ebersol to set them straight: "You should have no illusions," he told them. "She knows what she's about, and what she says she'll do, she'll do."

If Ebersol had been shocked when he first heard the news, after Brokaw's assessment, it finally sank in. "Jane," Ebersol finally told her, "you're just too important to the network. We can't let you go."

"Dick says he had blisters on his knees from begging Jane not to leave," said NBC's publicity director, Peggy Hubble, at the time.

As the negotiations dragged on, they only strengthened Jane's conviction that the mess that had resulted from all this had to be resolved, and it had to be resolved amicably. She still couldn't grasp the reality that NBC had any need of her. "Why would they want to have me on the payroll if I weren't doing the *Today* show?" she asked. The answer to that question most probably lies in the fact that if NBC had lost Jane Pauley after botching up one of their most profitable properties, as one observer put it, "Big heads would have rolled. No one would have survived unscathed."

Then something oddly fortuitous occurred. Jane got an idea for a prime-time special at almost precisely the same moment Brandon Tartikoff and Robert Wright cleared fifty-two hours of prime time for a magazine show for the network. Three weeks later, Jane signed a one-year extension to her contract, and everyone breathed a huge sigh of relief. In the midst of the *Today* show debacle, NBC had now emerged with a major female star, a news-magazine show, and—if they played their cards right with Jane, who could certainly fill in for Brokaw on a regular basis—a way to beef up their third-rated *Nightly News*.

The network had managed to keep Jane Pauley—even if she would depart the *Today* show, and now Ebersol, not shedding his glitzy *modus operandi* for a moment, decided that they should make the announcement of Jane's departure on the air, live during the *Today* show. The *pièce de résistance* was scheduled to take place the week of October 17, but consistent with the general tone that had prevailed throughout the disaster to date, an act of God would preempt it.

October 17, 1989. Dick Ebersol wanted to make sure that Deborah Norville really looked like a part of the team at all times. His gamble was that the anger which had been stirred up so fiercely by all the interfamily antics, the negative image the press had created of Deborah Norville as the successful interloper, would dissipate with time. So when the *Today* show went to Chicago to broadcast the show from there for a day, Ebersol made certain that Norville went along with the rest of the entire cast.

That would have been just fine, if the San Francisco earthquake of 1989 had not hit only hours after they all arrived in Chicago. Marty Ryan was there, along with Bryant and Jane and Deborah. Coby Atlas was the only producer in New York, and she was in charge of running the control room from there. Under normal circumstances, it would have been fine.

Coby was home, about to cash in for the night, when the phone call came. It was one of the men in the newsroom. "There's been an earthquake in San Francisco," he told her.

Coby, a native Californian, was not alarmed by this news. "Oh, big deal," she replied nonchalantly. "There are earthquakes in California all the time. Call me back if it's a big deal," and not thinking more about it, she hung up the phone.

Fifteen minutes later, her phone rang again. "It's a big deal," said the voice on the other end of the line.

"I'm on my way in," Coby said, jumping up. "I'm getting dressed, I'll be there in fifteen minutes."

When she arrived at the office around nine o'clock there was complete chaos. NBC News could not seem to get on the air. At around ten o'clock, Dick Ebersol came in, trying to decide, according to Coby, whether or not to bring the *Today* show back from Chicago. Technically, the decision should have been made by Gartner and Marty Ryan, but there was Ebersol trying to figure out what to do. Ryan had initially made a bad call by deciding to stay in Chicago. By the time Ebersol decided they should return to New York, they were unable to get a charter.

Here the old enmity between networks came in. ABC had a chartered plane to New York and would not let the *Today* cast on it. So the entire cast of the show, not to mention the executive producer, was all stuck in Chicago away from home base, while a major news story was unfolding.

By the time the *Today* show came on in the morning, things were as bad as they could possibly be. It was almost impossible for Coby to find out what, if anything, they could get out of San Francisco because of the earthquake damage. When she did find out, she had to make a decision and attempt to communicate it to Marty and Bryant and Jane and Deborah in Chicago, since the show still had to come out of there.

To make things even more difficult, since most of the lines were down, they did not know who they were going to get until seconds before they got them. It turned out to be a free-for-all. Whoever was there simply got on the air. Since NBC had botched the prime-time coverage the night before, they wanted the *Today* show to stay on the air for seven hours, which somehow they managed to do. The whole situation reflected the chaos that had been bubbling within the *Today* show since Ebersol had arrived on the scene.

Jane's on-air announcement of her upcoming and final departure from *Today* was postponed for ten days, until October 27. Then, according

to Ebersol's plan, two segments of the show were devoted to her emotional farewell, even though she did not even know at the time when
her last day would be. There seemed to be a need to simply say that it
was coming, to put an end to the rampant speculation that would not
die. So on October 27, the *Today* show opened as it had for the last
several weeks now, with Jane seated uncomfortably between Bryant
and Deborah. The shot looked like it should have a caption that read,
"What's wrong with this picture?"

Millions of viewers squirmed in their living rooms—or bedrooms,
bathrooms, or kitchens—while the latest installment of the soap opera
one observer had dubbed "Blood on the Sofa" unfolded before their
eyes.

Still, it was sad and ironic. Jane began by clearing up some mis-
perceptions. "It has hurt," she said, "to see two of my friends, Bryant
and Deborah, assigned roles in this that they did not play." She cleared
her throat and then said to Bryant, "I'll have to say that what I am
going to miss most is the pleasure I have taken in working with you."

The three of them looked about as comfortable as participants in the
Middle East peace talks. At least they were trying to convey goodwill.
All six eyes were moist, at moments.

"Too many of our dawns have been clouded with idle, often erro-
neous speculation, much to the detriment of all of us here," Gumbel
told his confused audience. He referred to Jane as "my buddy here,"
and said, "It goes without saying that I'm going to miss her." Then, he
added, "I personally am looking forward to sharing my first cup of
coffee with Deb, and I hope you are too."

Jane turned to the overwhelmed "Deb." It was now time to pass the
mantle once again to the new generation of *Today* show cohosts, as
Brokaw had done eight years earlier with Gumbel. "Deborah," she
intoned, "thirteen years ago I got a telegram from my predecessor,
Barbara Walters. She wished me good luck and a good alarm clock.
You are already a veteran of the dawn patrol. You already have my
respect and my friendship. Here's my alarm clock."

It was more than Deborah could bear. "Thanks. Oh brother!" she
exclaimed.

"Sister," Jane corrected her.

"Sister," said Norville, continuing, "Waking up is going to be the easy part, but the hard part is going to be following in your footsteps, 'cause they are awfully big shoes to fill. This will help." (She held up the clock.) "But Jane, doing it after you is going to be a nightmare. . . ."

She had no idea whatsoever how true that statement would turn out to be.

The ritual was over and behind them, finally. Nobody who was watching that day quite understood that when all the tears were dried, Jane would be back in the morning, plopped uncomfortably once again between the happy new couple, Deborah and Bryant. The next day, after the show, NBC got hundreds of phone calls, asking, in essence, isn't she ever going to leave?

It was not until December 29 that Jane Pauley presided over her last day on the *Today* show. Again, it was an emotional day, as the announcement of her departure nine weeks earlier had been. Now, after more than 3,000 shows, 12,000 interviews containing some 88,000 questions, after 70 trips and more than 200,000 miles of travel time in the call of duty, Jane Pauley was really leaving the *Today* show. This time she would not be back in the morning. And the *Today* show would never be the same.

Fourteen

NIGHTMARE AT 30 ROCK

Nobody dreamed it could get any worse, but from the morning Jane left, things sank even deeper. The whole miserable affair had resulted from the worst possible combination of circumstances. "Everything bad that could happen did," said an NBC executive. "Jane was more popular than anyone thought and Deborah was less likable and Bryant was less acceptable to the public. If any one of those things had not been quite so horrible it might not have plunged the way it did, but it was the worst-case scenario on every component. The audience finally said, 'We're not going to watch anymore.' "

Deborah had been right when she said to Jane on the air—for several million people to hear—that following in her footsteps was not going to be easy. She had wisely pointed out they would be big shoes to fill. Now they seemed to be getting bigger each day.

But the shoes were not Deborah's only problem. While she attempted—in vain, it appeared—to shed the dark, stifling cloak she had acquired as "the other woman," Jane was simultaneously being canonized as a saint. It was becoming painfully clear that in the eyes of the *Today* show viewers, Deborah simply could not do anything right.

Marty Ryan had not fared so well either. He had known when Dick Ebersol had arrived on the scene that the move did not bode well for him, that he would be stuck with Ebersol looking constantly over his shoulder, second-guessing him—to his face if he was lucky, behind his back if he was not. Within weeks, Ebersol had attempted to bring in a new man over him—David Nuell, from *Entertainment Tonight*. It looked for a moment as though the prophecy would be fulfilled. What Ebersol wanted was obviously to make the *Today* show more like *Entertainment Tonight*, but the Nuell deal had fallen through at the eleventh hour. Just days before David Nuell was supposed to start working at *Today*, the negotiations had abruptly fallen apart. NBC had taken the position that his demands had gotten out of hand, and they had thrown in the towel on him completely.

After they botched the Nuell appointment—they had already announced his arrival with great fanfare—they were left, once again, in an embarrassing position. This time, Ryan was informed that Gartner wanted to make a more drastic change. "They didn't know what to do and they looked stupid," explained a *Today* executive. Their solution this time was to get rid of Ryan and hire a new executive producer altogether—another friend of Ebersol's who had worked with him at ABC back in the seventies. Tom Capra, the son of the legendary movie director Frank Capra, took over the *Today* show on January 28, exactly four weeks after Deborah Norville had begun as cohost. Now that Cliff Kappler, Marty Ryan, and Michael Pressman had all been fired, this left Coby Atlas as the only person on the staff who knew how to get the *Today* show on the air. Although she was not offered the job of executive producer—partly because of her inability to play the necessary politics within the News Division, and partly because she was, after all, a woman—she was elevated to the position of senior producer.

In the increasingly macabre scheme of things, Deborah Norville was undoubtedly the biggest victim of all. She had never asked for any of this—Jane's job had been literally dumped in her lap. Now she had been permanently cast as the villain, the wicked witch who had demolished the precious "family." Soon even her staunchest supporters would begin to doubt that she was up to the job.

The ratings drop that followed the beginning of Norville's tenure was neither surprising nor unexpected. A loss in the ratings usually accompanies a change in the anchors of a show, as it had done with Bryant Gumbel and others before him. By the middle of February, only six weeks after Norville had taken Pauley's place, *Today* had lost an astounding 10 percent of its audience, an amount that was not only shocking, but financially devastating as well.

And *GMA* had gained a good piece of the audience *Today* had lost. It now had the clout to charge over ten thousand dollars more than its archrival for a thirty-second commercial, which meant that with twenty-eight network commercials on each program, *GMA* would be earning nearly three hundred thousand dollars more than *Today* every day, five days a week. After four solid years as the top-rated show, *Today* had slipped into second place in the blink of an eye—not with a whimper, but with a very loud bang.

For the most part, Deborah Norville was the one who got blamed—not only by the viewers but by her bosses as well, and the press continued to tear her apart. Her critics charged that she was too pushy, too brittle, too hard, too cold, too inexperienced. Her bosses were not quite sure exactly what was wrong, but the woman they had so passionately embraced just a few months earlier—their bright, new, young star, the very future of their network—now lay dying before a withering *Today* show audience as they stood by dumbly and gawked.

Deborah was totally devastated. Before long, she spent much of her time in the office crying. "Every day she'd get beaten up by the press," recalls a *Today* show staffer. "She never understood why everyone hated her. She didn't understand why the public hated her and the bosses had turned against her. They finally abandoned her like Typhoid Mary."

Another *Today* staffer summed it up well: "They were falling all over her one day," she said, "and the next day they hung her out to dry."

Norville felt, understandably, that she was in an impossible situation. "They want me to be like Jane," she told Coby Atlas one day, with tears streaming down her face. "What can I do? I love this show. I don't want to leave. I don't want to be forced out. What did I do wrong?"

Coby had tried to comfort Deborah, but the truth was not very comforting. "You didn't do anything wrong," Coby had told Deborah. "You have to understand how they think. They went to bed with a mistress and they woke up with a wife, and you're suffering the consequences of that. It's not your fault, but they don't like you anymore and there's really nothing you can do. When you're the glitzy prize, you tarnish very quickly. That's really what it boils down to."

The disaster—which *Time* magazine called "a public relations Chernobyl"—obviously encompassed more than Norville alone. But as *Time* pointed out, "one cannot ignore the whiff of a double standard here. After all, it was Bryant Gumbel who wrote the nasty memo about his co-workers at *Today*, but it was Pauley who had to watch her heir apparent being groomed on the couch next to her. Norville too was probably treated unfairly in the press. Would a man in the same position have been so rudely characterized as a conniving climber?"

It was Deborah Norville's image that had been irreparably damaged. The previous June, before Ebersol had come up with his ingenious plan, Deborah Norville had had no "negative factor" at all—a television measurement of popularity. When the public had begun to perceive her as a threat to Jane, her "negative factor" had risen alarmingly. Bryant's negative factor had also increased substantially. By March, the *Today* show had become the only morning show to have two anchors with significant negative ratings. In the February "sweeps," the crucial rating period that determines advertising rates for the months to come, *Today* plunged 22 percent in the ratings from the same period the year before, while *GMA* was up 7 percent and *CBS* gained 4 percent.

Nobody knew exactly what to do, but eventually they decided the smartest expenditure of energy would be to focus on Bryant Gumbel. "They decided they had to rehabilitate Bryant, to convince the world that if people only knew Bryant they'd love him," explains a *Today* executive.

It was an interesting strategy, and when the right opportunity came along, Bryant seized it, with NBC's blessing. What better forum to show the "real" Bryant Gumbel, than in a Barbara Walters interview? Gumbel, who had shrunk back from doing publicity of any kind since he had been burned so badly by the press throughout the episode of the now infamous memo, agreed to talk with Walters in an interview which was scheduled to run on March 16, one month after the disastrous February sweeps.

In the meantime, Jane Pauley's first special, *Changes*, based on stories about people who had undergone some sort of major upheaval in their lives, aired on March 13, three days before the Gumbel-Walters interview. Jane's popularity had continued to soar. Research by CBS at the time showed that she had one of the highest likability quotients—known as "Q ratings"—in television. *Changes* was well received by the audience and critics alike. "The critical factor would seem to be Pauley—persistent, compassionate and levelheaded," wrote Tom Shales. "No wonder we liked her in the morning. We're going to like her at night too."

Gumbel's showing with Walters was not as successful as Pauley's prime-time foray had been, in terms of accomplishing what he had set out to do. In typical style, the inimitable Walters did not go easy. She discussed the memo, and she brought up the fact that Bryant was being referred to as "arrogant" with increasing frequency. She also alluded to the story in *Sports Illustrated* that accused him so brutally of gross insensitivity to his mother, and she discussed the evolution of the Pauley-Norville affair.

Bryant handled everything coolly, but well. "I would say," he speculated about himself, "that Bryant Gumbel is an emotional guy, and where possible we should capitalize on it, and where it hurts us, we should try to minimize it . . . and he's not the one who should be the heavyweight, and so NBC should make the heavyweight decisions, and make sure that Bryant stays in the background." It was an unusually sensitive and perceptive evaluation, but one that was never acted upon.

When Barbara Walters questioned Bryant about Jane, he revealed more of his true feelings than a public-relations expert probably would have advised. "Did you want Jane Pauley to stay?" Walters asked. "I wanted Jane Pauley to be happy in what she did," replied Gumbel, smoothly evading the issue.

Maybe, Walters suggested, leading him, Jane would have been happy staying at the main desk and letting Deborah do the news. "You could have made it happen," she said to Bryant somewhat forcefully.

"I'm not sure I could have made it happen," he replied. "Barbara, I mean, you know, hindsight's perfect," he said, asserting that had he interfered, it might have been interpreted as trying to stunt Norville's career.

"If they could bring Jane Pauley back," asked Walters then, "if she would come back . . . would you like that? Would it help?"

"To take my place or Deborah's?" countered Bryant, successfully evading the issue once more. "Oh, I don't know," he said finally. "I think it's always difficult to rewrite history, Barbara. I think the idea of bringing Jane back right now, while certainly a pleasant one for a lot of people to consider, would be fraught with so many difficulties involved and so many hurt feelings, and so much discomfort for all included, including Jane, that I think it's kind of an unrealistic thing to consider."

That was all Bryant had to say on the subject. Around the time of the Walters interview, Gumbel and Ebersol were heard at 30 Rock, blaming Jane Pauley for getting them into the mess they were in. One staffer said they often alluded to the notion that if Jane had accepted things like a good soldier, none of the resultant catastrophe would have occurred. "Jane got blamed because she didn't play the game like everybody wanted," said the staffer. "So it was clearly her fault."

Allison Davis, who was now the permanent set writer at the *Today* show—which meant that she arrived at the studio at four o'clock each morning to write any neccssary changes in the show before it went on the air—was not known for being either timid or unopinionated. One morning, a few months after Jane had left the show, Allison was on her way down the corridor outside of studio 3B, headed for the ladies' room, when Dick Ebersol appeared and motioned her over. "Can I talk to you for a moment, Allison?" he asked her.

"Sure," Allison replied.

"I haven't asked you what you think about everything that's happened," Ebersol said to her.

"Dick," Allison replied, measuring her words carefully, "anyone who knows me knows never to ask me a question if they don't want to hear the truth." She continued towards the bathroom, but Ebersol reached out to stop her.

"I want the truth, Allison," he said.

Allison and Dick stood leaning against the wall of the corridor just a few feet from the door of the studio, within easy earshot of everyone inside. "Okay, then," Allison shrugged. "Let me tell you something. You fucked up royally, and frankly, I will tell you that what you've done to this show angers me."

Ebersol was speechless. He had not anticipated what he was hearing. "You know," Allison continued, "it was okay when you wanted to tweak this and tweak that, but when you started to make changes that affect my pocketbook and the food I'm putting on my table for my family and for my shelter, you started to fuck with me. When you started to fuck with the show, you started to fuck with me."

Becoming more excited as she spoke, she began to poke Ebersol in the ribs. The gathering crowd was captivated by the exchange, but afraid of what might happen next. Allison Davis was capable of almost anything. "Reserved" was not a word that was applicable to her. Everyone was glued to the conversation between them, which was rapidly increasing in volume. Ebersol struggled to explain his position. He brought up the well-worn question of the demographics. "They showed we needed a younger audience," he insisted, "and, frankly, Allison," he added heatedly, "I have to tell you that Bryant, who is an extraordinary talent, had voiced his frustration, and I thought that maybe I could be of help. I didn't know it was going to go this far. And Jane—"

Allison cut him off. "I don't want to hear about Jane," she told him. "And I don't want to hear any 'he said, she said,' or any of that kind of bullshit. You asked me what I think, and I think you all fucked up. You can't go around manipulating people like that—you simply cannot do that."

"I don't think I manipulated anybody," Ebersol shot back.

"Dick," Allison said, "this is where you and I part company, because nobody takes me for a fool." And with that, she turned and continued on her way down the hallway to the bathroom.

———

NBC's affiliate stations were as furious as Allison Davis was about what had happened to the *Today* show—and what was going on at NBC News in general. Besides losing Jane, who had now become the network's hottest star, they had lost a string of valuable correspondents over the last few years: Roger Mudd, John Hart, Ken Bode, Richard Valeriani, Steve Delaney, John Palmer, Chris Wallace, Connie Chung, and Bob Jamieson. On top of that, *Nightly News* had been in third place for thirty-six weeks out of the last year.

One of the biggest problems NBC was facing now was how to showcase Jane, whom they had clumsily managed to pummel into temporary oblivion. Momentarily, at least, television imitated life— and the full circle came around. Steve Friedman, who had left three years earlier to produce *USA Today on TV*, which had met a disastrous fate, earning the dubious distinction of being the largest failure in TV syndication history, was suddenly hired back by NBC to be the executive producer of *Nightly News*.

Friedman's appointment was an indirect attempt by the network to solve the Pauley problem, among other things. The annual meeting of the NBC affiliates—more than two hundred stations in all—was only two weeks away. The executives knew they were in for sharp criticism. Hiring Friedman as head of *Nightly News* could be strongly interpreted as signaling a major upcoming role for Jane Pauley in the program. At the time, Friedman insisted, "Nobody has ever said that I have to bring Jane onto the broadcast," but everyone knew her place there would be magnified. She had already become the primary substitute for *Nightly* and although it was clear that she and Brokaw would never split anchoring duties *per se*, the plan was to have Tom more frequently on location with breaking news stories, while Jane would read the news from the studio.

Negotiations were also progressing between NBC and Faith Daniels of *CBS Morning News*. They were trying to hire her away from CBS to become the anchor of *NBC News at Sunrise*, as well as the newsreader on *Today*, a job that was ironically open again.

These moves seemed to make sense, in light of the current problems. In the eyes of many, both inside NBC and out, what happened next did not. The focus on Bryant Gumbel had continued to grow, and concern had risen greatly because of his negative image. Bryant felt he was getting a bum rap, and he desperately wanted to bring someone onto the show who would "make him look like a nice guy," according to a *Today* executive. The person he thought could do this was his old pal, fellow baseball enthusiast—and maybe even father figure—Joe Garagiola, who had already put in four years on the *Today* show, having left in 1973.

When he was asked if he would take the job, Garagiola, who was comfortably ensconced in a nice home in Arizona with his wife, was as shocked as everyone else. "I don't ask why they put me in the lineup," he said after the deal was finalized. "I'm just happy they put me here." Then, when someone asked him where he thought he would sit, he humbly joked about his new place on the show: "I just hope it's in the building," he replied.

Why they put Garagiola in the lineup—or in the building, for that matter—was a question that many people were pondering. The original problem, after all, the very reason the blunders had been made in the first place, was that *Today* was losing young female viewers. Since Jane had left and Deborah had come in, that problem had gotten even worse. In the first five months of 1989, when Ebersol had first become concerned about the demographics, ABC had 1,460,000 female viewers between the ages of 18 and 49, while NBC had 1,150,000. Now, a year later, after the bumbling attempt to solve the problem, ABC's number had crept up to 1,490,000, while NBC's had slid to 990,000. How the addition of a pudgy, bald, sixty-four-year-old former baseball player was going to bring in more women in that age group was certainly a legitimate question.

Garagiola himself had no reason to ask it. NBC had made him a deal that was considerably more than the four thousand dollars he had made during his first year playing major league baseball forty-four years ago. They had agreed to pay him approximately $1 million, to supply him with a car and driver, an apartment in New York, and two first-class airline tickets a week for himself and his wife to commute between New York and Arizona. He was also given a highly unusual opportunity for the second-year renewal option on his contract. He alone would have the option to decide whether he would continue for a second year or not, something that was almost unheard of in the television business.

Michael Gartner made the announcement to the press on May 17, nineteen days prior to the affiliates' meeting, hoping this too might help defuse their ever-growing fury. He said that in order to restore a "sense of family" to the *Today* show, three new personalities would be added to the program, one of whom was Joe Garagiola. Gartner pointed out that the presence of Garagiola would mean some reduction in Norville's role in the program.

Bryant Gumbel offered his own opinion. "I don't know that I would call it a demotion," he said. "We think Joe's abilities will help Deborah make the transition into her role."

When Tom Capra, who had now been executive producer of *Today* for almost two months, was asked about Norville's future, he replied emphatically, "She's my guy. She's not on her way out," even though almost everyone on the show knew that Capra was lobbying hard to replace her. Then he added, "The ratings have slid because Jane left the show, not because of Deborah. She's a solid journalist. I believe the audience will like her as they are exposed to her. Joe will help the audience understand more about Deborah. He says things like 'Oh come on, you don't mean that.' He can bring out what is really going on with her." How Garagiola could accomplish that was very difficult for anyone to grasp.

The other two additions to the "family," Gartner announced, would be Faith Daniels, whom they had finally succeeded in hiring to do both *NBC News at Sunrise* and the news on *Today*, and Katie Couric, an NBC News correspondent who would become national correspondent for *Today* based in Washington. The new family was scheduled to gather for the first time on June 4, the same day the three-day meeting of the affiliates would begin.

It was obviously hoped that these additions would help stem the serious losses suffered by the show in recent months. To the chagrin of the network, *Today* had actually placed last in New York in the ratings the week before, not only behind its competition from the other two broadcast networks, but also behind a news/talk show on Fox Broadcasting, and cartoons on independent stations.

Gartner had one more rather momentous announcement to make. Dick Ebersol had decided to relinquish his duties as the executive in charge of *Today*. Ebersol had valiantly agreed to take the rap for the *Today* show debacle. "I clearly believe," Ebersol said, "that one of the best ways to put an end to this soap opera is for somebody to take responsibility for it. It's clear from research that the viewers are mad at us."

His official statement read as follows: "Almost all of the furor of recent months concerning *Today* has revolved around my decisions of last fall, and I believe that I must take the primary responsibility for those decisions. As a result, Deborah Norville has been wrongly and unfairly characterized, making it impossible for her to grow into the job gradually and win over the audience. My hope is that these new additions will enhance the sense of family and camaraderie and that the viewers will give Deborah the chance she deserves."

But most likely, Ebersol was not acting solely out of concern for Deborah Norville's career. As another NBC executive pointed out, "Ebersol cost the company about $40 million with his mistakes, to say nothing of all the terrible publicity."

Apparently the reality had finally begun to sink in for Ebersol, who nonetheless would stay on in his capacity as president of NBC Sports—concentrating on the 1992 Summer Olympics in Barcelona—and remain a vice president of the News Division. "Dick has really had a tough meeting with himself on all of this," said an NBC executive who knew him well. "He came in with the perception that Sports had things that needed to be done, but he says now he doesn't know how he could do both jobs. It was painful and depressing and distracting and preoccupying. He says this is the worst episode he's gone through and blames himself. He went into total shock and depression because as the events unfolded it became clear that either his choice was never going to work, or the way the situation was handled made it impossible for us to know the true answer."

Coby Atlas offered a different perspective: "When Ebersol took the blame for this, I always tried to stand up and say, 'There are four other men who should take equal credit and blame.' Because they all sat around and they all made this decision. I can come up with the most stupid idea—for example, 'Let's put Bruce Willis on instead of Bryant Gumbel'—and everybody should say, 'What a stupid idea.' If they all say to me, 'Let's get rid of Bryant, let's get Bruce Willis,' then they're as dumb as I am. It's not just Dick's fault. Dick came up with a really dumb idea and they all jumped up and applauded."

Michael Gartner himself is still overwhelmed at the magnitude of what he sees as a grand gesture on the part of Dick Ebersol. "He did it for me," says Gartner. "It was nobody's fault. It was a combination of history, of personalities, of all kinds of things. Dick is walking around with some real scars. None of what happened was his fault, but he stood up and did what I've never seen anybody in television do. He fell on his sword and he did it for me. It was the ultimate act of friendship. He did it to give me a clean slate."

———

The three-day affiliates' meeting, which took place in Washington, D.C., on June 4—the same day Garagiola made his debut on *Today*—was as bad as NBC had expected it to be. Michael Gartner was lambasted for the ragged performance of NBC News on everything ranging from the California earthquake to the fact that *Nightly News* was still third in the ratings, but the most serious focus of the affiliates' ire was what had happened to *Today*. Jane Pauley's departure was their greatest concern, and the entire NBC contingent was treated like ice, until Jane appeared as part of the presentation of NBC News—and they gave her a standing ovation.

After that, in a closed-door meeting away from both the press and the public, the top executives acknowledged that indeed they had made a grievous error. "You had a whole room full of guys saying, 'We screwed up,' " said a senior executive who was there.

The admission, however, did little to assuage the critical reception Joe Garagiola got after his return during the week of the affiliates' meeting. The avid *Today* follower and critic Tom Shales pointed out that Garagiola's attempts at folksy bonhomie seemed forced, "like the guy who runs around conventions with a squirting flower in his lapel." Shales was no more enthused about the rest of the additions. "Obviously the *Today* couches are getting awfully crowded, evident from opening group shots with the family assembled," he observed, "with Gumbel taking the fatherly position in the middle. The *Today* family is getting as populous as *The Waltons*, and the show's cast as big as that of *Twin Peaks*."

Still, Michael Gartner defends Joe Garagiola's role to this day. "Joe did every single thing he was asked to," he insists. "I believe that we would have had a worse situation without Joe. He was familiar. He was Uncle Joe. And it was never understood by any of us that he was coming in for the long pull. He was coming to help glue it together."

At the same time, Tom Capra clumsily attempted to fend off speculation about what the changes on *Today* really meant, when he was asked if adding Garagiola was not an admission that Gumbel and Norville were not working out. "Have you seen the ratings?" he growled back. "That's a stupid question! The ratings aren't very good; we've lost 15 to 20 percent of our audience in the past several weeks. We had to do something about the broadcast." What about simply *replacing* one of the other cast members, he was asked. "Well, we decided not to do that," he said.

This did little to stop the continuing speculation that Deborah Norville would soon be replaced. By this time she had been unfairly labeled by some as the Dan Quayle of TV journalism, and her critics still complained that she was hard to take with her "desperate, dizzy, chirpy grin." Privately, NBC executives were admitting that she was fundamentally miscast as a *Today* show host.

———

Oddly enough, I, of all people, became one of the first guests to try out *Today*'s new family, when I was scheduled to appear on the show to publicize Harold's book, *The Dark Romance of Dian Fossey*, when it was published after his death. It struck me then—with the force of a hurricane—how different things appeared from the other side of the camera.

I was still reeling from my husband's death more than a year before. He had not quite completed the book, and I had promised him that I would make sure it was finished, knowing it could never be as good as he would have made it. Somehow it had gotten done, and now, ironically, I was about to talk about it on *Today*.

In spite of the fact that for four years I had booked people on the show, made their hotel and limo arrangements, met them in the greenroom, escorted them to the studio, and tried to gauge what kind of guest they would be, this was a whole different ball game. Now the bookers were doing it to me! They had put me up at the Berkshire Hotel the night before, on Fifty-second and Madison, only blocks from 30 Rock—the place countless *Today* guests had stayed throughout the years. They had offered to pick me up in a limo to take me to the studio in the morning, as they do with all of their guests to make sure that they get there on time, but the weather was beautiful and I decided to walk. I would have felt silly taking a limo two blocks, even in a snowstorm. I was nervous and apprehensive. And more than anything, I wanted to do a good job for Harold.

I did not sleep much the night before. I was scheduled to appear in the last half hour of *Today*, at 8:37, and I was told to be there an hour early for hair and makeup. I had watched hundreds of guests get powdered and coiffed, but I was shocked when I sat down in the chair myself and the hairdresser descended upon me like an attack dog before I could tell her I was happy with my hair the way I had done it myself—at least, I was as happy as I was going to get. She brushed it out frantically before I could stop her, and then she started over from scratch. When she was finished, I looked a lot like Imelda Marcos.

I tried to be cool. It should have been second nature to me after all the hours I had spent observing, but that clearly had nothing to do with my current situation. I went to the greenroom where I was supposed to go like all the other guests to wait until I was called. The familiar bagels and donuts sat there in the familiar cardboard box, next to the familiar metal institutional-size coffeepot filled with the infamous NBC coffee—at that hour of the morning people would drink any-thing. I poured myself a cup, and then I sat down on the same couch in the greenroom where the Pointer Sisters had slept, and tried to watch the show on the monitor in front of me. A couple of other guests were in the greenroom, too, but I had no idea who they were. My first secretary, Nancy Fields, who now worked for Willard, came by. I was glad to see her. She commented right away on how strange my hair looked, confirming my worst suspicions. Well, what did it matter, I thought to myself. The ratings were down. That meant only around four million people were going to see me.

Finally, just before 8:30, a young production assistant came in and escorted me into the studio, where I met Deborah Norville for the first time. A taped piece was running and she was near the door of the studio, away from the set. She looked stunning—taller, blonder, even prettier in person—as diametrically opposed to me as was humanly possible. She knew who I was and that I had worked on *Today* and she had actually read Harold's book. And she had loved it. That endeared her to me immediately.

She left to take her seat on the set and I waited for my turn, struggling to suppress any feelings I had, which seemed to be ranging from simple nervousness to abject fear. Jim Straka, the stage manager, who had been there when I had worked there, came and escorted me into my chair opposite Deborah during the commercial preceding my segment. Suddenly I was being interviewed by Deborah Norville. For the next five minutes, I was on automatic pilot. The five-minute interview seemed like five days. When it was over, I did not remember one thing I had said. I did not even realize, until I finally got the nerve to look at the tape many months later, that Deborah had called the movie that was based on Harold's book *Gorillas in the Midst*.

In July, almost one year to the day after Dick Ebersol had taken over the *Today* show, the ratings hit a seven-year low. With a 3.0 rating and 16 share, it was the worst Nielsen showing since the dismal summer of 1983—the summer my troubles with Elizabeth Taylor were in full bloom. *Today* was now down 24 percent from the same week the year before, while *GMA* had gained 14 percent in the same time period. Gartner conceded at the time that by year's end, the program's problems would cost the network and their affiliates more than $20 million.

Then something happened that caused NBC staffers to wonder just what it was about the *Today* show couch: On September 4, Deborah Norville announced that she was expecting a baby in March. NBC said simultaneously that she would remain on the show as long as her doctor recommended she do so. Even from the beginning, Norville's pregnancy did not work to her advantage as Jane Pauley's pregnancy had. Nothing seemed to soften her image, and things continued to go downhill. "Deborah's instincts about what's good for her are just awful," observed an NBC executive. "After a while, she had been so badly burned that she became very skeptical and lacked trust."

There was little reason for her to do otherwise. She had a difficult pregnancy, and in the last few months of it the war with Iraq began. "I didn't feel like I could slack off," Norville said later. "Because of the war everyone was working such awful hours, and I didn't feel like, because I was pregnant, I could say, 'Be nice, let me go home.' "

Not only was Norville exhausted, but in the last month of her pregnancy she developed toxemia, a serious complication that made her blood pressure skyrocket. Her doctor told her that she should stop working, unless she could lie down and put her feet up between interviews. She asked Bryant, who had a small office with a couch just steps from the studio, if he would mind if she used it to rest between segments. He refused. Deborah left *Today* on her maternity leave at the end of February, just days before her son, Karl Nickolai, was born on February 27, the same day the war with Iraq ended.

Katie Couric was named to fill in for Deborah during her maternity leave. The minute the easygoing, ultra-natural Couric took her place on the now-infamous couch, the ratings went up instantly. In Norville's last week on the show, *Today* had had a 3.8 rating. In Couric's first week, the ratings increased to 4.3. After a month, *Today* had moved to within three-tenths of a rating point behind *GMA*, the closest it had been in nine months.

Couric was not your run-of-the-mill morning-show anchor. Her father was a newspaper reporter, and she had a solid journalistic background—having worked her way up through the ranks from ABC News to CNN to NBC. (She had gone to Saudi Arabia during the Gulf War for NBC.) She was totally real and unassuming. Besides that, she was not even blond.

Her mere presence on the set with Bryant Gumbel seemed to ease the suffocating tension that had been flooding the *Today* show set like a sea of thick pea soup. She seemed the perfect antidote to the crippling, negative signals that had been emanating uncontrollably from the Gumbel-Norville team. It was also quite clear that the petite, tomboyish Couric, despite the girl-next-door image she exuded, would stand up to Bryant Gumbel. Even she admitted, "I feel I can cut him down to size."

Shortly after Norville departed for her maternity leave, there was another brouhaha involving Bryant and the press. This time it was *Spy* magazine, an irreverent periodical which some called snotty, that did a negative piece about Gumbel and his role in the *Today* debacle. Although *Spy* did not have the clout of *Time* and *Newsweek*, it was still read by many, and it was visible enough to cause concern among the executives at the network, especially since the article it published dealt with not only Gumbel's derisive attitude towards women, but also the way he had often referred to Jane Pauley. It said, in part:

> When Gumbel's old chum, Dick Ebersol, then the senior vice president in charge of *Today*, moved to replace Jane Pauley with Norville (egged on, it is said, by the antipathy of his wife, Susan Saint James, toward Pauley), Gumbel was not displeased. His feelings for Pauley can be summed up by his charming pet name for her—*cunt*, as in "Jesus, that cunt was really on Pluto today."

The *Spy* piece went on to allude to one of Gumbel's alleged extramarital liaisons, which caused even more consternation within NBC's Press Department.

Someone had to warn NBC president Robert Wright of the upcoming *Spy* article, and the unpleasant task fell to a senior vice president. "I had to say to him, 'Boss, look,'" recalls the executive, "'there's a memo in a magazine coming out next week with a story about two of our employees. One of the people to whom we pay more than two million dollars a year has called the other employee to whom we also pay two million dollars a year a cunt. And that's not the worst thing in the article.' "

Wright listened intently to the news, and then replied calmly, "Oh, really? Top it." The executive informed him of the rest of the content of the article, which was picked up the minute the magazine hit the stands by *USA Today* and the *National Enquirer*, among others.

It was not long after the appearance of the *Spy* piece that Deborah, perhaps in an attempt to promote her image as a new mother, gave an interview to *People* magazine. She allowed herself to be photographed breastfeeding her new son for the article. "I hope I'm glowing when I go back to work," Norville told *People*. "I do think that people will look at me differently—certainly the mothers out there. I feel like I joined some exclusive sorority. So forgive me if I don't wax poetic on the subject of Bryant Gumbel, the press and all that, but it seems so unimportant to me. Let's talk about life."

In spite of her attempts, the *People* reporter insisted on talking about *Today*. Deborah tried her best to be diplomatic about her recent professional experience, concluding, "It was more painful than childbirth. No comparison." She admitted it had taken a great toll on her. "I can't tell you how depressed I was," she said.

Less than two weeks after the *People* article appeared, NBC announced that it had named Katie Couric as permanent cohost of *Today*. Deborah Norville would not be returning. NBC executives were said to have found the breastfeeding photo self-serving and embarrassing. But the real reason for the move was the bottom line— ratings—which had risen steadily with Katie.

The day before, on April 4, Michael Gartner had gathered the staff of *Today* shortly after the broadcast and made the announcement. Within moments, the news that the thirty-three-year-old Norville would be spending the next year at home with her new baby was flashed across the NBC in-house cable system, signaling what network executives hoped would be the end of the worst chapter in the history of the *Today* show.

With typical grace, Bryant Gumbel made the announcement on the air. "Katie is now a permanent fixture up here, a member of our family, an especially welcome one," he said. "Deborah Norville is not."

Then, ironically, Katie announced almost immediately that she too was pregnant and would be going on maternity leave in July. *Today* show staffers continued to wonder—or marvel—about that couch.

In a statement to the press, Michael Gartner said, "Deborah is a terrific anchor and reporter and has done excellent work for NBC News over the years—from *NBC News at Sunrise* to *Today* to reporting some of the most popular specials on NBC. I respect her decision to devote herself full time to her family at this point."

An NBC executive explained, "They did offer her other things, that's not a secret—things that she didn't want to do. Once they made the decision to take her off the *Today* show, she did want to stay home with her kid."

Regarding Katie, Norville told a reporter at the time, "I wish her lots of luck. And a healthy baby. Do you want me to give her the alarm clock that Jane gave me? She obviously already has one that works."

Norville also made a statement to the press: "During the past month away from my day-to-day responsibilities, I've had time to reflect on the tumultuous last year and a half. And perhaps my personal situation—being a new mother away from the spotlight—has allowed me to see clearly what I want to do: give my son the best possible start on life, and practice good journalism. There is plenty of time for the latter, but I'll get only one chance to do the former. I have advised NBC News that I would like to take the next year to spend time with my family, and to plot the best course for my professional future."

A senior NBC executive tried to explain the obvious disparity: "They ruined Deborah Norville's career," he said. "Eighteen months ago, she was the hot anchor at NBC. She had an unlimited, boundless future. And now she's dead meat and they're paying her three and a half million bucks not to talk."

And so, with Jane Pauley, Deborah Norville, and Dick Ebersol gone from the *Today* show, it appeared that the chapter of the great debacle had come to a close. Bryant Gumbel was, for the moment at least, the undisputed king of the morning.

But only for the moment. Katie's popularity continued to build steadily, and her power grew proportionately. She captivated the audience with her down-to-earth style. Who else could have conversed as easily with General Norman Schwarzkopf as with Warren Beatty, or grilled presidential contender Ross Perot for two hours only weeks after fitting a condom on a model of a penis with total equanimity for a story relating to AIDS after Magic Johnson's disclosure that he was HIV positive—all between seven and nine in the morning?

Katie's ways were working well, certainly in terms of the ratings. Within a year after she took over, *Today*'s ratings had climbed an astonishing 20 percent. For the first quarter of 1992, *Today* was the only morning program with increased ratings, up 5 percent from the year before, while both ABC and CBS dipped a jolting 12 percent. Katie was duly rewarded with a new five-year contract that more than doubled her original salary to a sum of over $1 million a year. By May 1992, the week after the riots stemming from the verdict in the Rodney King case in Los Angeles, *Today* beat *GMA* for the third time that year, by the biggest margin to date—two-tenths of a rating point.

Last June, as the presidential campaign heated up and *Today* cleverly blew away the competition by offering a full two hours to each of the contenders, the show was on top three weeks out of four. After the long, dry stretch of total domination by *GMA*, an element of *déjà vu* was surfacing. The battle for the morning was escalating once more. The hysterical war was raging white-hot again.

There was, however, one more factor in *Today*'s new equation for success: a twenty-six-year-old, balding, brilliant, sometimes maniacal young man by the name of Jeff Zucker. Although Zucker was not officially made executive producer of *Today* until the end of 1991, he had virtually been running the show since he had been named supervising producer under Tom Capra months earlier. Capra, who was considered by most staffers to be uninvolved and ineffective, had announced he would be leaving *Today* to assume a production job at

NBC Entertainment. That is when the Zucker quotient started to build.

Jeff Zucker was a Harvard graduate headed for law school at the University of Virginia (which was also Katie Couric's alma mater) when he was offered a job as a researcher for NBC Sports during the 1988 Olympics in Seoul—yes, the same Olympics during which Bryant Gumbel wrote his infamous memo. There, Zucker did research for the NBC commentators, including Bob Costas, Jane Pauley, and Bryant Gumbel. He quickly impressed them all. Jane ushered Zucker onto the *Today* show in the capacity of writer, and he became Katie Couric's producer when she joined the show as Washington correspondent.

In the months that followed, Bryant Gumbel also became a strong backer of Zucker's and they established a close relationship. When Gumbel's contract came up for renewal in December 1991, his insistence that Zucker be promoted to executive producer was said to be a factor in the negotiations. Zucker was promoted and Gumbel signed a three-year contract after months of difficult negotiations, during which NBC floated the name of sports commentator Bob Costas as a possible Gumbel replacement. (NBC reportedly retained the option to dump Gumbel after one year.) Zucker soon became known around the *Today* offices as "Doogie Howser," after the adolescent TV doctor, and as "Miles," after the neurotic wonderboy producer on *Murphy Brown*. Ironically, he was astonishingly like Steve Friedman in many ways. Some said he patterned himself after Friedman and, not surprisingly, Friedman thought the world of Zucker.

But nobody was Jeff Zucker's champion more than Michael Gartner himself. Gartner admits he backed "Zuck" in the face of controversy within the News Division. "I held the line on it," he says. "I said, 'Look, this guy is terrific.' The reason I was so adamant was because the same exact thing happened to me when I was a kid. I was given a huge job at *The Wall Street Journal*, and there were probably a million people saying, 'Don't give him this job,' and I realized when they gave it to me that, by God, I was going to work so hard to show all those people they were wrong. I kind of saw myself in Zuck. I knew he was smart, I knew he would work hard, and he's young enough to take risks."

Zucker served another function. The executives at NBC were able to point to him as proof that now that Gumbel's services were no longer needed in every aspect of the show, Gumbel could pull back, relax, and concentrate on his role as anchor. He could remove his fingers from every last piece of the pie, an image that had hurt him.

The combination of Couric and Gumbel seems to work, in front of the cameras at least. Katie is not shy and she keeps Bryant in line. "I'm not intimidated by him," she says, although she gets irritated when he talks about her looks. "It's sexist. I don't think Bryant would think it was funny if I said his recent hairstyle made him look like Bart Simpson," she said after Bryant tried a new look.

Bryant is enthusiastic about his new partner. "She comes prepared and she's fun to be with," he says.

Michael Gartner admits he has seen a positive change in Bryant Gumbel. "Bryant Gumbel has been absolutely sensational for the past year," he says. "He's always been a sensational journalist, but now he is also a real team player and has been ever since Zuck took over."

It is even more significant that *Today* appears to have learned from its mistakes, on paper, at least. Three out of the top four people on the show now are women. Ironically, Karen Curry has been appointed the executive producer in charge of morning programming at NBC, and she is, if only technically, the one to whom Jeff Zucker reports.

"We're making enormous efforts right now," says Michael Gartner, who emphasizes that he still relies on Dick Ebersol daily for counsel and advice. "*Today* was the number-one problem around here and we sat down and we attacked it with a system and a plan that has worked. We knew we had to bring back a sense of family and stability. And that is what we have done."

Today's emphasis has also tilted back towards news and journalism, which has always been its strongest suit, and viewers are coming back. Travel remains a significant part of the equation, too. *Today* will broadcast live from Africa in November 1992, after the election. But as Michael Gartner points out, "It's a long haul up. One thing about television—there are no quick fixes."

Still, if *Today* is a microcosm of life, as it often seems to be, nothing stays the same. Only one thing is certain. You never know what will happen next. Will Bryant tire of Katie as he has of all of his other cohosts? Will Katie tire of Bryant? Will a Hollywood studio—Disney or Paramount, perhaps—acquire NBC and the *Today* show? Will NBC choose to renew its option on Gumbel's contract after one year? Will Bob Costas ever say yes to NBC's offer to him of Bryant's job? Will it matter by the time he does?

Will *Today* regain—and maintain—first place one more time in the battle for the morning?

Stay tuned . . .

E p i l o g u e

Bryant Gumbel is still anchor of *Today*.

Katie Couric is still co-anchor of *Today* with Bryant Gumbel. She has a daughter, Ellie.

Jane Pauley's first post-*Today* show, *Real Life with Jane Pauley*, was canceled. She is currently anchor of *Dateline NBC*, with cohost Stone Phillips.

Deborah Norville has a radio talk show on ABC and is negotiating with CNN for an afternoon talk show.

Steve Friedman is still executive producer of *Nightly News*, but is enmeshed in controversy, as always.

Karen Curry has been made the executive producer of morning programming at NBC.

Chris Wallace is a correspondent for ABC News.

John Palmer was the anchor of cable television's *World Monitor News* show until it folded after one season.

David Hartman's television career ended with his departure from *GMA*.

Dick Ebersol was in charge of the 1992 Olympics in Barcelona and is still president of NBC Sports.

Michael Gartner is still president of NBC News and is the godfather of Dick Ebersol's youngest child.

Willard Scott signed a new four-year contract in 1992.

Faith Daniels was replaced as news anchor on *Today* by Margaret Larson. She is host of her own show, *Closeup*, on NBC.

Marty Ryan was hired by ABC to be executive producer of the *Home* show on ABC.

Coby Atlas left *Today* to produce documentaries for Gary David Goldberg's documentary-film company, Vu Productions, in Hollywood.

Scott Goldstein won two Emmys and two Golden Globes for *LA. Law*, and is currently supervising producer/director of *Doogie Howser, M.D.*

Marianne Haggerty is talent producer for Jane Pauley's show, *Dateline NBC*.

Allison Davis just gave birth to her second child.

Joe Garagiola's latest stint at *Today* ended in spring 1992.

Mariette Hartley is between television projects.

Ellin Sanger is talent executive at ABC's *20/20*.

Priscilla Presley's career is flourishing.

Elizabeth Taylor is still married to her eighth husband, Larry Fortensky.

Index

ABOUT THE AUTHOR

A former *People* magazine and *Washington Post* writer, JUDY KESSLER was the talent coordinator of *Today* from 1980 to 1984. She was subsequently a producer for *Entertainment Tonight* and Norman Lear's Act III Productions, and coproduced the film *Gorillas in the Mist*. A graduate of Stanford University, she lives in Los Angeles.